UNDERCOVER

UNDERCOVER

THE POPULATION OF MY LIFE: VOLUME II

RONALD E. MARKSITY

Deeds Publishing | Athens

Copyright © 2021 — Ronald E. Marksity

ALL RIGHTS RESERVED—No part of this book may be reproduced in any form or by any electronic or mechanical means, including information storage and retrieval systems, without permission in writing from the authors, except by a reviewer who may quote brief passages in a review.

Published by Deeds Publishing in Athens, GA
www.deedspublishing.com

Printed in The United States of America

Cover design by Mark Babcock.

ISBN 978-1-950794-57-7

Books are available in quantity for promotional or premium use. For information, email info@deedspublishing.com.

First Edition, 2021

10 9 8 7 6 5 4 3 2 1

To

Baba
Maria Vukich
my maternal grandmother.

Her guidance and love
prepared me to live this.

CONTENTS

End Of Summer	1
Western Hills High School	5
Mike	13
The Seventh Grade	21
Temporary Roommates	27
Holidays	31
1956: Second Half Of The 7th Grade	37
Summer Squirrel	45
Gamble Nippert Junior High School	49
Mr. Cheeseman And Mr. Schmalfuss	51
The Eighth Grade	55
The Other Eighth Grade	61
Undercover	65
Mr. Stevens	71
September 1957, The Ninth Grade	75
Imagine That	81
Eddie Heuer	85
The Ninth Grade: Continued	89
Is There A Chill In Here?	93
Tournament	97
The Wreck Of Justice	101

September 1958: The Tenth Grade	109
Petar Dejurdjev	113
The Uncle And His Nephew	117
Physical Roommate	123
Aimlessly Bullseye	127
Don Schmidt	131
You Drive	137
My Cousin Donald	143
Gone	149
Mrs. Lewis	153
Chasnitza	157
Canada	171
Normal Is A Place I'll Never Even Visit	179
The Rest Of The 10th Grade	185
Hawthorne, Without The Seven Gables	191
Summer 1959 And Beyond	195
The Matriarch: In Her Garden	199
Mr. Findlay	205
The Flamenco Tattoo	207
Handler	219
Meanwhile	223

The Breakthrough	229
The Reverend E. J. Bruton	239
By The Way	245
The Matriarch: The Burden	253
President, Mayor, Governor	263
Partner—Tutor	273
Life With Pete	279
Freshman Year	297
Continuing Education	305
Cathie	315
Buy The Barracuda	321
My Barracuda	325
The Proposition	329
Preparations	333
The Drive	341
Maelstrom	347
Out And In	355
Departure	367
Foul Air	377
Benefactor	383
The Bus To Reality	393
Final Debriefing	401
Epilogue	405

END OF SUMMER

Sprawled in the grass of our front yard looking up at the stark white clouds trundling across the brilliant blue sky I was excited; tomorrow was the first Tuesday of September 1955 and the start of school. I couldn't believe it was almost a full year ago that I was in the sixth grade having to make decisions. Looking back, I was happy and sure about all of them.

By Thanksgiving I had respectfully declined the invitation to attend Walnut Hills High School and "…participate in the breakthrough application of college preparatory education." Instead, I enrolled in Western Hills High School.

After Christmas I completely stopped attending The Peniel Missionary Assembly. This was an easy decision to make and only involved me and The Something Bigger that had been with me since before I was born. I had an immutable, personal relationship with God. A connectedness that was built on both experience and faith and didn't require attending a converted store front or a cathedral.

When I graduated from Westwood Elementary, my normal priorities became my summer plans. Summer became chores, save, paperboy, save, practice the accordion, save, help Uncle

Charlie, save, and as much time as possible at the tennis courts. It was successful, my tennis steadily improved, and I had saved enough money to cover my needs during the coming school year.

Three weeks ago, when I told Art that I was going to stop delivering papers, I was glad and sad. Glad to have worked for him and sad to stop. It was a tough meeting for me, but as I should have expected, he put a spin on it that enabled me to keep the glad and drop the sad. Looking at me with approval, and wanting to be sure I saw that approval, he smiled and said, "It was good having you work for me, but there is more for you to have."

And last week when I told Uncle Charlie I was going to stop helping him, I was neither glad nor sad, I was just done. I had bad feelings about working for him, feelings I couldn't explain. So, he picked that time to surprise me by volunteering to take me to school each day. My first reaction was that he would try to use the rides to make me obligated, but when he pointed out that he would pass our house and West Hi was on his way to work anyway, I took him up on his offer.

…and then Duke was all over me because I wasn't reacting to Olga's call, it was time for supper, mine and his.

I was surprised by Uncle Charlie's offer, but I was flabbergasted by the offer that was served with supper. George and Olga had decided that as I was entering the seventh grade, it was no longer appropriate for me to be spanked. To this point I got spanked when I knowingly did something wrong. In those few instances I could remember, I clearly was delinquent and deserved to be held accountable. George used either a belt or a wooden cooking spoon which is much more effective as a tool of discipline when referred to in Serbian, a 'va-re-a-cha', with the 'r' rolled and a hard 'cha'. This was certainly a big endorsement of my maturing, but like all things from Olga and George, it wasn't free. Now, I would have to discipline myself, but no matter how hard I tried, I couldn't see a belt or vareacha as part of my self-discipline. The supper was tastier than usual.

As I went to bed that evening, I felt ready for Western Hills High School. The feeling didn't last.

WESTERN HILLS HIGH SCHOOL

The next morning at the curb, Uncle Charlie's bright yellow Chevy pick-up, with "Glenway Chevrolet Service" painted all over it, came into view. I hopped in and off we went, neither speaking, me because I knew he wouldn't, and he because he didn't. This morning I was glad Uncle Charlie preferred silence because there was a lot to think about.

What was West Hi like? I honestly couldn't remember ever being there. Maybe I forgot or was having some kind of mental block, but the truth in my mind was that this was going to be the first time I saw the place.

While I struggled with my memory, we rode Ferguson Road until we crossed Queen City Avenue and cleared a little rise and whoa! There were cars everywhere. I mean a traffic jam at seven, early in the morning. Where were all those cars going? As we crept forward, I craned my neck and saw they were jamming a parking lot and then we were stopped. I was getting out and there were people all around...little kids, big kids, huge kids, or were they kids and adults and cars and girls and boys. They were swirling around and past me. and then the pick-up was pulling away. As it did so, Western Hills High School came into view—and that was the end of my being ready for the seventh grade.

My mouth fell open, the place was monstrous, four times, the place was four times as big as Westwood Elementary. It was clear as day, there was one entire Westwood on each end of two Westwoods across the middle.

I was going to have to cross the street and go inside. Where? How? What...fortunately others were moving, and I let myself become part of their flow. For the next, I don't have a clue, I let myself be part of the horde. Before we got to the main entrance, we passed the U-shaped driveway whose island of vegetation looked like a national park.

Our horde didn't have to breach the monster because it welcomed us with open doors. Once inside, our mass was gone, the horde was nowhere to be seen, swallowed by the monster's cavernous innards.

Alone without the horde, I was glad I had read the information sent me and memorized my homeroom number. The signs were easy to follow but I navigated slowly because there was so much to see, all of it new to me. When I finally saw the room, I was a lost boy found, until I entered and was lost again. I was yet to see one person I knew!

Okay, there's one from Westwood...hello, over here. Now some more. Not a bunch but enough to know...the bell shut down the noise and ushered in orientation.

Good, the direction signs will be up until we know how to get around. "Fill out this form." Seat assignments and lockers...Ah ha. They do it by alphabetical...with the last names...and I need a combination lock for the wall locker me and some other M, or maybe L since I'm Ma, would share...or he or she might have one already. "Please complete this questionnaire." "Here are the required classes, for a sound foundation of well-rounded learning."..."and electives"—what's that mean? "Extracurricular"—huh? Tests, grades, report cards. "Now read and sign these three." Look for the cafeteria, library, band room, bookstore...Principal's Office, Nurse's Office, Athletic Offices...she's gonna point out a post office before she's done....gymnasium, auditorium, nauta...something and outside track and football field and baseball fields and tennis courts and wait! Tennis courts? Is that true? "...and pass around these school bus schedules and..."

It may be lunch time but I ain't going anywhere, I'll sit outside near my next class. That orientation helped, but that can't be all of it. Those four rooms were only half my schedule and I've got to learn how to get from one to another or I'll be late for all of them. I still can't remember which of those stairwells I need to take to...stairwell, I can't even remember which section of the building...that couldn't have been lunch time.

"No sir, I was just thinking for a moment, nothing's wrong." He was the last class of the day, my eighth, and what was wrong was my life had been swirling around me since that yellow pickup pulled away from the curb. I was sitting there because in that seat the swirling had finally stopped.

"Good, but be careful, you don't want to miss your bus." He must be kidding. I've never been on a school bus, and I've already had more 'new' than I can handle in one day. No, no, I'll just take my time and walk home.

As I left West Hi there was a river of walkers that included all the varieties I had been overwhelmed with since morning. Could it have been this morning? After Queen City Avenue, the river lost volume and became a stream. By the time I hit Boudinot, it was a trickle and long before I got to Daytona, I was the last drop.

I don't know how long it took but it wasn't long enough for me to digest day one.

Uncle Charlie and the second day led to more of the same. The traffic jam and horde were there, as was the monster whose innards consumed more bodies than I could imagine and where everything about people, classes, and facilities swamped my capacity for handling 'new'. And so it went, the first two weeks at Western Hills. On the third Wednesday, things changed.

The blazing yellow pick-up was right on time, and I prepared myself for another ride. Uncle Charlie didn't like to talk but that is not to say riding with him was dull. As I knew from working with him on his farm, he was a notorious tailgater and these last two weeks proved he kept at it on his way to work. He made me push my imaginary brake almost every morning. He was a real maniac behind another vehicle. Over the years, I had seen that his actions were premeditated and cruel, he wanted to aggravate the other drivers, he tailgated with purpose.

This morning, the man he was tailgating slammed on his brakes and we rear ended him big time. Uncle Charlie told me to stay put. Traffic adjusted and soon the police came. It was unbelievable, he was blaming the other driver, lying flat out to the policeman. The man of silence became a waterfall of words. The policeman would not be fooled and cited Charlie. My quiet Uncle cursed that policeman all the way to school. When he dropped me off, I told him that if the policeman had not cited him, I would have told the policeman the truth, and I was glad he didn't get away with it. He drove off without a word or blink. Walking to homeroom I thought, for a man who didn't talk, he was very able at lying. It took a lot of practice to lie so naturally. I also admitted he enjoyed making me push my imaginary brake and enjoyed it even more because I knew that he enjoyed it.

All day at school I kept thinking about Uncle Charlie, the bad feelings I had about working with him were based on more than my intuition. Walking home, I knew there was something deeper and more concrete about him that I couldn't explain. And I was strangely glad I couldn't explain it. When I went to bed, the picture of him talking to the policeman kept me awake. Next morning, as he dropped me off, I told him that was the last time I would ride with him and walked away, without a word or blink.

By the time I got home that afternoon, I had decided I would ride my bike to school. I left early the next morning and when I finally got to the bicycle racks, I would have kissed the ground but there was the usual multitude waiting for something to look at. More than half the ride had been pure terror and I was all sweaty. Riding home was another matter, it was lonely compared to the morning and faster than walking, much faster. Plus, the fact I was sweaty didn't matter.

The next morning, Friday, I gave it another try. Stupid! It was just plain dangerous. On the ride home all I could think of was, "Now what?" I certainly wasn't getting back in that truck with Uncle Quiet after just getting away from him. But what? I would have to work on it, it was going to be a long weekend.

Long, with an early start. Olga and her interrogation face were waiting for me when I got home. I guessed my treatment of her beloved brother had put my neck in a noose and braced for the worst. Surprise, all she wanted to know was when I decided to ride my bike to school, not why. I decided I'd offer the why before Uncle Tailgate talked to her. When I was done, she said, "You sure?" First self-discipline instead of spanking and now this, I could get happy with growing up.

But that happy was on hold because it didn't help me get to school Monday. I spent the weekend on the problem. Riding with Charlie was out. The bike deserved more consideration, what were my options? I could ride earlier in the morning, try some different routes, change clothes to handle the sweating. Not bad, but what about when it gets cold? Why can't I just think one step at a time. I had to try something else, the bike wouldn't do. Maybe a different driver. Oh yes, mister inhibited is going to introduce himself to someone in the neighborhood who drives past West High and arrange for a ride to school. Idiot.

The weekend zoomed by, and Sunday found me nervous, I had no way to school. The solution must have been sitting on a bench in my brain waiting for me to notice. It must have got bored sitting there because at one moment I heard, "Ride the bus."

Oh no, not the bus! I cannot, repeat, cannot, ride the bus. I have never been on a school bus. What do you do on a school bus, how do you act? Where can you sit and where can't you sit? What are the rules? I had heard people talking about this in scary terms. A school bus is not like the street cars to McMicken where I was comfortable riding with adults. I would be riding with kids, I'm uncomfortable with kids. I was upset and that confirmed it was the answer, I was going to ride a school bus.

Like a sheep led to shearing, I got out the paperwork. Locations and schedules for pick-ups and drop-offs gave me all I needed to take my first school bus ride the next morning.

But there was a lot of time till morning, and I spent it nervous, then worried, and then sweaty. I truly was unable to relate to kids. I was just too different from them, and a school bus might be the place where I couldn't keep my differences undercover. I had done just fine at Westwood, nobody knew me, well maybe the gym teachers who helped me avoid going swimming, but otherwise…and then I got quiet.

I was convicted, I was all tied up with I and wasn't relating to my experience. Whenever I needed help, I always got it and more by calling on My Father. Good Lord, how could I have forgotten that it was never about I, it is always about You. I got down on my knees and prayed. Afterward, in bed, I was asleep before the echo of my last words was gone. "Goodnight God."

Monday morning, kids from Westwood and even those who didn't know me were shocked to see me on the bus. These were the same kids who had jeered at me in the yellow pick-up or as I walked home. Getting off with the others, as if I was one of them, I was looking forward to the ride home. Turning into homeroom, I was ready for the seventh grade.

MIKE

I could not imagine calling an adult by their first name, but Mr. Voinovich didn't think of himself as Mister and made a point about his last name. "When I was in the Marines, they used my last name. It was always, Voi-no-vich you son-ofa-bitch." He told me to call him Mike.

Our relationship began when I was in grade school but I'm not really sure when they moved in next door. Mike and his nice Serbian wife Rosie may have been there when we moved in. Eventually there were boys, Mike and Frank, then a daughter Donna and finally a Collie.

I'm not sure where Mike worked or what he did. The only thing I know about his family is he had a relative, who received a medal for saving a woman's life after dragging her out of Lake Erie. The relative went into politics.

At first, our relationship consisted of saying hello anytime we saw each other. My being comfortable with adults enabled me to expand the relationship to me following Mike around as he worked in his yard or garage. During this period, he discovered I actually lived the words to live by, "Children should be seen and not heard." and became comfortable with me.

I liked listening to Mike from day one. He was different from other adults. He seemed to talk in straight lines, no turns, or even slight bends. Some described him as rough, crude. I thought he was direct. What was lucky and what few people knew, was that Mike talked to me. Imagine…I had the chance to spend time with an ex-Marine who was Serbian, lived next door, and talked to me.

One summer, his nephew from Chicago came to visit. He was a little older than me and just came over to our house and introduced himself. As you know, my background had rules about going to a house uninvited and about inviting people to our house. His didn't. In time, he just took me into Mike's house as if I were invited. It was the first time I was in the house next door or any house on Daytona other than ours. I learned that the Voinovich's lived differently from us.

I was welcome and no one thought a thing about their visitor bringing a visitor. There were things all over the place and you were allowed to sit anywhere. I sat on the edge of the couch by the coffee table. I remember because there were magazines on the table. CONFIDENTIAL, STAG, MEN'S LIFE, a pile of nudist magazines and more like them. There were half dressed women on the covers, and I wondered what was inside. Mike saw me and as if reading my mind said, "The only way to know is to look."

They were mostly woman in bikini bottoms. In CONFIDENTIAL there were black bars over their chests but in the others there were no black bars. I had never seen anything like it. Mike applauded my discovery and from then on, he talked about anything having to do with sex as if it were perfectly natural and normal. What a notion? I had never heard anyone in my family talk about sex…period, never mind natural or normal.

Mike spent a lot of time in his garage. Like ours, it was a free standing two car at the rear of the lot. Unlike Uncle Charlie, who had something specific for the evolution of his farm/estate whenever he went into this garage/workshop, Mike tinkered in his garage. Tinkering was entirely new to me. It had no direction, no purpose, no clear-cut end, or beneficial result. To my amazement, Mike's tinkering was for fun. Unfortunately, I never got the hang of it, but I did come to learn tinkering in his garage was Mike's private place.

On this day, I'd been in his garage watching him work when he needed something. I offered to get it. A funny look crossed his face as he sent me to the cabinet in the basement bathroom. I found the bathroom and opened the door. There was no cabinet but there was a calendar. Over the toilet was Marilyn Monroe laying on the red satin drape. The calendar that caused Edgar Bergen to ask, "Miss Monroe, what did you have on at the time you posed for the calendar?" She replied, "The radio." I didn't notice the radio.

By this time, Mike was behind me laughing and then he began a routine that every time thereafter, once started, kept going. Marilyn walks past the two and Bergen asks Charlie, "Charlie, did you see that." "Oh yes, how could you miss 'em?" "Them?" "Yes, them." "Well Charlie what does them look like to you?" "Them look like two puppies fighting in a sack." Monroe hears this and turns around. She wiggles, points at McCarthy, and says, "Come over here." He can barely be heard as he says, "How can I come over there, when I just came over here?" I wasn't exactly sure what that meant but Mike was laughing up a storm and it was easy to follow. In time, I knew exactly what that meant. From that day on, Mike was my mentor in matters sexual, matters he made natural and normal.

One day coming home from junior high, I heard a commotion in Mike's back yard. When I got there his collie was lying on her side by a big hole next to the garage. She was beautiful and I knew how much he liked her from watching the two of them. Now he was trying to kill her with a shovel. He couldn't make himself hit her hard enough and was just crippling her. He asked if I would help, I couldn't. About to hit her again, he almost went to his knees, hesitated, then told her he'd be right back.

He returned with a handgun and shot her in the head. He put the gun aside, picked up some kind of cover, and cradled that dog like a baby. He settled the wrapped dog in the hole and cussed under his breath as he laid the ground on top of her. He wasn't shoveling, he was comforting. When all the ground was in place, he turned his attention to her blood. It was on the grass, and he tried to hose it away. In time, not satisfied with the job, he stopped and sat down next to me. We sat some time. He whispered, "God. I couldn't watch her suffer any more. I loved that damned dog too much." Later, he got up and went inside, taking the gun with him. Later, I learned how sick the collie was, he had been caring for her himself over the past several months after the vet gave up on her.

As time passed, Mike and I spent time together regularly. He taught me by demonstration what it meant to be together with no agenda, goal, topic, or anything specific. Just be together.

It was a hot summer day, Mike had been in his garage and as soon as he saw me walking up our driveway yelled for me to join him, I did. I sensed there was something special in his head, I had never seen him like this. He sounded almost like a teacher. This was not an off the cuff talk, he had prepared and was dead serious. I wasn't sure what to do, so I did what I did best, I listened.

It took over an hour, he was trying to help me. It was time for me to understand about women. I assumed this was going to be about the birds and bees like some guys said their fathers gave them. Mike explained he'd been thinking about it and wanted to do it formal. I was surprised at the build-up he was going through when I realized, he needed the build-up. He was actually beating around the bush to ensure he did it right. His mannerisms, speech, and the fact this was so important to him made me more nervous than excited. Finally, he put his arm on my shoulder and spelled it out. Once he was satisfied he had given me what I needed, he let out a huge sigh and went back to tinkering, expecting me to go home. I did.

That was his truth. Only he could share it. I didn't know what to think. I was in over my head and let it ride. Years later, I realized how much he trusted and cared for me, this was his private heart, his personal self, and he had shared it with the kid next door. It would take even more years before I fully understood his message.

By the time I was in high school, Mike knew about my plan to make the Army a career. That became the focus of our talks and he shared some of his combat experiences fighting Japs in the jungles of the Pacific. Hearing war stories was nothing new for me. It was natural for adults to talk to me and frequently they talked about their combat experiences. My various roommates all shared their war stories. Some did so willingly, while others did so unwillingly, only sharing because they couldn't control their dreams or the fact they talked in their sleep. But Mike was my first exposure to someone who had been in the Pacific Theater.

Coming home late one evening, I noticed the lights were on in Mike's garage and decided to say hello. I found him more than preoccupied, he was not in his garage, he was in a different place. I had never seen him like this and he, looking straight at me, couldn't see me. Eventually he noticed me and when our eyes met, it was as if we knew each other's thoughts. He was in his past. I was okay to be there. Did I want to be there? Yes. Was I sure? Yes. He believed me. And, although he didn't know why, something told him I could be there. Then we were quiet, me waiting.

When he started, he wasn't talking, he was lamenting gutturally and shivering. He was back in a Pacific jungle fighting Japanese. The head count after a night patrol revealed five Marines were missing. A squad was put together and sent to look for them. Marine Mike Voinovich was a member of that squad sent out to find his buddies. They found all five hanging by their hands in a stand of trees. The sun made it hard to see. When they were cut down it was even harder to see. Each had been skinned alive from fingernails to toenails and then hung up to die.

While he relived his horror, I kept my eyes on him. Then he stopped making sounds. He stopped shivering. He was somewhere else. He was back with me. He was back in his garage. He was resting. He was okay. He wondered how it was I could handle such a horror but didn't want to know, he had enough horror in his head.

As always, I knew I had this experience under The Almighty Auspices watching over me. I didn't know why I needed this experience, but now knew why I had an earlier experience. I was able to stand with Mike as he relived his horror, because as he relived his, I relived mine. His jungle was my playground where at age seven I watched Favorite, without a nose or ear, ribs broken, lung punctured, face red mush with white bones shining out, as Sneaky Mean tried to beat him to death.

Such horrors should not happen. If they happen, they should not be acknowledged, evil needs no confirmation. When forced to be acknowledged, they should be forgotten. But when they happen, those who lived them can't forget. I have never forgotten the playground and believe me, I have tried. How could Mike forget the jungle, I have never forgotten it after only hearing of it in his garage.

    I don't remember us talking again. I do remember Mike, he is unforgettable. We both knew the sharing of this incident confirmed the bond between us. A bond never mentioned until now, yet just as strong as then.

THE SEVENTH GRADE

It seemed that riding the school bus took me behind the curtain of my inhibitions, and just as Dorothy found there was no wizard, I found there was no monster. Western Hills High School became the stage on which I played the seventh grade.

I loved the books. There was a lot of reading to do which was great, assignments asking me to do what I loved. My best memories of 64 E. McMicken were of the library on the corner and now, each class seemed to be contributing to the growth of my own library.

There were bodies everywhere. Bodies of all shapes and sizes. Bodies pushing, rushing, running, whispering, talking, yelling, too many bodies, in a hurry, making noise. Did they know what they were doing? Did they know where they were going? They acted like they knew for sure.

The classrooms were big. The desks were big. The lockers, hallways, stairs, lobby, grounds, everything was big. I didn't know if the bathrooms were big, I didn't go to the bathroom at school.

The eighth and ninth graders were not just big, they were different. They didn't know much. I mean, for example, they didn't know the answers to any of my questions. What other explanation could there be for them to just laugh when I asked them something?

There were so many teachers and coaches and advisors and specialists and staff, all adults I could relate to, but they didn't want to relate or didn't have time or something else...anyway, it seemed being comfortable with adults wasn't worth a plug nickel in the seventh grade at West Hi.

The place was bright wherever you were. Each classroom had a wall of windows so that even on cloudy days you could read without lights but there were lights on all the time. Lots of lights.

As for the senior high kids, they were too much for me. A lot of them were bigger than the adults I grew up with and, imagine this, these senior high kids were the cause of the morning traffic jams. These senior high kids drove to school in their cars. Kids didn't seem to be the right description.

It was six not four! West Hi was six Westwoods, two side by side, one on each end and two more centered behind for the gym, swimorium, music facilities, and auditorium.

Once I could get around, I found places for quiet and alone time where I maintained my bearings. In short order I was able to attend to the classes I had been attending. I did

love learning, the teachers were really good, and the classes were fulfilling. The tests and such were straight arrow, no tricks, or traps. All I had to do was listen and take notes in class and then read the stuff assigned, the answers to the tests were right there. This is not to say I always found them.

The first time I saw the gym, I wondered how many people were in gym class that it had to be so big. I learned they played basketball games there and filled it up, full to overflowing. And then, thank You, thank You, thank You, I learned the best thing. That word was natatorium and meant swimming place and swimming was an elective! I had heard right, elective. HA, I elect nat-to. I gave thanks again, no need to negotiate about my inhibitions and hope for teachers as understanding as those at Westwood.

Oh no, we had to take showers after gym class! This was not Westwood and the idea the gym teachers would let me out of taking showers was not an idea. I had learned to wear shorts and t-shirts at Westwood but my inhibitions about being naked continued past the seventh grade. So, I kept my feelings undercover and got in early or waited till late and managed never to be in the showers with anyone else. This took a lot of maneuvering. I loved gym even though it was the most pressure filled class of my first seven years in school.

English, would I ever get the hang of English. I hadn't done my thinking in Serbian since the third grade but when it came to English, especially punctuation, I couldn't think at all.

Shop class had me stumped. Can the teacher really tear a Cincinnati telephone book in half?

The library was huge, but I didn't spend time there. No, when I needed a library, I'd walk up Daytona to my good friend the Westwood Library. It was more my size; I knew where everything was, and the librarians knew me.

The first time we had assembly I was flabbergasted. I was thinking of The Peniel Missionary Assembly and The Assembly of God and boy was I surprised. The auditorium for assembly was bigger than a church, it could have been a tabernacle. I enjoyed assembles, there was so much to watch without being watched.

I had never seen so many kids in all of my whole lifetime. I couldn't get over the kids. Some were bigger than adults, just huge, and it wasn't just the senior hi kids, one eighth grader I talked to was bigger than Uncle Nicky.

I thought it was a joke when we toured the "music facilities." Rooms didn't describe that joint or the hardware. Did West Hi really have its own orchestra, band, choir, combos, and music show? After that tour, I knew one thing, this was not like practicing on my front porch. I would keep the fact I can play the accordion undercover, deep undercover.

Today, I was coming up the stairs and just before I reached the landing, the big guy in front of me hit the big guy in front of him in the side of the face. The hit guy fell forward and the guy who hit him jumped on top and punched him in the head again and then they were struggling to hit each other...I had to struggle to get back down the steps. Kids were actually trying to get up close to see what was going on. Once free, I took the hall and another way to my next class.

I couldn't get this out of my mind, kids wanting to see a fight. Compared to the fight in the playground on McMicken this was a waltz, but it scared me plenty. What scared me was no one else seemed to know how a fight could end up.

Everyone talked about how big the cafeteria was, too big to be called a lunchroom, but I never went to look. I brought my lunch and eating in some quiet place, alone, was the lunch break for me. Plus, some of the things Olga fixed or left for me to fix for my lunch might not have been understood by Americans.

There was a bookstore. Why there was a bookstore was beyond me. Why would anyone buy books when they gave us the ones we needed for classes and there was a huge library where the books were free. I never found the bookstore, probably because I never looked for it.

I saw it but had trouble believing it, he tore a Cincinnati phone book in half, just as easy as I tear a piece of notebook paper. However, in addition to his reputation for tearing phone books in half, which I had witnessed and was deserved, he was known for throwing things at students who weren't paying attention, things like hammers and screwdrivers. I knew about my attention but worried about the attention of those around me, what if his aim wasn't so hot.

What a day today in gym class. The teacher asked if we had any physical skills or talents, and I didn't keep tennis undercover. Mr. Otten, the coach of the tennis team, set it up for us to hit together. I couldn't believe it. Plus, oh man, the courts...there were three concrete, six clay, and two grass. I had never played on grass. Mr. Otten really said, from what he saw I would definitely make the tennis team. I'm going to get the chance to play on a team. I love this place!

Life was good and I was comfortable with my routine. Bus in the morning for a full day of school and back on the bus to home. I never went back until the next day. I never participated in any after school activities. I never attended any functions, school or social. I heard the band, choir, and actors practice and rehearse, but never went to see them. I saw the football team and then the basketball team as they went to practice or play but never went to watch them. Bus to school, bus home, nothing else. I had a routine for home as well, homework, chores, accordion practice, and whenever possible playing tennis against my old friend the green board or with anyone who invited me.

Such were my first months in the seventh grade and as fall approached, I was a happy fellow.

TEMPORARY ROOMMATES

Funny to put it that way. Since Uncle Steve, back in the third grade, having a temporary roommate was as much a routine of my life as chores and Duke. Back then, Olga and George explained that The Lord had blessed us, we had our health and lived well in a nice neighborhood, now it was time to practice our faith and share our blessings. There were many people coming to America who had no place to go. They were called DPs for Displaced Persons. We could help them by opening our hearts and home. And then they introduced Steve Klajic, who became my first roommate and happened to be a relative of some sort.

Since then, there had been a regular flow of DPs from mainly Slavic countries. This one, the gentleman sitting in our living room when I came home from school in late October was a Serb. Short and stocky, he had a very dark complexion and was seriously balding. The oddest thing about him was that he held his head in a manner that made it appear his head was in his shoulders rather than on them. This is not to say he was funny, there was nothing about him that was funny. In fact, I had the unhappy feeling he had not seen anything funny for a very long time.

I don't remember his name, I remember almost none of their

names, but I can't forget them. As with most of those who came before him, his eyes were the page on which his story was written. Tired. Disbelieving. Were we sincere that he was welcome to stay with us? Shocked, were Olga and George really going to help him get a job? Overwhelmed, was he really not the only one who needed help and were there really no strings or payments-due attached?

He immediately displayed the characteristics common to his predecessors and those who followed him, he was quiet, cautious, and nice. He spoke no American and when he discovered I spoke Serbian I saw not a smile, that seemed to be too big a stretch for his tired face, but the attempt at a smile. I gave him the best smile I had and showed him his side of my dresser, desk, and closet. He assured me he had nothing to put anywhere but under his bed, the one opposite mine. His hands were most interesting, rough, thick, dark, and no matter how often or hard he washed them, the creases and lines never came up flesh colored. I wondered if they were scarred.

He was with us for a little over a week and then moved on to the job and place that Olga and George had found for him. This was how it went with all my roommates. Where they were from and how long they stayed varied, but getting jobs and housing never varied, all were successfully placed.

After he left, I thought of this part of my life's routine. I was very thankful for my roommates. I knew I was young and that I wasn't grasping all they had to offer, but I felt somehow, someway, later I would realize the full scope of their lessons.

This last gentleman had been one of the easy ones. When roommates started popping up regularly, I quickly learned they all had dark spots in their past. These were horrific, tragic, wrenching, haunting, or combinations thereof and were the results of war, capture, torture, or just plain evil. They all had to get these dark spots out of their systems and our place seemed to be the place for this to happen. It made sense, Olga and George and their ministry were truly heaven sent, if not heaven itself. And I was their roommate, a Serbian speaking boy with the reputation of being seen and not heard. These releases of their past took one of two avenues. The easy ones sat up and told me their stories because they knew they had to release the pressure. It wasn't that they were telling me their stories, it was that the circumstances provided the only thing they needed, a human with his mouth closed. The hard ones didn't want to let it out, so release came via nightmares, talking in their sleep, and screams and cries from the other side of my room. I was humbled by the opportunity to listen to them, easy or hard.

Thinking about the man who just left, I started to be embarrassed because I really didn't know how many there had been since Uncle Steve. More embarrassing, I only remembered one name, Steve Sverchev. He was an engineer of some sort and the most refined of all my roommates. He got a big job at the Cincinnati Milling Machine Company and later presented me with a stereo system that he had built. That system was so professional that I used the speakers for the next 48 years. But no names for the others.

Finally, recalling the faces of my roommates, there was one thing they all had in common in exactly the same manner, they loved America. I liked that and was sincere in wondering when my next roommate would arrive. I knew he would not be the last.

HOLIDAYS

It was Thanksgiving and I had plans for the break but found myself unsettled. I wanted to know why I was so different from those at school. No question I was different. I didn't think like those around me, heck, I didn't do anything like those around me. So, instead of enjoying my plans, I spent the Thanksgiving break trying to figure things out. I never had problems being different and there were countless examples of my difference.

For most other kids, summer vacation meant they didn't have to go to school. For me summer vacation meant I didn't get to go to school. My schools were generally better than where we lived. Summer vacation for most others meant they were free to do whatever they desired, time to have fun. Since I didn't get an allowance, summer was the time to make money and put aside funds for school. Specifically, enough aside so that I could act like the other kids during school.

The other kids were American and thought and acted accordingly. I was American but was reared Serbian. I needed school to continue assimilating Americana, which was the key to my future.

During school, most guys didn't think about classes too much. I did. Learning gave me a sense of accomplishment and more importantly, being able to learn with Americans gave me optimism that I could become Americanized. For those around me, the other kids and maybe the adults, school opening was an event but certainly not the biggest of the year. For me, except for tennis, school opening was the biggest event of the year. I could stop working, resume my education, refocus my study of Americana, and I got presents. Neat things like a new notebook, clothes, pencils, or gym shoes.

Thanksgiving was another example of my being different. For me, Thanksgiving was the Westwood food drive, puppet show, pilgrim's pageant, and a family get together for a nice big turkey dinner. That was not what I saw and heard from others. Others didn't see Thanksgiving as an independent event, or two days off school, or a four-day break, or a celebration of a wonderful tradition, or all of the above. For others, Thanksgiving was a holiday, a part of The Holidays.

The Holidays was an entire category in the lives of others. They planned for them, often long in advance, and did all kinds of things, usually with their families. The Holidays could start anytime. Like a circle, they had no beginning or end, they were there all year. After Thanksgiving came Christmas, New Year's Eve, New Year's Day, President's Day, Easter, Memorial Day, Summer Vacation, and Summer Vacation had two holidays in it, The Fourth of July and Labor Day. I hadn't caught my breath when I learned that Summer Vacation was more than being off school, it was for going somewhere, doing something, usually for one to two weeks. This must cost a fortune. I was very sure we could never afford The Holidays part of Americana.

Okay, that's how others did it, but what about us? I reflected on my holiday experiences starting with The Peniel Missionary Assembly. The year looked like this from the back of our church.

We did not celebrate Thanksgiving. Thanksgiving was not a holiday; giving and being thankful was what it was like every service every week.

We did celebrate Christmas. The birth of Jesus. The arrival of Our Forgiveness. Mankind's Loophole from that moment to this and all the moments to follow. I loved Christmas. The congregations during Christmas at our church brought to life the meaning of hope, peace, love. I was blessed to grow up among people who had almost nothing to hope for, people who were unfamiliar with peace, people who escaped hate and as a result saw a good life as an absence of hate rather than the presence of love. Watching such brothers and sisters rejoice at Christmas, give of themselves, love others, and be at peace, made Christmas the best times of my life.

Easter was the holiest and most serious time at The Peniel Missionary Assembly. Easter was lilies from Brother Neville's generosity, I never knew an Easter without his flowers carpeting the altar. I loved standing on the stoop holding the church door open and sharing with brothers and sisters, "Christ has risen." "Verily, He has risen." This was another time being bilingual was a blessing. I may have been wrong, but I thought each attendee got an inner smile sharing the exchange in their language. Even though the gift we had been given deserved eternal celebrating, I didn't feel Easter to be a celebration as much as a reminder of the huge responsibility that came with Christ's sacrifice.

Well, that was our Peniel Missionary Assembly version of The Holidays and—can you believe it—the end of my Thanksgiving break. I decided I would have to live with the fact I was different regarding Thanksgiving and The Holidays.

The next morning, I was back at school and my routines, bus to school, bus home, chores, homework, accordion, but no tennis, the weather was deep fall. Fine, but this was on the surface, there was something else. Others had their way about The Holidays, and we had our church way, but I had my private way. A way which began in the second grade, came in small doses, was delivered by Aunt Rosie, and kept growing. A secular way that I kept undercover.

When I was in the second grade, Aunt Rosie took me Christmas shopping. It was winter and very cold, but perfect to me because I had never been Christmas shopping before. Actually, I had never been shopping like it went with Aunt Rosie. With Olga and George, shopping was finding the best deal on a specific thing I needed. With Aunt Rosie, shopping was looking around and, this was unbelievable to me, considering not what was the best deal but what would I like to get for someone. The decorations in the stores flabbergasted me. Closing my eyes I see the crowds, elevators with operators dressed up like Christmas characters, stores knee-deep with wonders, and Rosie bundling us along. And I hear that swooosih of a capsule flying through the overhead tubes full of orders for presents. Shopping with Aunt Rosie became a tradition I loved.

From my spot as a seventh grader, I had to admit Christmas presents were a big thing to me, underwear, socks, shoes, clothes, and all brand new! But back in the fourth grade, in addition to things to wear, Rosie and Lou gave me a baseball glove and ball. A rubber ball that looked just like a real hardball. It was perfect for throwing against our bricks and then running to catch the flies. From then on, not only would I get new clothes, but Rosie and Lou would get me something special. I wore out the Lone Ranger's silver six shooters in the looked-like-leather-to-me black holsters.

This undercover way of celebrating was to continue to high

school and beyond. As an example, Olga and George never decorated. In the beginning they couldn't afford it and later that was just the way it was. Sometime in High School, the day after Christmas I went to Walgreen's and bought a tree stand, two light strands and all the ornaments left. The next year I got a tree and while Olga and George were out, decorated the place. They didn't say a word when they got home. I said, "Merry Christmas." Until I left for the Army, I did the same thing every year. The ornaments were four inches in diameter and metallic pinks, golds, blues, and greens. Eight survived and go on our tree every year.

It was a warm feeling thinking about my secret secular way of Christmas, when the phone rang. It was Rosie asking if I wanted to go shopping Saturday. Only then did I realize the Christmas break was upon me and tomorrow was my last day of school

Christmas came and went so fast it was a blur, but I made a point of focusing on how the Vukich family celebrated the event. In so doing, I reflected on how we celebrated The Holidays in general.

Thanksgiving was supposed to be observed at the Botts. It was difficult to go to the home of Uncle Charlie and his second wife until they moved to the farm. This difficulty was not the modest size of their house, the excuse they offered and all accepted, the difficulty was the proximity of her parents who had no use for foreigners. Once the Botts moved, the location was physically comfortable, but the atmosphere was not. Thanksgiving was at the Botts because it was expected to be there, not because it was welcomed.

Christmas was at the Golusin's and you couldn't find a better setting. Old three-story house that made you think of Dickens. Don's train set running round a huge tree in the bay window area of the dining room. A table, big enough so everyone would sit together, in front of the blazing five-foot-wide fireplace with all kinds of grand food and take as much as you want.

There was nothing special about New Year's Eve, but New Year's Eve Day was another matter. It was set aside for the making of the chasnitza and the general preparation for the next day...year.

New Year's Day was at the Bakers. The men standing around in the kitchen drinking shots of Four Roses while stealing fat off the duck. The women finding ways to serve the feast in that tiny kitchen. It made me think of how The Botts house was plenty big, it was their hearts that were of modest size. Lou asleep on the couch while TV football occupied the eyes and ears.

Once we were settled on Daytona, Easter was at the Marksity's, where Olga made us recognize every ceremony and tradition from the Bible, America, Serbian Orthodoxy, and her imagination. It was not imagination to dive into the feast.

In our family, the tutza (toot-za) of hard-boiled eggs was a true Easter event. Everyone made hard-boiled eggs and decorated them as they wished, but the key was to try and get the hardest egg. To tutza, one holds his egg in his fist and another hits it with his egg. Whichever egg cracks goes to him that cracked it. Who held and how to hold, and who hit and how to hit, and how often and where to hit, and was it cracked and...there was no end to the machinations, but in the end, some had no eggs and some had more than enough. The competitiveness of the clan was evidenced in this tradition and became a legend the Easter Uncle Lou decorated an egg-shaped rock and cracked up everybody.

So that was it. The family didn't observe any other holidays. Yeah, Rosie and Lou had gone to Yugoslavia once or twice, but those trips were more as duties to the "old country" than for holiday. I was glad I was no longer unsettled and set out to enjoy the rest of The Holiday.

1956: SECOND HALF OF THE 7TH GRADE

I came to think of the Thanksgiving, Christmas, and New Year that just passed as The Season of the Family. Over the past five weeks I had watched, listened, and formed my own opinions of my relatives and how I would relate to each. This gave me a sort of confidence and I headed back to school ready to continue absorbing Americana.

January and February were cold, gray, and white, like winter should be and I was comfortable in my routine. Bus to school, bus home, chores, a new roommate, homework, the accordion, and Duke. Life was grand, plus spring was coming and bringing tennis.

It was early March and my temporary roommate had already moved out as he had been placed in both a job and flat. Duke and I were walking when we heard a car turn onto the street we were approaching. The tires and engine seemed to be screaming, got louder as the car accelerated and kept getting louder until THUD...then nothing but the horn blaring. I ran to the corner and saw the car four houses up on the left. As I got closer, I saw that the car was wrapped around a tree and, once there, was surprised that the driver, who was stuck behind the wheel, was smiling, and seemed fine. I asked him if he was okay and then there were other people and Duke and I stepped aside. The other people were unanimously angry with the driver, as were the Police when they arrived. As we headed home, I couldn't figure out the driver's behavior or attitude. I was scared from hearing the accident and seeing the tree in the middle of his hood. But he was unusually happy and not at all concerned, as if he was surprised to be getting so much attention while people worked to get him out.

April was around the corner, tennis was about to start, and I was in high cotton wondering if I could actually make the tennis team as Coach Otten had prophesied. Such were my thoughts the day my bike hit a spot of sand and sent me flying until, like the car, I hit with a thud. There was a sharp-edged lump under the skin of my left forearm which was very red. At home, Olga and George agreed it was broken and, as you know our beliefs, prayed for healing. I joined and added private thanks that it was not my tennis arm. They made a sling and we waited. The next day it was past dark red and on the way to purple. Over the next day and a half, it went a little green and kept getting darker until it was black. It was the afternoon of the day it turned black that Danny and Lucille Krison, from Detroit, rang our doorbell.

As I heard Olga welcome them, I got uneasy. We had been to Detroit for church related work and to visit relatives so often that when I heard Detroit I saw Nine Mile Road, a thoroughfare where Slavs sat on their ample front porches and watched the world across the few feet of their front lawns. Behind these houses were an alley and yards and trees and stand-alone garages.

During the Detroit visits, the religious experiences had been wonderful while the relatives made me uneasy.

Genealogy was not our family's strong suit. Who came from where by whom depended on the speaker. Each speaker had his or her version which they tended to change for no reason. Nonetheless, I tried to produce a family tree and over the years of visits to Detroit I saw constant mutation.

It started, when from out of the blue came Grozda and Melorad Krison. She was introduced as my "aunt," but her husband Melorad was not introduced as my "uncle." Next came a phalanx of Slavs who were relatives for reasons I didn't understand with titles I couldn't fathom. So help me, there was a name for someone who married the second cousin of a third brother of a good friend. Later, Melorad was identified as not Grozda's first husband and then Danny was introduced as their son and my "uncle", until his wife Lucille was introduced as my "aunt" and Danny became my "cousin." At one point in this I became Grozda's "half nephew" and Melorad's visitor. Then it got complicated.

Everyone knew George was an orphan, but in Detroit he introduced Grozda as his sister, no wait, he made an adjustment, she was his half-sister. She and my father had the same mother but different fathers. No, wait again, they had the same father but different mothers. Finally, one year George concluded they definitely had the same father. Fine, however that didn't address the fact that Danny and Lucille were not called nephew and niece. Nor did any of this prepare me for the next several years during which I was to meet George's half-brother Wally, who was about a foot taller than George and my "half-uncle." Wally was Grozda's half-brother as they had the same father but different mothers. So the three "halfs" had different mothers but the same father. Finally, again from out of nowhere, came my father's much older "Uncle George" and his umpteenth wife Cookie and how I related to them was never discussed.

Such were my "relatives" in Detroit and, frustrated, I decided this was just one of those Serbian Things no one would explain. I gave up on Serbian Thing after the following. Olga took me with her as she ministered at an orphanage, and I learned that orphans were children with no relatives. I asked a worker if I had heard right, and he explained that the definition of orphan was no relatives. This didn't fit my experience, so on the way home I asked Olga how George could be an orphan and yet have relatives. She gave me her song and dance that meant she wasn't going to answer. I never did learn the answer from Olga or George, I learned the answer from The U.S. Government while I was teaching at USAINTS but that comes later. For now, I was pulled back into the present as Danny and Lucille were ushered into our house and I realized I still wasn't sure what to call them. So, I just said "Hi".

They said "Hi" back and seeing my sling looked at my arm. Olga had no chance to protest and George no time to support her as my uncle cousin half-uncle half-cousin and aunt cousin, loaded me into the car and we went directly to the hospital. The doctors were none too pleased with the condition of my arm and shared their displeasure before aligning and setting it.

I felt much better on the way home from the hospital and settled in the back seat, looked at my benefactors. As it had been the first time I saw her in Detroit, one look at Lucille and I was a goner. She was not dark or Yugoslavian or any other 'slavian, she was an American blonde, a gorgeous American blonde. Tall, she was taller than Danny and taller than my other relatives. Different, one time she made something called a taco which by Serbian standards was a lot of work with not much result, but I didn't care, Aunt Lucille was a beautiful maiden, and I had a crush on her from day one.

Danny was dark, square, hairy, and loud. He was constantly in motion and nothing like any of my uncles or cousins. He was open and seemed to be having fun all the time, to really be enjoying life. In addition to his view of living, he showed me other new things. The neighbor boy with the comic book collection that almost filled his basement. Fast pitch softball and how to be a player, coach, manager, and promoter of the league, Danny was tireless. He worked for FORD in a great job and on one of our visits set up a tour of the assembly plant, which remains one of the most memorable experiences of my young life. But I felt something undercover that made me not quite believe everything he said. I figured it could be his being so different from my relatives in Cincinnati who took themselves seriously and expected to be taken seriously, while Danny Krison didn't take himself seriously. To his credit, he treated me like an equal, despite the vast difference in our ages. But, to my discredit, I couldn't find the way to comfortably like him. No mater, he liked him enough for both of us.

I snapped out of my reverie when we got home but promised myself that during their visit, I would study Danny and Lucille. We had spent some time together and I knew some of their characteristics, but now I wanted more. So, I took an undercover perspective and made sure they wouldn't know I was studying them. Everything I saw merely emphasized the way they had always been in my eyes.

I had never seen a couple like them. They were constantly aware of each other and subtle in consistently displaying affection such as brushing against each other, holding hands, hugging, and even kissing. This was their norm and was reflected in how they ate, drank, conversed, and did things or did nothing together. I came to understand that Danny and Lucille were in love and their interaction was my first example of such a thing.

They shopped in a manner beyond my imagination. Shopping was not just for need; shopping was an activity that might be undertaken at any time and just for fun. Once out, if Danny decided he wanted something, he bought it. If Lucille thought it might be nice to try something, she bought it. Neither weighed the options for doing without or getting a substitute or deciding because of price.

They treated me in a completely unique fashion, they treated me as if I were something special…special just because I was a kid. They never considered me an adult and from the first time we met until now, with me in the seventh grade, their idea of what it meant to be a kid was all to my benefit, and wonder. They questioned me and then Olga and George. Why did I have so many chores? How come I didn't get an allowance? They were aware of Olga and George taking people in and admired them for doing so, but why wasn't room made available for the Displaced Personnel in the basement? Why did I have to share my room? They enjoyed hearing me play the accordion they had given me but were flabbergasted that I was made to practice on the front porch. Did Olga think I was a side-show? What exactly did Olga and George think? How could they have let my arm turn black and not do something? Where did they find a dog that was part fox? Their questions reflected their ideas about kids…kids were people.

Having the Krison's in the house for a few days was a unique dose of Americana and I wished they could have stayed longer. But they couldn't and the reason they couldn't bewildered me. They had not come to visit us; they had stopped to see us on their way West. They had sold their house and were moving from Detroit to a new home in Arizona. Not just a new home but an entirely new life. What could have motivated Danny to leave his great job with FORD and his roots in Detroit and move, sight unseen, to Arizona? The following is how I understood what he told us.

He had been working on a project team studying a new type of carburetor. In the recent past the project team had developed a carburetor system that would permit a car to get near 50 miles per gallon. For some reason I couldn't understand, FORD didn't want to build cars that could get near 50 miles per gallon. Danny and the other project team members were given lump sum bonuses on the conditions that they forgot the project, left Detroit, and never mentioned anything about this again. So, as Danny put it, this project was the reason his new life was being funded, it was the carburetor that made him rich.

I don't remember seeing the Krison's again, but over the years Olga kept me informed as they settled in Arizona where he established a successful insurance practice and they lived well, with a second home in the mountains and some children.

Today, Lucille remains the tall, beautiful blonde and Danny the hyperactive enigma and I realize I never had an adult conversation with either and wouldn't know them if we passed on the street. No matter, they will always be the people who gave me countless lessons on Americana and the couple God used to heal my arm.

As for the arm, from the moment the bike hit the pavement, I knew I would be taken care of. The fact I was taken care of in this roundabout way merely confirmed my faith. The arm healed perfectly but there was no audition for any tennis team. However, Mr. Otten earned my loyalty when he allowed me to hit with some players even though I had the cast and couldn't serve. And then BANG...Summer was outside, and I had successfully completed the Seventh Grade at Western Hills High School.

SUMMER SQUIRREL

As the seventh grade ended, it hit me that I was out of work! I had to find a way to make money, enough money to fund me through the eighth grade. I let everyone know I was looking for work and several neighbors offered me odd jobs, I like to think it was because of my work as their paperboy. When Uncle Lou offered me the job of cutting his grass, I had a good start.

One odd job was helping some of the neighborhood do-it-yourselfers as a go-fer. It turned out that I had a special talent, holding a light. With Uncle Charlie I learned to shine the light on the work spot, not just in the general direction of the work. One man said my helper-ship was grounds for me to strike out on my own. Doing what? He was sure I'd think of something. I was sure it was amazing that people would pay me to hold a light and be a go-fer.

A few weeks passed and I wasn't making enough money. I didn't know what I was going to do when along came Olga's friend Vi Todorov, who knew I loved books. She subscribed to Reader's Digest Condensed Books and on this day wondered if I wanted the one she had just finished. I was elated and she gave me four more. They were all the same size and had looks-like-leather binding on the spine. I knew they would look classy on bookshelves so, money aside, I decided to build a setting for my books.

Great, now how do I build bookshelves? Easy, I go to the hardware store. It was 1956, our neighborhood was open, safe, and self-sufficient. I never had a key to our house because we never locked the doors. We had a milkman, breadman, and a man who came to sharpen our knives. Within walking distance, we had Westwood Elementary, a savings and loan, library, grocery store, gas station, drug store, bakery, barber shops, several streetcar stops and the hardware store which was run by Sally and Milt, who I knew would help me. They were patient and understood my need to do everything as cheaply as possible. They set me up with the materials and directions for making my bookshelves.

It was hard because George didn't have good tools while Olga had opinions. She made me paint the bookshelves light blue, to match the walls of my room because we had light blue paint and paint cost money and not using paint we had while spending money on new paint was…blah blah blah…In the end, light blue or no, my little library was standing proud.

I went to the hardware store to return things I hadn't used and everything since Vi Todorov gave me her book came together. I noticed the rows of numbers, 0 to 9 made in all types of styles and materials. I asked Milt what the numbers were for. He explained several uses, including house numbering. What? People made signs to show their addresses. Sure enough. Did Milt and Sally think people would pay for a handmade sign? Oh definitely. The rest was easy.

Building the bookshelves had introduced me to pine boards and gave me experience with saws and screws. Among George's tools I found an old wood-burning set and the results were 1 x 6 x 10-inch street number signs that had fancy zig-zag cuts on the ends, wood-burned accents, four inch reflecting numbers and were fastened to a stake to be driven into the ground. When I showed them to Milt and Sally, they agreed that I could sell them to all the homes in Cincinnati. Okay, maybe not all but a bunch. With the odd jobs, grass cutting, and signs, I squirreled enough away for the eighth grade and some extra for my undercover savings account at the Westwood Homestead Savings and Loan. I kept this account from Olga and George, I didn't want them borrowing for the needy.

Incidentally, over the years Vi Todorov lined my library with rows of looks-like-leather volumes. I like to believe it was more than coincidence that she married Steve Sverchev, the temporary roommate who made my stereo system. In fact, I fantasized that they found each other as a reward for their generosity toward me. Finally, I must admit that after I read one of the books in the first volume Vi gave me and realized what condensed meant, I never read another. But I was grateful for her volumes and those looks-like-leather spines on my light blue bookshelves were a library to me, my library.

For the rest of the summer, my routine was chores, jobs, and tennis, without the cast. Life was grand, and then I got the letter. Actually, the letter was addressed to George and Olga but as soon as they saw it was from The Cincinnati Public Schools, they gave it to me. As I read it, I was back at West High near the end of the seventh grade when I couldn't understand what was going on. For months, time was spent on rumors and discussions about some big announcement. It never came, until now. I was not going back to Western Hills High; I was going to Gamble Junior High. Life was grander.

Not too long after receiving the letter, I made myself remember my first days at West High. I would not repeat that experience. Instead, I would be familiar with my new school way before the first day of class.

It took a few bike trips, but I finally found Gamble Nippert Junior High and the moment is etched in my brain. Having left busy Montana Avenue, I rode through a quiet residential side street, cleared a rise, and experienced Arthur holding Excalibur and The Pilgrims sighting land. The golden bricked vision flowed over the expanse of hilly terrain making it difficult to determine if the ground or the building was there first. The classrooms, offices, and auditorium were supported by land on both ends and a gymnasium and lunchroom in the middle…and…Gamble wasn't my new school; it was a new school. Brand spanking new!

During subsequent trips I learned Gamble Nippert abutted The Westwood Commons, a huge recreational complex with baseball fields, tennis courts, swimming pool, playground, and picnic areas. I learned there would be no ninth graders as the place needed fine tuning and our class would do that, thank us very much. We would be the senior class for the next two years. I found all the ways for getting there and back and unlike West High, I could walk, or bike, and a bus would be a waste of time and money. I walked the tennis courts to let them know I was coming and by the first day of class, going to Gamble was like going to play with an old friend.

GAMBLE NIPPERT JUNIOR HIGH SCHOOL

During the opening convocation, reference was made to some company called P&G which stood for Procter and Gamble and Nippert was someone, I wasn't sure who, but whoever they were, some very nice people had built a palace for our school.

It's as hard to describe as it was to experience, everything was new. New bricks, windows, floors, doors, sidewalks, walls, rooms...every place and everything had never been used. And everything was not just new, it was the best of the new. Big desks where you could relax in the rounded backs of chairs that swiveled and whose tops pulled up to hold your gear. Desks without even one stain, carving, or missing chip. Smells, people get all twitchy over the smell of a new car, imagine the smells in and around our new palace. Hall lockers with no dings, dents, scratches, missing hooks, or broken shelves. For awhile, every time you used something, it was the first time that something was used. The books were the best editions, and you turned each page for the first time. Everything worked and I honestly can't remember anything that needed fine tuning.

The palace may not have required fine tuning, but there was still plenty our class had to do. Pick the school colors. Agree what we would call ourselves, and then pick the uniforms for each sport. Develop songs for ceremony and competition. Decide on the mandate and design for a school newspaper. Determine student government activities, establish criteria for our Gamble Annual, and more. First, we got a new palace and then we got to pick everything for us to live in it, everything for us and every class that would follow.

As for me, last year's habit of bus to school then bus to home and no involvement, was replaced by total submergence. This started immediately after my class schedule was finalized and tryouts for the nonexistent football team were announced.

MR. CHEESEMAN AND MR. SCHMALFUSS

Mr. Cheeseman and Mr. Schmalfuss greeted those of us who were trying out for football, behind the school at the base of the path to The Commons. We were told what they would expect from us and what we could expect from them. It seemed they wanted to scare us, but I couldn't feel anything but excitement.

The next day I had my papers signed and my gym gear on as we met again behind the school. Once we were assembled and the paperwork collected, Mr. Cheeseman and Mr. Schmalfuss led us up the path. When we reached the top, we found that the outfields of baseball diamonds two and three had been converted into a football field with goal posts, line markings, and even some bleachers, this was going to be our home field.

Mr. Schmalfuss announced, "Now, let's see which of you will play on this field. Laps around the diamonds start that way." Once moving it was fun and then Halas ran by me and said, "Come on Marks, a chain is only as strong as its weakest link." Everyone within earshot was familiar with his phrase and cheered us on.

Not only was I not familiar with his phrase I had never played football. I had never even been to a football game. The only exposure I had to football was the TV time at Uncles Lou's on holidays.

I needn't have worried. While my contemporaries had learned from their fathers, older brothers, uncles, and cousins, I learned from Mr. Cheeseman and Mr. Schmalfuss. To this day I practice the warmups, calisthenics, and flexibility exercises they introduced. They taught me everything from the names of each position to how both offense and defense function. Then they coached me on specific points of my position as I became the center because I had quick feet and could pull to block.

I was very happy I made the team but what came next was better, that's when we Gamble Warriors got our brand-new equipment and scarlet and gray uniforms. Every single item I put on was directly from out of the box. As we headed to the field, I knew I was wearing the best clothes I had ever worn. From the first we played with heart and hope but we were only seventh and eighth graders. Some of the opponent's ninth graders bewildered us, but with the coaches we had, I knew we would just get better.

Of course, from day one I kept my little secret undercover. The secret of how I didn't swim in grade school and spent the entire seventh grade showering without anyone seeing me. Somehow Mr. Cheeseman and Mr. Schmalfuss understood my situation. Almost as if they knew that living with the Matriarch and the Reverends had made me extremely shy about my body and embarrassed with the bodies of others. They broached the matter of my self consciousness and soon after football started, I was taking showers like everybody else.

During my two years at Gamble, Mr. Cheeseman and Mr.

Schmalfuss played the roles of my American father, uncles, cousins, mentors, and opened my life to the joy and wonders of sports beyond tennis. They changed my life and remain the criteria I use for evaluating any coach.

THE EIGHTH GRADE

Not too long after football season started, the music teacher pulled me aside and suggested I try out for the choir that was being formed. I couldn't relate to this idea but took it as a compliment. After some thought I decided to give it a try, what did I have to lose? Me in a choir, ha. They must have needed bodies because I made the choir, some sort of tenor. We practiced regularly and in some ways it was easier than football practice and in some ways it was harder. There were a bunch of girls in the choir.

Football season was ending and tryouts for basketball were announced. It seemed the football team was going to morph into the basketball team as most of us on the football team tried out. I made the team as a backup guard, way backup. I also, once again, got to unpack my spanking new uniform. The scarlet with gray trim was dynamite. I even bought myself a pair of basketball shoes, high tops, but not Converse, those were out of my price range.

Thanksgiving was dead ahead, and a lot of time was devoted to how Gamble would celebrate. I pushed for the puppets like at Westwood Elementary but got shot down, the majority felt puppets were too baby-like. The Thanksgiving Program we presented was a success, the choir sounded good, and we got food to the less fortunate.

I had a temporary roommate for a time after Thanksgiving. To be honest, I was so busy at Gamble I hardly even spoke with him. It would be more honest to say, I was so busy I didn't notice him. Anyway, he was successfully placed, and I was glad for that.

From the first days at West High, I kept my accordion playing undercover, but somehow the Gamble music teacher found out I played. He felt an accordion would be a nifty addition to a dance band he was putting together. I was surprised with how easily I said I'd give it a try. He gave me some music and explained we would start after the holidays, I explained I would start practicing now.

Over Christmas, Baba and I were together more than we had been for some time. I used the opportunity to reflect on The Matriarch and recalled how by the time we moved to Daytona, she no longer was The Matriarch. She hadn't relinquished her position or lost it to a coup, she provided leadership as the best leaders do — until the followers can lead themselves. A few years after we moved to Daytona, Baba started staying with her other children, but mostly she stayed with us.

The Holidays were one big vacation, time without requirements, but I was just as happy going back to Gamble and just enough time for all the requirements.

As the eighth-grade winter rushed by, I came to realize I had stopped my study of Americana. It had been wonderful to learn, digest, and assimilate Americana by watching those around me be themselves, but now I felt I was American enough to be myself.

Choir, dance band, and tennis filled the days of classes which were going fine, particularly gym. When Coaches Cheeseman and Schmalfuss started us through the track and field events, my lack of knowledge or experience was very evident. When they were done, I had an understanding and appreciation of track and field events and athletes.

Unlike football or track and field, I was confident in tennis and thought nothing of the fact our first team included a girl. With tennis, Mr. Cheeseman coached me very specifically. He noticed that when I hit my backhand, I was twisting my head toward the ball to the point of disturbing the stroke. He suggested I go to an eye doctor. It was the right suggestion, my first ever visit to an eye doctor revealed that my right eye was lazy, 20/400, and I was twisting my head so I could see the ball with my 20/10 left eye. The correction was for me to wear glasses and a patch over the left eye to force the right eye to work. I put up with that rig for almost three weeks after which I used the glasses and pitched the patch. On the court, I adapted the position of my feet for the backhand stroke to compensate for twisting my head.

It had to be mid-May because Tommy from California was at the door. When he came it was only at this time of year and he stayed with Baba Mitza and Elia. I found this odd because he didn't speak Serbian and they spoke little American. During past visits we spent some time together but this year I was ready for more. I wanted some clarity about our mutated family tree.

He was one or two years older, and we had originally been introduced as cousins. Why? Because Baba Mitza was the "sort of Aunt" my father George, the orphan, came to see when he arrived in America and she and Elia lived down the street, however we didn't associate with them. Well, that sure made us cousins.

It wasn't clear if Mitza and Elia were married, and neither was it clear whether they were Tommy's grandparents or aunt and uncle. That wasn't clear because their relationship with Bill

Vukovich wasn't clear. Were they his parents, aunt and uncle, or something else?

Bill Vukovich was a famous race car driver who brought Tommy with him for the Memorial Day Indianapolis 500. Tommy's mother was in divorce limbo and Tommy never made it clear if Vukovich was his father or uncle or something else. I never believed I knew Tommy's real last name.

Having achieved this level of clarity we did other things together, things I never imagined doing. He'd lead us to places I was too timid to go, like expensive stores and places we weren't supposed to go, like construction sites. The fact we weren't supposed to be someplace was the very thing that made him go there. Nothing mattered to him, nothing inhibited him, he was a daredevil.

He had special experiences starting with being on the race circuit and around the cars, he had even done some laps at Indy. He lived in California, but on the circuit, he stayed with relatives or friends, like Baba Mitza and Elia, or by himself. He found it normal that his parents were divorced but hated the amount of time he had to spend alone. I loved being alone, but Tommy had to have constant contact and attention. It wasn't clear if he had been in jail or juvenile detention, but that's where he became an avid reader. He gave me his paperback set of THE WORLD'S GREATEST BOOKS and I gave him my undivided attention.

It was a good visit, but I knew it would be our last. If I stuck with him the chances of getting into trouble were 100 percent. There was a sadness about him, his life was exotic but also migratory, running from one not-quite-his-home to another. It was too bad we couldn't solve the ambiguous mess that was our family tree, if we were actually related that is. I don't remember seeing him again.

At Gamble, things were winding down and I focused on making money over the coming summer. I had street number signs to sell, a few odd jobs, and Uncle Lou's grass to cut, but it wasn't enough. While ordering sign materials from Milt and Sally, I told them I needed a job. When I went to pick up my order they had some news, their brother was willing to interview me about some work.

Sally, Milt, and Howard owned the Sunoco gas station on the corner of Glenmore and Montana and run by Howard. They owned the house next door where they lived together, and they owned the hardware store next to the house. They were The Schneider's, and this was their empire, but they acted more like workers than rulers. They were honest, kind, sincere, and helpful to anyone and everyone. I never understood why none ever married, they would have been the best of parents. As it was, the three of them were inseparable and provided service and integrity to the neighborhood.

I believe that Howard hiring me was a done deal because of the recommendation from Sally and Milt. He said he could use me Saturdays as a general helper. That seemed like a step up from go-fer and I was thankful. Thankful grew when he explained it could be for up to twelve hours some Saturdays. Thankful exploded when he said I could start this coming Saturday, there were still two weeks of school. But when he told me the hourly wage I'd earn, Eureka — summer was set! That Saturday was the start of eight years of employment with Howard, who was a tutor who trusted me from day one and more a friend than a boss. Our friendship lasted way beyond eight years.

THE OTHER EIGHTH GRADE

It was warm the September day I saw them. I was sure they weren't teachers; they were dressed too well in dark suits with ties and white shirts. The coaches seemed comfortable with them, so I was too.

They waited until what we were doing was over and then called me by name. I responded and they motioned for us to meet. As the rest of the team and coaches left for the showers, I left to meet them.

They didn't give me their names. They did give me questions. Are you Ronald Marksity? Is your grandmother Maria Vukich? Are you a student here at Gamble Junior High? Are your parents George and Olga? Do your parents run the Peniel Missionary Assembly on McMicken Avenue?

I answered as I would to any adults. Unlike any adults I was used to, they were indifferent to my sincerity to answer as best I could.

They asked more questions, but I didn't answer, not because I was afraid, but because I was hurt. If these strangers were not going to give me credit for answering their questions, I would not answer any more of their questions. As I headed for the locker room and showers, they headed for wherever it was they had come from.

The second contact was a while later. I remember this visit very clearly because they contacted me at home when no one else was there. I was playing fantasy baseball in our driveway beside the house. This game involved bouncing a rubber baseball off the bricks and trying to catch it cleanly. I didn't see them at first. But finally, I noticed them standing in the driveway. It was the same two suits. They maneuvered me to the backyard and suggested I sit on the back porch steps.

I don't remember their approach verbatim but do remember the message. "Young man you're quite the tennis player. It would be a shame if you couldn't play anymore. It would be a shame if you had to leave this area and live in a foster home. It would be a shame if your parents had to be deported. It would be a shame if your parents had to go to jail. It would be a shame…"…They continued cataloguing an endless possibility of shames awaiting me.

After they were satisfied they had my attention, they made their pitch. "Your parents are assisting and harboring known enemy collaborators. They are using their church as a cover. If you want your parents to stay out of jail and the three of you to stay together, you are going to have to work for us. Who "us" was, seemed to be a secret. It was no secret that these two suits were serious.

I listened, heard them out, and didn't say a word. What word could I think to say?

They looked at me as if inspecting an insect and concluded, "Think about what we've told you. We will be in contact." They turned and again headed for wherever it was they had come from.

If you're waiting for my reaction, don't. I had no reaction. It was all beyond me.

Weeks passed. This time there was only one suit. White shirt and tie. I knew he was one of the "us" the first two had been referring to. He too came when I was alone. But his approach was different. Oh, so different.

"Hello Ron. Yes, I'm with the first two who visited you. But we're all not the same."

I didn't say a thing but couldn't avoid giving him a look. He didn't miss it.

"Okay, we dress alike but that's only on the outside. What's the game?"

I explained my fantasy baseball. He wanted to watch. I didn't want to play just then.

He asked if we could talk somewhere. I said sure, and he asked where I would be most comfortable.

"Anywhere."

"Fine, let's sit here."... and he sat down in the grass that separated the two strips of concrete that were our driveway, in his suit, with his white shirt and tie.

He told me his name. He said he was with the Federal Bureau of Investigation.

"Yes, the FBI."

The other two were also FBI. He was apologetic about their manners and hoped I could overlook them and deal with him. He put me at ease. He wanted us to talk because that was the only way we could get anywhere that would be mutually beneficial. He was sincere. He did not look at me as if inspecting an insect. He looked at me as if I could help him—and that was the hook.

I could help him. I could help my parents. I could help The

FBI. I could help my country. I could help myself. And all I had to do was go undercover.

It was 1956. I was 13 and in the eighth grade.

UNDERCOVER

When we met for our chat, he set the tone and got us started.

"So, we both think you could help me out. Good. You know we're in this together."

I wasn't so sure but didn't feel the need to say so. He went on.

"There's really nothing to it. You just kind of keep your eyes and ears open. See who comes and goes. Remember if you hear anything that sounds interesting. Just anything. Don't worry about what it means, if it sounds interesting, remember it. You don't have to get everything perfect so there's no need to ever write anything down. Just trust your feelings and your memory.

"Anyway, all you're really doing is keeping your wits about you and taking in what's going on around you. Then, occasionally, we'll sit down and have a session. You can tell me all you've been remembering and that's the way we'll get this mess all straightened out."

***

This was the start of our sessions. The places where we met are vague in my memory, but the atmospheres are crystal clear. Daytime, always in the open. Calm. Seemingly cool, regardless it was summer. Quiet. Seemingly warm, regardless it was winter.

* * *

No matter where we met, these first sit-downs were very general. We talked casually about Baba, Olga, George, and other family members, covering backgrounds and what they were like. We reviewed The Peniel Missionary Assembly and its relationship with the community. We just talked.

* * *

As time passed, I saw he had a gift for asking questions. The gift was making me think he asked because he was interested in what I had to say and not for another purpose.

"So, your parents have been taking in boarders? Oh, not boarders because they didn't—yes, couldn't—pay any rent. So these people, you know to call them DP, as Displaced Person, very good and accurate. So various people, displaced from Eastern Europe, have been staying, on and off, with your parents. Oh, not with them, in fact they stayed with you, in your room. Nice of you to share your room with a stranger, or various strangers. Go on." And on I would go.

* * *

Over the following months, in various increments, I told him my reality. He was a good listener. By demonstration, he taught me how much can be learned by listening.

"I see. Mr. Vukich. Interesting story. But you don't know how long he was in the concentration camp?"

"You pronounce it Sphere-chev? I don't think I'd ever get that language down."

"Oh, so Mr. Vukich was actually a relative? Second cousin of a... You know I don't think I know the name for that relationship."

"And Mr. Sphere-chev was an expert with electronics."

"Were you ever afraid of any of these roommates? Really? Not just a little? I'm glad. A young man shouldn't be afraid in his own home. Nobody should."

"So, your parents helped most of these roommates get jobs. That is a very Christian thing to do. How did they manage that if you don't mind repeating?"

"Mr. Klajic. Another relative even harder than Mr. Vukich to line up with my knowledge of family trees. Played the guitar and mandolin. Great singing voice. Barber."

"So, several of your roommates ended up being employed by The Milling Machine Company? Did your parents have a contact there? That would be good to know, but don't bother about it just yet."

"And Mr. Klajic was a Serbian who met the lady he eventually married while he was a prisoner in Germany? She was a German. What a wonderful development. Imagine that."

So it went. Nothing dramatic. No pressure.

***

He was doing a great job of making me feel comfortable. He was doing a greater job of making me believe I was doing the right thing. Our meetings became part of my life's routine. All I had to do was keep my eyes and ears open. However, in that last session, did he say, "Oh, it's possible that something may come of this later, but not just now."

* * *

Our work continued and I learned he was a very good listener in a completely different way. By demonstration, he taught me how much can be said by listening. By listening he didn't make statements. The statements he didn't make were the most pregnant, foreboding what would obviously have to come. His listening forced me to fill in the blanks, anticipate, and be anxious. During this period, he taught me that letting the other person think up the possibilities, resulted in possibilities far worse than any I could concoct.

For now, let's talk, was enough. When would that change? When would I have to do something more? What would that something be? I could feel myself sinking into and becoming one with an entirely different way to live. I had always been a good watcher, Baba, my parents, and the church saw to that. Now, I was becoming a good listener. Soon, he would handle me into becoming a good reporter.

* * *

As he taught by demonstration and I learned by participation, our interaction evolved. Before the first year was up, I had developed a pattern for my work. After each of our sessions, I made a mental summary of everything I could remember. I let the data percolate. I played the session back. I relived it. Only then would I make my decisions. Decisions that became the plans for what

I would do, how, where, and when. I lived my plans and kept everything inside until our next session.

* * *

He was a good evaluator. He accepted both my successes and my failures. His recognition of both plus and minus fit my concept of how life should be lived. Had he only acknowledged the good or the bad things I did, he would have lost credibility in my mind. He was insistent that credibility was the life blood of our interactions.

* * *

However, make no mistake, ours was not a relationship. This was not a maturing cooperation. This was not the development of mutual respect based on working together. This was nothing but a Handler and his implement.

* * *

We never discussed anything personal...families, what I'd been doing, how are you feeling, how 'bout those Reds, what he'd been doing, Merry Christmas, it sure has been hot, nothing. Nothing went beyond Handler and implement and as the gardener's handling of the hoe makes the hoe work the soil, his handling of me made me proficient in security, never write anything down, need to know, it's not just what you say and who you say it to, it's how you say it, codes, how to contact, how to break contact, fall backs, covers, contingencies, and more. Much more.

One example typifies our work. He needed some phone numbers. I had already filled in that blank and had the numbers memorized. When we met, I was ready but didn't know how he would take the information. Just before I started reporting the numbers, he took out a small school style tablet and pencil. Not a leather note pad but a cardboard spiral. Not a pen that fit permanent notes but a simple short pencil with a used eraser. He flipped the cover back and announced we could go over the math I had been struggling with. As I recited the numbers, he turned them into a math problem. Later, as I reviewed his act, I had to smile. It really did make perfect sense to anyone watching, that the tutor would help his pupil and repeat very carefully the numbers of the problem.

* * *

As Handler and implement we were a secret, and I was very good at keeping secrets. He was very good at being a Handler. How good he was, was one of his secrets. He let me see his mastery little by little. How he did this was another of his secrets. He shared everything I needed, but only what I needed, at precisely the instant before I needed it. He was more than just a master handler, he was a virtuoso, who would make even this implement perform.

By this time, I realized that I had been right and wrong. Ours was not a relationship of friends or teammates, but it was a relationship. We had a working relationship that was very much alive and growing with the accumulation of experience and then — exactly as he predicted, "Oh, it's possible that something may come of this later, but not just now." Later was now.

He began stepping up our activity, very smoothly and in small increments, so that I might not notice. I noticed.

MR. STEVENS

It was the first day of the second year in Gamble Junior High's history and as ninth graders, we were still the senior class. I noticed the car because it looked new, even though it wasn't. I didn't remember it from last year, but whose ever it was really took care of it. When the driver got out, he was a new teacher, not from last year. As he went from his car to the building, anyone could just tell by the way he moved, he was a tough man. Tough and very strong. The guy was strong and tough and took care of his car, I liked that.

Later that first day, I entered a classroom and discovered he was going to be one of my teachers. His name was Mr. Stevens. I was excited and wanted to find out how a tough guy like him got into teaching junior high. He called the class to order and by the time the bell rang there was no question he was going to be in charge all year. I liked that.

I was right to be excited to be in his class. It was clear he knew his stuff and his knowledge of the subject constantly seemed to grow, the more we learned the more he knew. He was a good teacher. His classes were organized and easy to follow, his reviews filled in the blanks, his exercises demanding and when done right were rewarding. He was a good teacher who was hard and fair. I liked that.

I was not the only one who liked him. Mr. Stevens created a sense of commitment in our class, commitment to paying attention. No one talked about him or treated him as they did other teachers. An example was those who tended to be teacher's pets. The usual way to teacher's pet was to help the teacher with whatever might be needed. No one ever approached Mr. Stevens this way. It was very clear from the first time you met him, he didn't need any help and would not take kindly to being offered any. He seemed to be in a category all his own, tough, devoted to his job, and sincere to help us learn his subject.

My appreciation for him was increased more than a little by his car. I had noticed him because his car was an older model yet looked new. I don't remember seeing it dirty. As the year passed, I became familiar with his car. I liked cars and his was real exotic. The transmission could be operated by pushing buttons and the brake and gas—accelerator—could also be controlled by brake and gas handles near the steering wheel. I had never seen a set up like that before.

I found I watched him more than any other teacher I ever had. I also took every opportunity to talk with him outside of class. Over the year we talked a lot. He had a view of life and the work ethic that fit my Baba's, but he was American, male, and very educated. The most important thing about his philosophy, what drew me to him, was that we both believed people should do the best they can with what they have and that we are not all equal. Knowing Mr. Stevens helped me express a belief I had before I met him, a belief that has never left me. We deserve equal opportunity but are not equal. I was to meet few people who did as much with what they had or were equal to Mr. Stevens.

However, the thing about him that impressed me the most was his sensitivity. He was tough and competent alright, but he was also very human. Very strangely aware of what it was like to be a junior high girl, a ninth-grade boy. Somehow or other, he had never lost those perspectives and was able to relate to us better than any other teacher. He could show that he cared about how someone felt. More amazing, sometimes he showed that he actually felt how someone felt.

When the year was over, my time at Gamble was too. I wished that Mr. Stevens was going with me to West High, I may have been a little jealous that next year some other kids were going to be in his class while I'd be long gone. Anyway, nothing could take away what he taught me in and out of the classroom. I knew I would never forget him.

Oh, but I did forget to mention he had a disease as a youngster and was terribly crippled. He parked his specially equipped car next to an entrance door and hung his briefcase on a hook built on one of the two custom designed crutches he needed to move. I apologize to the reader for omitting this and to him for including it, he would take great exception to even the idea that his physical self should be mentioned.

As would all of us students. Kids can be mean and as a teacher Mr. Stevens presented two targets for cruel humor, but he was never targeted. He didn't get that type of treatment because he wasn't disfigured or crippled to himself, or to us. He just moved differently, physically slower than most, but mentally and emotionally he moved faster than most. He made us junior high kids do more than not mistreat him, he made us treat him as just another person.

I was taught to treat adults respectfully. Teachers, policemen, firemen, were special adults. Mr. Stevens was a special teacher. I didn't treat him respectfully because he was an adult or a teacher or even a special teacher. I treated him respectfully because I respected him. Mr. Stevens was one of my heroes. He still is.

SEPTEMBER 1957, THE NINTH GRADE

It was hard to believe we had been at Gamble last year because everything still looked new. English, Algebra, Biology, Latin, World Geography, Mechanical Drawing, and Phys Ed. were a nice load and enjoyable. Our football team improved while the choir and dance band started to sound like musicians. I worked Saturdays at the gas station, stopped cutting Uncle Lou's grass and dropped the street number signs, everybody who was going to buy one had one. As for the FBI, my Handler and I continued our meetings and my education. So, things were going smoothly until...

"It's a point of honor." That's what I was telling myself. Jimmy Wickman was a school mate from day one and his father was the coach of our Class C Knothole team, but on this day, he was treating some girl in a manner I didn't approve of, it's fitting I can't remember who or how, and I asked him to stop. When he said, "Make me." we agreed I'd try after school. By the end of school there was a mob waiting to see the spectacle.

It wasn't much of a spectacle unless you liked punishments.

George had taught me the techniques of The Marquis of Queensbury, while Jimmy's dad had taught him the bob-and-weave. So, I stood up straight with my fists in front of my face and Jimmy bounced around and beat on me from every-which-way, for a long time. I may not have had any training, but I did have a hard head. After considerable time, Floyd Knight, a classmate who was bigger than anyone and had the reputation of being a hard case, stepped between us and said, "Okay, you're not going to be able to knock him down and you're not going to be able to just keep bleeding, so let's call it over." And we did.

The mob broke up, Floyd said it looked like I'd be okay, but I'd probably have a scar over my left eye and suggested I wash off and go home. Riding my bicycle home, and bleeding all the way, the first thing I felt was embarrassment. Then I felt stupid, and the embarrassment magnified. Not stupid for losing but stupid for doing something I had already been taught never to do, fight. I learned that lesson in the playground on McMicken.

I kept it all from Olga and George by means of another bike accident. I wanted them to see I was trying to be upbeat, but I knew I was, "Lucky I didn't break my arm again."

Hum... They seemed to be spending a lot of time looking at the bike. Finally, George offered, "Yes, it is even more luck that your bike doesn't have a dent, not even a scratch."

"Well, I hit the concrete while RoadMaster landed in the grass." Hum... they're not done looking at the bike. They got to leave it alone.

"Will this blood come out of my shirt?" That did the trick and, "Of course. And out of your pants and the rest. Let's go downstairs to the washer..."

On the way to the basement, it hit me. Wait a minute. What just happened? Did it happen? It did. The Reverend Olga

Marksity can't read me anymore. This will take some getting used to!

It turned out Floyd was right; I was going to have a scar. I already had a scar from fighting for the honor of girls at Mary Whitehurst's birthday party when I got a mug stuck on my face. Stupid, embarrassed, scared but lucky, I didn't have a session with my Handler until I looked okay.

Thanksgiving came and the preparations, skits, songs, and collections for those in need created a good feeling that lingered into December.

With football finished, I was on to basketball. I was getting more playing time because the quick feet and hands of tennis made me a good defender or, as Mr. Schmalfuss put it, "You're a real pain." We did much better than we had in football and felt ready for "Gamble's First Annual Student-Teacher Basketball Game." The entire place was excited. The gym filled up before the last bell stopped ringing. The other teachers were merely bodies to fill out the team of Cheeseman and Schmalfuss. At the tip-off, Cheeseman demonstrated what the term height advantage looked like and just keep pouring them in till the half.

Our team captain decided to put me on Cheeseman and see how big a pain I could be. As the second half opened, he was shocked to see me guarding him and I stole the ball. The crowd was as shocked as Cheeseman, tennis boy had picked Goliath's pocket. The next time down the court I managed to keep him from getting the ball and from then on, I stuck to him like glue. Our offense started hitting, and the game was actually tied when I managed to punch another pass away from Cheeseman and learned Schmalfuss had been right. I was a pain and Cheeseman had had enough. As we headed up court, he put his arm over me from the side and picked me up by the uniform.

The place went nuts and it took me a bit to realize I was being carried up court like a rag doll. As he carried me, the noise increased and there was no question Cheeseman and his package were the center of attention. I'm not certain when, but at a point I got the feeling something was wrong and then a teacher from the stands ran on court and Cheeseman let me down. That's when I felt cold, real cold in a place that was not supposed to feel cold. Seems when Cheeseman picked me up, he pulled more than just my uniform and all of me was plain to see by everyone in the stands and, for some of them, up very close. I don't remember who won the game.

A few days after what I called my little exposition, Mr. Cheeseman called me into his office after basketball practice. He was sorry for what happened during the Teacher—Student game and wanted to know if I was okay. I thanked him for his concern and explained that I had been embarrassed a lot of times in my life just by being different, while this time there was a real reason to be embarrassed. We shook and that was that.

As time passed, I realized that was not that. Mr. Cheeseman had accepted my not swimming at Westwood and showering in private at West Hi and helped me adjust and shower like all the others at Gamble. He told me what a jockstrap was and where to buy one and we laughed when I told him the clerk had to explain how to size and wear one. He taught me what a letter sweater was, where I could buy one, and how to display the letter and the little insignia for football, basketball, and tennis. Mr. Cheeseman sincerely cared about my feelings, and I didn't take the time to tell him what he had done for me.

The Christmas break was days away and I was truly anxious about my parts in our pageant. When it happened, I felt like all the talents of my classmates seemed to peak and the choir, orchestra, and program were marvelous. The best for me was when those of us in the choir entered the dimly lit packed auditorium from the rear doors, singing and carrying candles made of cones of construction paper taped to flashlights. They really did look like candles and the mood was magic.

The holidays came and went, school resumed, basketball ended, and I enjoyed a real winter season with plenty of snow like on the day Norton and I were walking after school and some people on the bus started razzing us. We looked at each other and started making snowballs. On my third throw I hit the window where the group that was yelling at us stood, and they hit the deck as the window shattered. Norton and I took off, satisfied because we had scared the kids on the bus and scared because I had broken the window. When we stopped before going our separate ways home, Norton and I agreed to deny everything.

Later that evening, Olga called me downstairs and when I hit the landing, I saw a policeman standing in the front room. What in the world? That didn't faze him, he got right to the point and asked if I had thrown snowballs at a school bus. I came clean faster than a speeding bullet. He liked that, but then asked if I was willing to go with him to visit my pal Norton? Sure, but why? Seems Norton denied our actions and wouldn't even identify his accomplice. Oh, oh, poor Norton having me as his accomplice.

I rode along with him and as soon as Norton saw us, he was cooked. Of course, the policeman didn't need anything from either of us because the kids on the bus and others had identified us. Fortunately, no one was hurt but we had upset a bunch of people, including the bus driver, some teachers, and this policeman. Before we left Norton's, the officer announced we were going to have a reunion, in Juvenile Court.

For me the entire episode was fear, humiliation, and—what

seemed to be my new friend—embarrassment. From the moment we ran off until the policeman came to our door was the worst time in my life. I learned I could never lead a life of crime. The shame, the absolute self-hatred, and the guilt for what I had done ate at me. Throwing the snowballs was okay, breaking the window was a bad break but, running away and not standing up to my responsibility were not okay. Baba must never know what I had done, or more correctly, what I hadn't done. My behavior ignored all the precepts of honor and personal duty she had taught me. I was in hell.

By taking us to Juvenile Court, the authorities and our parents were trying to teach us a lesson, to put the fear of the law in us. That was okay. However, not one of them could see that I had very little fear left for the law. All my fear was for me. I was questioning my inner worth. Was I honorable or not? The depth of my dismay made being in court a surface issue. Finally, it ended as we accomplices promised we had learned our lesson and the judge sent us home. Whoa!

IMAGINE THAT

A few weeks after I put the snowball through the school bus window, I had a scheduled meeting with my Handler. Going into it I was excited. In a bunch more weeks I would be going to Court because I screwed up, but this day I was going to our session with proof I could do well. I had gathered all the information he had been fishing for and uncovered some related facts he wasn't expecting.

After we got settled, I noticed he seemed rumpled, I had never seen him anything but cool, calm, and collected. As we went over my material, I was somewhat disappointed because he didn't seem as impressed as I imagined he would be, but I felt sure that when I gave him the unexpected material he would come around. Not so. In fact, when I finished, it was clear he was fit to be tied.

"So, is there anything else you have for me today?"

I hadn't expected that. "No sir.…ah"

"What? What is ah?"

"Ah nothing."

He was nowhere near cool, calm, or collected. Something was sure wrong with him, but I didn't know what, so I decided to hit him straight on.

"Well, I felt this was particularly good work and you don't seem too happy."

"Okay, you're right, it is good work. The extra, coming as facts, was very good. But is that all?"

My history taught me, when in doubt, shut up. He waited. I was very good at this, but he wasn't playing.

"One last time, you got anything else you think I should know?"

Mum's the word.

For the next too long he "mentioned" the school bus. Oh, he acted neutral, neither blaming nor criticizing, merely emphasizing that I was on my own, which was the worst thing he could have done because it made me guess where he stood.

Then he lectured, as if to a class full, on being completely open with each other…all the time…and the pitfalls of holding back…and trust…and no surprises…and I recall the phrase, "incredibly stupid" being mentioned and the question, "We did speak about keeping a low profile?" being asked.

He concluded in a most severe manner. "This is not school or church or a game. I'm not giving grades or keeping score. This is getting a job done and we don't have time for you to be self-conscious about anything, particularly anything that draws attention to you. I expect you to make mistakes but if I don't know, I can't help. Keep me informed."

When we agreed to the place and time of our next session, I was very glad to be on my way.

Once on my way, the session began to percolate in my mind and the brew that resulted was bitter, humbling, and a real wake-me-upper. I didn't want him to know I had screwed up. How naive was I? It never occurred to me that he would know what was happening with me, that he would keep some sort of track of

me, have his eye on me...he was The FBI for the love of God, he had to have his eye on me, but I had not imagined that.
 Imagine that.

EDDIE HEUER

One day someone pointed to a group standing together and said, "Those are hoods." I had never heard that term used to describe people. I didn't know what it meant but nodded as if I did. Afterward, I thought about them being "hoods" and was stuck. I had read about hoodlums. Was this a relative? I'd have to keep my eyes open.

The "hoods" stuck together. But so did the "brains", the "musicians", the "teacher's pets" and so on. The guy "hoods" had greasy hair, heavy shoes, dark jeans, black t-shirts with cigarettes rolled up in the sleeves, and combed their hair a lot. The "sports guys" had flat tops, loafers, tan cotton pants, white t-shirts under madras button-down shirts, and punched each other in the arms a lot. The girl "hoods" cussed a lot, wore leather shoes, tight short skirts, flashy tops, and their hair wild. The "in crowd" girls wore plain white gym shoes and socks, skirts with pleats, full blouses, their hair in ponytails, and whispered a lot. Everybody had a uniform and a way to act.

This was not helping me learn about "hoods".

As it turned out, help was on the way. Help from teachers, school staff, students except for "hoods," and even some parents.

It was interesting that all this help made the same pitch. "Hoods" were trouble. Lived in tough, not so nice neighborhoods. Didn't do their homework. Didn't participate in any school activities. The girls put-out, and the guys were dirty fighters. They all had bad attitudes and even worse parents. Watch out.

This help didn't help. I had seen nothing firsthand that backed up their pitch. My neighborhood had been 64 E. McMicken. You could call that a tough and not so nice neighborhood. Some of the "hoods" had jobs and I knew that can put a crick in participating in school activities. I knew kids that weren't "hoods" who didn't do their homework. I didn't know too much about putting out. I knew any fight was dirty. I decided "hoods" were just other kids. I liked some of their actions more than some actions of the other "groups". I didn't belong in any group and was at peace about "those hoods".

Eddie Heuer (hoy-er) was a "hood". That didn't mean a thing to me. To me, Eddie was just like all the other American kids, someone who could help me learn more of Americana. However, I did see him more than most kids at school because he spent a lot of time going to and from the Principal's Office. He was short and skinny with a sharp angular face and wary eyes. He was light complexioned with medium brown hair, but he looked darker because of the stuff he spread in his hair and all black "uniform of those hoods" which he wore religiously.

There was one thing about Eddie that made him stand out, even from all the other "hoods". A thing that gave him notoriety. A thing the help always managed to point out. Eddie Heuer's parents were—the D word. There was considerable debate by the "in crowd" whether divorce did, or did not, make the kids bastards.

It was a school day, and we were moving between classes.

We were defying nature as currents of us moved between banks formed by the walls and lockers. Two currents going opposite ways in the same channel, yet both currents flowing freely. I knew this from experience, not because I was aware. In fact, this day I was unaware of everything except...? Hum...yes, that's it and there's no getting around it. I had become fanny focused.

It was good that the current was carrying me to my next class because I was not headed there. I was headed wherever the backside of the girl in front of me was headed. Once it, she, caught my attention, I couldn't take my eyes off it...her. I had maneuvered to get behind her and soon realized her rear had a personality all its own. It was amazing. In addition to moving side to side, it moved up and down at the same time. Side to side, up and down, side to side, up and down. At a certain moment I believed I was watching an entire dance troup made up of two round spheres. If they look like that, how do they feel?

Suddenly, I was holding the right sphere in my left hand and moving across to the left one, which I squeezed. That woke me, but I hadn't been dreaming. I did have her left sphere in my left hand, and I was feeling around. But my left hand was in the right hand of Eddie Heuer who had seen me transfixed by her rear, realized I wasn't going to do anything, and decided to do it for me.

I looked over at Eddie who was smiling at me, but before I could speak the girl spun around and was facing us. She looked at the two of us but didn't see me. She only saw Eddie and immediately smacked him upside the head.

"No! I'm sorry, it wasn't him, it was me, I'm sorry, it was me."

She totally ignored me. First, she didn't see me, now she didn't hear me. In the meantime, Eddie had let go of my hand. The girl tried to smack him again, but he caught her hand and told her it was worth one, but no more. She cussed at him, and he laughed at her. She and her friends agreed he was a creep. He asked me if I agreed she had a great ass. Then they were gone. Lost in the currents. I remained like an abandoned wreck, impeding the current's flow. The entire incident took no more than ten seconds. As time passed, I learned there is no correlation between the length and impact of an experience.

Before Eddie took action, I couldn't imagine touching a girl. Had he not taken action, I would not have touched the girl. The right thing was not to touch girls. But the wrong thing, touching, had consequences that were right for me. Eddie Heuer knew I wanted to touch her before I knew I wanted to touch her. His action exposed me to me.

He seemed to know about me, the house that was me, and the rooms of my house. He went to the large Female Room occupied by The Matriarch and The Reverend and turned the lights on. Baba and Olga were not alone. There were countless females. They were everywhere like snowflakes in a blizzard. It was too much for me and I closed the door. I had to admit, the thought of being caught in that blizzard unsettled me.

Eddie opened the door of my Female Room and showed me it was actually my Sex Room. I had passed that door many times but never opened it. Eddie showed me I was going to have to enter that room and I'd better get prepared. His action made it clear that I could no longer brush off what was happening to the "fanny focused" me.

Eddie Heuer and I spent ten seconds of our lives together during this incident. I can't remember talking with him before or after those ten seconds. But during those ten seconds, "that hood" Eddie Heuer taught me more about myself than anyone with whom I went to school.

THE NINTH GRADE: CONTINUED

We were deep into spring, tennis was in full bloom, and I guess it was the compliment of being asked that made me agree to play intramural softball, it would take time I could use on tennis. I wasn't fast, but my good hands and quick feet were perfect at second base. Hitting was a piece of cake, as I considered it tennis. No need to try and hit the ball a mile, just forehand for the lefties and backhand for the righties. I just poked the balls where they weren't, there would be games between my making an out. It was fun and we were playing for the league title when I let a ball go through my legs and instead of the game being over, it went on, and we lost. That my error cost our team was an experience I never wanted to repeat, and tennis became even more inviting. At tennis my errors only cost me.

One day at lunch, someone told me our World Geography teacher wanted to see me. Heading to her room I wondered why. When I got there, she closed the door, and I knew it was serious. Where was my end of year Term Paper? In the stack where you told us to put them. But mine wasn't in that stack, in fact mine was nowhere to be found. I was flustered, how could this be, I knew exactly where I put it, here, let me show you...and then I realized she never even considered that I hadn't turned it in. Her seriousness was over who would steal my work and why. We discussed these questions but couldn't find answers. In fact, no matter how we or others tried, we never found out who or why. On my final report card, she gave me an A for the term. That she never doubted my word was worth more than a bag of As.

I couldn't get over my term paper being stolen. It was so different from anything I understood. Whoever had done it thought in a way I couldn't imagine. No matter how I tried, I couldn't identify which kids would have done such a thing, but I knew in my heart, whoever it was, was very different from me. In this way, over time, I was reminded that it was I who was different and always had been.

Take kids. The kids I grew up with were not my friends, they were people I watched. They played the roles of mentors and tutors and educated me in Americana, but I never cared what they thought of me, they were kids. When this year started, I realized I had digested and assimilated Americana by watching them be themselves and was now comfortable with myself as an American. As such, they had nothing more to teach and I watched them with a different purpose. Now I watched them to evaluate, form opinions, and determine what I did and did not want to mimic. More different was that I still didn't care what they thought of me.

It was unnecessary for me to catalogue the 'different' of my background; a non-denominational church in the Slavic ghetto run by an ex-tailor and a faith healer would just be the start. But I did catalogue my identities. I was three nationalities, with three names and three languages. Zoran was a Yugoslavian who spoke Serbian. Ronnie was an American who spoke American. Little Brother Marksity was Non-Denominational and spoke Biblican. Oh, yea, I'm not different, there were lots of Biblicans at Gamble.

From day one, Olga and George told me, "When you go to England you can speak English. Here, you will learn American. You will speak American, write American, be American." But in fact, the Bible was my first language, whether in Serbian or in American. At the Peniel Missionary Assembly, everyone I associated with talked Bible and everything I read and heard was from the Bible, so I thought and spoke in Biblican.

My Biblican library had one book, the 1934 edition of The New Chain-Reference Bible, in its third improved edition, with self-pronouncing text, published by B.B. Kirkbride Bible Company, Indianapolis, Indiana. But listening to any Bible readings in services, church school, prayer meetings, and other gatherings taught me to hear with complete understanding so that thou shalt, disobedience, grace, wisdom, blessing, naysayers, whereby, unto thee, behold, marvel, thus, whence, spake, henceforth, prophesied, covenant, hasten, intercessor, ye, exaltation, carnal, sanctify, discern, abide, beseech, verily, and more, were all as normal to my lips and ears as American or Serbian.

Furthermore, as a Biblican, I had a different sense of geography. My maps were those appearing in my Bible. Not only did I see everything from the Far East to the Middle East as India, I saw the Middle East as it was in the time of Christ, not as it was in 1958.

So what?

American, Biblican, Serbian, so I had three identities, so what? I no longer thought of who took my term paper, that was one in my pile of experiences during the ninth grade. I was different and happy to be so. This realization became part of me, and I felt a new sense of independence that became tangible self-confidence.

As the school year came to a close, I was honestly a little sad but unable to explain why. Was it because of the experience of being in a brand-new place, the academics, the sports, the dance band, the choir, the teachers, the...yes, all that and more? My two years at Gamble had been full of life. In fact—my feelings flew in the face of the prophesy for me in our Gamble Annual, "Sarcastic humorist Ron Marksity is on another successful tour." I was proud to be in The First Ninth Grade Graduation Class at Gamble Nippert Junior High School.

IS THERE A CHILL IN HERE?

As a result of his stepping up our activity, our work together evolved. Now we met regularly, and our approach was no longer general.

"Okay, let's just look at The Peniel Missionary Assembly. You feel your parents started it for very admirable reasons but I'm not certain I understand exactly what happened. How about you start with this Reverend Nash, who you mentioned was Pastor of The Assembly of God, and your mother's mentor."

This was typical of his routine. If I had mentioned Reverend Nash, it was once and in passing. In fact, I wasn't sure I had ever mentioned The Reverend. No matter, he caught it and I knew we were going to pick and pick and pick until anything I might have thought about Reverend Nash was chewed up and digested.

It was now normal for us to have agendas for our meetings, agreements about information we were targeting, and schedules for the collection and evaluation of that information.

Most recently, information about my temporary roommates dominated his focus and he was driving me up the wall over these people. I mean some of them had been my roommates six years ago, while others had only been my roommates for days. No matter, he wanted to know everything about everyone. Part of what irked me was that for each, his pattern was the same.

We'd start with how was he referred to The Reverends Marksity, name, nationality, what country, state, sector, or region did he come from, physical descriptions, skills, education or training, types of jobs in the past, and end with a rundown of his visit from when he arrived to when he departed. Then, we'd do it all again. Finally, I had had enough.

"Look, this makes no sense. We go over these people, whether I remember anything or not, and over them and over them. In all cases, there are ten times more questions I can't answer than I can answer. Plus, you ask the same things regardless the time and situation of their stays with me. You do know I didn't sit up and grill these guys. If you don't trust my answers, let's just knock this whole thing off."

He was immediately and genuinely apologetic and perhaps because of this, he gave me a rare treat, a preview.

"Okay, that is a good point. You're doing a good job and I know it's not easy. But listen, later, no telling when, you'll understand more about this technique of reporting and believe me it will serve us both well."

I didn't have a clue what he was talking about, but I was glad that our work moved on. After my outburst, he began to bring pictures to some of our sessions. I learned to study them, search for recognition, be sensitive to recall, and just say anything that the pictures stimulated. This was more to my liking, but I didn't do that well, I couldn't identify almost any of them. For the few I could identify, he wanted detailed information and we frequently inched our way through sessions.

"So, this last roommate, who moved out what was it, six weeks ago, let's focus on him today. He's the one with the interesting hands.

"No. Oh, he was earlier. Okay. Well, that's the one I want to review.

"You said his hands were rough, thick, dark, and no matter how often or hard he washed them, the creases and lines never came up flesh colored. Did I get it right?

"Good. So, have you ever seen hands like that before?

"What made you think they were scars?

"You don't know? Hum…Well, have you ever seen skin like that before? Anywhere? On anyone?"

"Never? Hum…

"Okay, let's look at the rest of him. Did he have any other physical characteristics that might be considered different?

"Yes, I do remember. You did mention his head seeming to sit on his shoulders without a neck. Did you ever have the opportunity to see his neck?

"If you had seen it, do you imagine it might have the same markings as his hands?

…and on and on and…

In time, regarding my temporary roommates, I began to notice that he was more interested in some than others. Our focus and emphasis might have looked equal for each, but he was not equal with each. Those that interested him most affected the intensity of his eyes and the precision of his comments. The way he reacted to these men had changed as a result of our sessions.

And then, after our last two sessions, I noticed that the way I related to my temporary roommates had changed. For some reason, I didn't think about them as I did before I met him. It didn't make a difference if they had shared my room six years or six weeks ago, if they had stayed for months or days, if they were Serb, or young, or old, it was all the same. I had lost something.

Comparing my feelings for them before and after working for The Bureau, I saw that this undercover process had altered my perspective toward them, but I could find no reason for this, no explanation. As far as I knew, we had uncovered nothing covert, nothing more than raw suspicion.

It was as if we dissected them and hung them out to dry and by participating in this dissection, I had lost some of my warmth for them, and more. After our work on them, I was drained of everything I had felt for them and couldn't find my old feelings. I was left with nothing but a void where memories had been, a fragile shell, empty on the inside. I was strangely lonely, oddly sad.

Is there a chill in here, or is it me that's turning cold?

TOURNAMENT

The Western Hills Press, June 13, 1958. "The first annual junior tennis tournament, sponsored by the Western Hills Junior Chamber of Commerce, was played at the Western Hills High School Courts. The tournament was open to all boys in the Western Hills area. Winners in each division will represent the area in the State Jaycees Tournament at Delaware in July. Ron Marksity was the champion in the boys' division."

It was a great feeling to read the newspaper. This happened because my aunt Margaret brought a cake and the clippings of my success to our house. She dropped them off saying, correctly, that Olga and George would never notice such a moment. Then she left. She didn't want to celebrate with us. She wanted to remind everyone that Olga and George weren't normal parents. What she did was nice. How she did it, was just plain mean to George and Olga. To me it was just fine, I would never have thought to look in the paper for a notice about myself, plus, we didn't get a paper. Olga really liked the cake.

I practiced like crazy preparing for the State Tournament. In July, I rode up to the tournament with a nice gentleman from the Jaycees and never did see the winner of the junior division. Once there I was on my own and immediately found I had never been as different or out of place in my life. The other players had huge bags with multiple racquets, shoes, outfits for playing and warming up, different types of powders for their hands and feet, other gear I couldn't identify and, many of them had coaches. I had one racquet, the pair of shoes I was wearing, and a change of t-shirts.

But the real difference was with the other players. Many of them knew each other, they were on some sort of tournament circuit. All of them played cards while waiting for their matches, I learned the favorite game was hearts. I didn't know how to play hearts or any card games and couldn't imagine playing any game before a match. On the courts they chatted with each other as they warmed up and often during their matches. They discussed statistics of who should win and why and made it all sound predetermined. There was no question they could play but their approach to tennis was that it was a game. Imagine, friendly banter with your opponent.

As for me, the guy I played didn't know me and didn't want to. It was a terrible mismatch. In addition to a great flat serve and superior ground-strokes he had a slice serve, something I had never even seen before. I swear, it hit the court and took an immediate left turn away from me. Next to my cross-court forehand my serve was my best weapon. Mr. Magic Serve had to concentrate for my first serve but beyond that, nada. I never saw his net play; he didn't have time to include it in my destruction, but I did see his fans. I had never played tennis with people watching and my opponent had a bunch of people who followed him around to watch. Midway through my slaughter, some of these people were laughing and began to throw balloons on the court.

On the way home, the nice gentleman tried to convince me that the fans were just having fun and the balloons got away from them, "Ron, there were just a few people watching your match." It wasn't till years later that the joke about paranoia closed this chapter. You know, the football fan up in the bleachers who is convinced, "Those players in that huddle are talking about me." Anyway, for the rest of the summer, the specter of laughter and balloons added motivation to my practice and conditioning. For the rest of my tennis playing, I refused to notice who was watching or what they were doing.

THE WRECK OF JUSTICE

The important stuff of this summer, tennis, began in the spring as I prepared for the Jaycees District Tourney and shifted into high gear after I took my whooping in July at Delaware. From then on, any spare minute was tennis, anyone, anywhere, anytime.

The secondary priority, making money, started as soon as school was out. But thanks to Howard giving me my job, things were different. I was no longer trying to get enough money to cover my expenses for the next school year and maybe squirrel away some extra, because now the gas station was providing a real income.

At home, my chores stayed the same, but my activities changed. After the dance band gave its last performance, I announced to Olga that once I graduated the ninth grade, there would be no more accordion practice or playing. Her look said, "Oh, I know you'll want to reconsider this later." And my words said, "Oh, I know you need to find another way to recreate your image of life in — the old country." I didn't miss that porch or squeezebox one time.

As for other things that might come up this summer, I'd just have to Handler them in a confidential way.

As for today, it was a gorgeous early afternoon, and I was on my walk to work. Clear sky, perfect temperature, low humidity, and the traffic on Montana Avenue was the typical unhurried summer traffic of patient mothers and school free children.

As I approached the corner of Dartmouth, a side street, the moment was blown away by the sudden screaming of tires and roaring of an over revved engine. Looking left I saw the car barreling toward me. It accelerated through the stop sign, into the intersection and bashed broadside into a four-door sedan with a mother and child. The impact drove the cars across the lanes and into a front yard.

I was the first to the cars. Amazingly, the injuries were relatively minor. However, it appeared the child was never going to stop crying.

The crazy driver was not an adult but certainly older than me. His was such an obvious fault that I was shocked by his attitude. He seemed more upset with not being able to continue to where he was going than with having caused an accident. He didn't ask about the people in the car he hit and didn't even seem concerned about his car.

I got some of the observers to help me manage the traffic flow around the wreck. I didn't worry about being late to work. I knew Howard would understand. I would stay and testify for the authorities. I would meet my responsibilities as a citizen and eyewitness.

The police came. They checked the condition of the participants, took over traffic control, gathered things from both drivers, and started asking questions. Everyone pointed to me because either I was there before them or, I was closer to the crash.

When the policemen came to me, I met my responsibilities. In no uncertain terms I reported the clear-cut picture of what happened. They wanted to make sure, I was sure. I let them know surely, I was sure. After all, I was standing on the corner of the intersection less than ten yards from the impact. In fact, I was almost in the crash. Finally, they took my name and number and said I would be notified about the next step.

After talking to me, the police talked to a few other bystanders and the lady driver. It all seemed cut and dried. I was about to head for work when I noticed the police talking with the crazy driver and that their mood changed. I decided not to go to work just then. When they finished talking to the driver, they started asking questions of people they had already questioned. They tried to find other people to question. Oddly, they didn't come to talk to me a second time. I thought they didn't see me, or figured I had left for work, so I went to show myself. No, they had nothing else to ask me. I was free to go.

It was still a gorgeous afternoon. The clear sky, perfect temperature, and low humidity were still real but, I had a funny feeling. Finally, I decided that my feeling was because I had just seen an accident. I walked up Montana to the gas station. Everyone was riveted by my report and Howard approved my tardiness.

Sometime later, I was notified that I was to appear in court. This was going to be my first visit to the Court House, and I was full of anticipation. I was going to the seat of Justice. I was getting the opportunity to do my duty as a citizen.

The appointed day arrived, and I found myself on the street in front of the Court House. The first impression was gratifying. I liked the building. It met my expectations. It looked like I wanted it to look. It was serious, solid, and secure but not overbearing, cold, or indifferent. As I entered and found my way to the courtroom, my first impression was reinforced. It was reassuring to see a routine atmosphere and feel an underlying presence of accountability. As I stood in front of the courtroom, I felt justice was on the other side of the door. Inside, the room was not crowded but seemed full.

Our case was called first. As I listened, I was distracted by almost all of the experience but, as time passed, I became acclimated and could concentrate. The more I concentrated, the more that funny feeling I had at the scene came back. There was a lot of talk about what a good young man this was. The young man who had run a stop sign while speeding and broadsided a mommy with her kid. There was discussion that perhaps the lady could have been a more defensive driver. I wondered how you could be more defensive while driving in the right of way of a major thoroughfare and some kid speeds through the stop sign of a feeder street and broadsides you? Well, let them say what they will, when I get my turn to testify the facts will be all too clear.

My turn came. There were some general questions and then the lady driver's attorney asked me to tell what I had seen. I told the truth as it happened. The attorney thanked me and sat down.

The other attorney got up and repeated some of the previously asked general questions. I answered as before. He then asked me to repeat what I had seen. I answered as before. Then he asked me if I was sure. I was shocked and sat looking at him. He again asked me if I was sure. I was no longer shocked, I was upset. I looked him in the eye and asked him why he would ask such a stupid question when I was ten feet away from the impact and had just answered the same question twice.

The judge suggested I be more respectful towards the attorney.

The attorney suggested I might have mistaken what I saw. I suggested he might be more respectful towards me because I was not stupid and no, I was not mistaken, I was on the corner of Montana and Dartmouth when that guy sped through a stop sign and broadsided that lady and...

The judge interrupted me and said that was all. I was stunned. I tried to ask him a question, but he pointed to the seats, told me to be quiet and go sit down.

I sat down and waited to see justice served.

In his summation, the Judge said that it was impossible to determine who was at fault because of the lack of eyewitnesses. I couldn't control myself. I jumped up and yelled, "I was standing right there." The Judge turned to me and said, "One more outburst from you and I'll put you in contempt."

He continued that the young man had no previous serious record and was known to be good natured. He added that, as a judge with years of experience, he felt the young man was sorry for the accident and sincere in his commitment to drive responsibly in the future. He concluded with, "...and finally, because the only eyewitness is a minor, I rule in favor of the defendant."

This was injustice and I started to stand up when I felt myself encircled in a huge black bear hug. It was the bailiff who had been standing behind me. As he manhandled me, I could tell this was not meant as restraint, this was meant as rescue. He hustled me out of the courtroom and whispered, "Calm down, I'll explain."

The doors shut behind us and we were in the main corridor. He put me down and motioned for me to follow him. I did and we stopped in a window alcove. He looked me in the eye. I was touched because I realized he believed me and cared about me. He began, "You could have gotten in trouble in there. That bastard would have sent you to jail. Don't you know who that driver is? Now get out of here before you get into trouble." He turned and walked back toward the courtroom. I hope that my face and gestures showed the respect and appreciation I had for him.

I watched him until the courtroom door closed behind him and then found my way out of the building. The place had changed. I didn't feel justice behind the door of any courtroom I passed. There was no underlying presence of accountability, and the routine atmosphere seemed a charade covering reality. On the outside the place was still serious, solid, and secure, but only for those who knew the secret code, for the rest of us, it was indifferent.

I felt nothing but contempt for the court and this increased as the week passed. I could think of the judge only as, Your Dishonor. No matter, I still wanted to ask him a question. I wanted to hear him explain how several years earlier I was old enough to begin working undercover for the FBI but now I was too young to see a wreck ten yards in front of me.

The following Saturday I returned to work at the gas station. As the day passed, whenever there was the opportunity, we talked about the wreck and trial. Everyone, even some customers, were interested and there was a lot of lively discussion. Most agreed this had been a real screw job for the lady driver. But I noticed Howard and Whitey were not sharing everything on their minds. As it turned out, it made sense that Howard didn't say anything because he hated giving anyone any bad news. Whitey did the dirty work of education.

Whitey waited until we were alone and then asked me what happened. As I was relating my experience he began to laugh. I had heard this laugh a lot as I was growing up because it was the laugh of someone unlike me. Someone not optimistic, idealistic, naïve, and inexperienced. Someone realistic, seasoned, mature and experienced. As I talked, Whitey laughed less and less. By the time I finished my story, Whitey had stopped laughing.

I suppose Whitey saw from the look on my face that I didn't know what he was laughing about. He stood up and said, "Ron my boy, the bailiff was right. You could have gotten yourself in big trouble. You really don't know what happened." As he paused, he closed the door leading to the service bay as if to make sure another worker didn't interrupt us. He got real serious and said, "You really don't know who that driver is, do you?" He waited, as if giving me a moment to disagree, then grinned and began to laugh. Between the laughter he announced, "Ron, the son-of-a-bitch is the son-of-a-judge."

SEPTEMBER 1958: THE TENTH GRADE

I was ready to return to West High for the tenth grade, even though it had been a great summer. I had a sense that time was moving on and I had to keep up.

It seemed to me that I had spent more time at the West High tennis courts over this summer than I had spent at West High as a seventh grader. Whether I had or not, the time was paying off. My game was steadily improving, and I was looking forward to competing for a spot on the varsity.

As for my finances, as planned I worked at the gas station and as predicted I made more than enough money for my tenth-grade expenses and to add to my private account. What wasn't planned or predicted was my business. Maybe the neighbor who said my helper-ship was grounds for me to strike out on my own and when I asked, doing what, said he was sure I'd think of something, had prophesied.

It started when I made a comment to a customer that his car could use a wax job and he asked if I could do it. Howard sold me whitewall solvent, pre-wax cleaner, paste wax, chrome cleaner, and chrome polish at cost. Customers would drop their cars off at our house by eight and pick them up after five. I cleaned out and vacuumed the interior and trunk, washed the exterior, and treated the white-walls, pre-waxed the exterior—this was a coat of cleaner that prepared the finish for the paste wax step, cleaned and polished all the chrome, and topped it off with spotless windows and mirrors. It was wonderful. The exercise of five workovers of each car was like a tennis workout for income. My expenses were about $2 per car, and I charged $15. And everyone gave me a tip that at least covered my expenses. I did fifteen cars over the summer and all my customers referred me to others. I was fourteen and had options for making money!

With school approaching, Olga and George agreed with my reasoning that a fellow in Senior High shouldn't be burdened with weekly household chores. However, since I liked cutting grass, raking leaves, and shoveling snow and coal, I volunteered to do those whenever I had time.

When school started, it was nothing like the seventh grade. So many people offered me rides that getting to and from was a matter of choice. Now, I was in one of the cars that caused the traffic jams at seven early in the morning. And the place that, "…was six times as big as Westwood Elementary" was no longer monstrous. Rather, it seemed like a kindly aunt who was happy to have her nephew back for a visit, though both knew it would only be for a limited time.

In homeroom, it didn't take long to understand my class schedule was set up according to the "College Preparatory" program and consisted of English II, Latin II, Plane Geometry, World History, Mechanical Drawing, Phys Ed, and Health. During the first few days, I got a feeling I had some solid teachers and great subjects. It was interesting that the workload for this college prep business, which was supposed to be heavy, seemed nothing more than an extension of my summer reading, in fact I may have read more in the summer than I was going to read in school. Nice.

Finally, unlike the eighth and ninth grades at Gamble, there was no football team, choir, basketball team, dance band, or intramural any things on my agenda, tennis was my sole extracurricular activity. Unless you knew that I was now starting my third year undercover for The FBI and you considered that an extracurricular activity. But, of course, no one knew that. No one.

PETAR DEJURDJEV

The doorbell interrupted my homework. I remembered Olga said they were expecting another Yugoslavian who had been referred to them. I figured I'd better head downstairs to meet him since he could be my next roommate. Before I hit the bottom of the steps, I saw him and immediately knew he was absolutely different from all the other DPs in absolutely every way.

Introductions all around and as Petar Dejurdjev began to tell us about himself, I found an end of the couch where I could demonstrate I knew, "Children should be seen and not heard."

He started by explaining how he knew to come here. It seemed Olga and George had a wonderful reputation for helping people, DPs in general and Slavs in particular.

He was very well dressed. Everything fit together or matched or, anyway, his clothes were really nice.

I refocused and learned that the people who referred him said he should be totally honest with the Reverends Marksity so, the truth was he was hoping they could help h…

What kind of watch is that? That's the most gold of a gold watch I've ever seen.

I forced myself to pay attention as he started on his background because asking for help was a one-way street to sharing my room. He was originally from …

I don't get that ring. What is it? If he would just turn his hand. A horseshoe? The ring is a horseshoe. Hum. But what, what are, Oh my Lord. Are those diamonds in that horseshoe? They gotta be!

I checked to be sure my jaw wasn't sitting on my chest and hoped no one had noticed me. Refocusing on his monologue was a challenge, I mean he's decked out, his watch is a gold ingot, and he's wearing a diamond filled horseshoe ring.

I got myself together as he was talking about the war. He said he had participated but I could feel he was downplaying the specifics. As he skimmed the topic, he used too many terms and nuances I had learned from previous roommates who had participated and realized he had seen a lot more than he was sharing.

He moved on to review his work experiences. He had always loved horses and at an early age found he had a knack with them. From working with them he earned the chance to ride and became a successful jockey. His knack with horses coupled with his riding experiences earned him a position as a jockey for Tito …

WHAT!!! TITO! JOSIP BROZ TITO! I forgot everything else.

This Petar sitting in our living room had met Josip Broz Tito? Marshal Josip Broz Tito, the incredibly gifted diplomat, military professional, and statesman who was able to unite seven naturally antagonistic elements into a united group, into Yugoslavia. This Petar had worked for The Leader of Yugoslavia!

Leader or Dictator, as you like it, Minister of Defense Josip Broz Tito was the man who had the vision and made it a reality. I knew about this from the family, those temporary roommates who had experienced life under him, and The Encyclopedia

Britannica. There was even a prophetic fact only those of us who spoke Serbian knew about Tito. In Serbian, Tito is pronounced "tea-toug" and translates literally into "you-do that."

A mark of Prime Minister Tito's leadership was that no matter how things went, which way he leaned at any given time, his people, both military and civilian, were more loyal to him than to any way he leaned. He was able to walk a tightrope between Russia and America, playing one against the other to get the best for his people. And this man in the great outfit with the watch and ring, had worked for him.

I knew myself, that was all my mind was going to handle, I was totally discombobulated. The session continued, agreements were reached, arrangements established, and the session concluded with goodbyes all round. But none of that was in my mind's grasp. I went back upstairs to do my homework, but no homework was done. I had just met a man who knew and had worked for Josip Broz Tito, The President of Yugoslavia.

THE UNCLE AND HIS NEPHEW

While we were sitting people didn't notice us, but once we started strolling anyone could notice us. We needed not to be noticed. It didn't feel right that people might take us for father and son, maybe because I didn't know how to wear the hat of a son. It felt much better if, as we strolled, people took us for an uncle and his nephew. We were strolling because I had so much to report we got tired of sitting. He had never asked so many questions before, pointed, specific questions.

There was another reason we were strolling. I had done my best in reporting everything I remembered about the meeting with Petar Dejurdjev. Then, I admitted that after the Tito bomb, I was totally discombobulated and had missed the rest of the visit. People like him weren't titled Handlers for nothing and that is what mine was doing to me when he suggested we take a stroll.

"You have to be a little easy on yourself. You've done a great job. If you don't remember another point, we have plenty to work with. Your descriptions of his clothes and jewelry, his holding back about his war experiences, those are great. For example, because of your descriptions, I see a lot of questions. Why does a guy who is, what did you say, "decked out"', why does a guy who is decked out like that ask for help? What does he want? What does he need? See, you did an excellent job."

We strolled, looked around, and both felt better. We didn't chat, we had been debriefing a long time. We hit a drinking fountain and in time he started up.

"You know I mean it when I say you did a great job?"

He gave me time to digest this and reinforced his compliment by establishing eye contact and then waiting for me to admit I knew. Only after I said I knew he meant it; did he continue. Look at that uncle mentoring his nephew.

"Okay then. But, you know, I bet you're a lot better than you think. You have extraordinary powers of observation and I'm beginning to think your memory is also superior. I'll bet your mind recorded things you don't even realize it was recording. You know anything about how our brains work?"

I sure didn't.

He then gave me a simple primer, exactly what I needed, precisely when—in this case—we needed it. His handling of me was becoming recognizable. He expected I knew our brains ran our bodies even though we weren't aware our brains were doing so. He was pretty sure I knew our brains did other things we weren't aware they were doing. His point was that one of the things our brains do, that we are unaware of, is record almost everything going on around us, all the time. He was certain my brain was doing just that the entire time I was with Petar Dejurdjev and if I wanted, we could try to see what my brain recorded.

I wanted.

"To start, don't try to remember. Don't press yourself. Just relax, let it come to you. Don't look for it. It will come to you from, you don't know where. Don't wait for it. It will come to you at its time. Just know it will come to you. All you have to do is accept it will come and be alert to when it does."

The uncle and his nephew were finished with their stroll. Anyone looking at us would see the fatigue of satisfaction from time well spent together. My fatigue was from what I had to bring to the debriefing. His fatigue was from what he had to do with what he took from the debriefing. Our mutual satisfaction came from looking forward to future sessions where we would debrief my brain.

* * *

It was at supper when Olga asked, "Weren't the colors of that boat he was driving marvelous?" that it came to me. It was the huge '98', the top of the 1956 Oldsmobile line, two tones of light and dark green, light interior, absolutely mint condition, and Ohio plates.

* * *

As I was leaving for school, George offered, "Got a call from Pete last night, said he would be here next week." And it came to me. Pete Johnson. In order to fit in better in The US, Petar Dejurdjev went by the name Pete Johnson. In fact, it was possible we were the only people in The US who knew Pete Johnson was really Petar Dejurdjev. I didn't know any other DPs who changed their names or had two names. Like I said, absolutely different in absolutely every way.

***

And so it went. Things came to me and for several sessions to follow we learned what had gone on in the visit with Petar Dejurdjev, as we debriefed my brain.

These debriefings started with a bang. I had not just met a man who had worked for the President of Yugoslavia, I had a new roommate who was working for The President of Yugoslavia. President Tito loved horses and wanted his Yugoslavia to have the reputation and reality of world class horses. Petar's riding as his jockey and distinguished service in the war, saw a relationship develop between the horseman and The Marshal, Minister of Defense, Prime Minister, President. Now, Pete Johnson was charged with finding the best horses possible and getting them to Yugoslavia where subsequent breeding and attention would see the realization of Tito's dream.

It was agreed that Pete would become the next of my roommates but that he would come and go as his assignment for President Tito required. He didn't need an apartment if he was going to be on the road tracking down horseflesh most of the time.

As for arrangements, Olga and George didn't want him to pay for their assisting him, helping was what they did. Plus, Olga was The Matriarch's daughter and pure Serb. This was a unique opportunity to be of service to "the old country." Pete read them correctly and didn't push the point. I had an intuition that as time passed, he would make it up to them, one way or another.

***

After the last session during which we focused on my first meeting with Petar Pete, several things were clear. What I learned and experienced about the workings of my brain would become invaluable way past the near future. I learned how to listen without pressure, to listen while trusting my subconscious. My subconscious had not been discombobulated and I gained confidence that my brain would do things even when I couldn't. And I found I could be uncle and nephew all by myself. I was the nephew and all I had to do was trust my uncle brain.

* * *

It was subtle and came to me over time. I didn't recognize it at first. Then I remembered and it was no longer subtle. He had said, "Okay,...I know it's not easy. But listen, later, no telling when, you'll understand more about this technique of reporting and believe me it will serve us both well." My Handler had been right and my trust in him increased.

PHYSICAL ROOMMATE

I was home alone when he arrived. I smiled to myself that it was indeed a green-on-green 1956 Oldsmobile '98'. The trunk was really big but only held a valise, smallish suitcase, and a long sort of bag. I offered to help him, and he said I could take the valise.

As we made it up the steps, he said he was glad I was letting him join me. His words jumped out at me, "I was letting him..." From that instant, there was never a question of Mr. Johnson or Mr. Dejurdjev between us. Between us it was Pete and Ron and by the time we entered my room, our relationship was set for me, and I was completely comfortable with Pete.

I put the valise on the floor next to his bed and showed him the left side of the chest of drawers, including the top, I had cleared for him. He put the suitcase down and I showed him his half of the closet. He hung up the bag and began to take out clothes on hangers. All his clothes were very nice and there were a lot of them in that bag, certainly more than enough for half my closet. When the bag was empty, he made sure his clothes were pushed together so they didn't go past half the closet. He wanted me to know he knew this was my room.

When he was finished putting all his things away, he slid the suitcase and bag under his bed and wondered if I really could spare all the space I'd given him, it was awfully generous of me. I smiled and he accepted that as my answer. The truth was that when you have just a few things to hang in your closet, you hang them equidistant from each other. When you have few clothes, you spread them through your drawers. As for your few books and personal items, you space them on the surfaces available. I was not so much generous as experienced with having little, I couldn't even fill the space I had left. And I did the same for all my roommates.

We spent the rest of the time till Olga and George got home looking around the house, yard, and garage. He was very interested in where he could clean his car. By the time they got home, he and I had history.

During this first stay, his physical presence dominated my attention. He was not much taller than me or Olga or George, about five four. He was not a coordinated boy full of physical potential, or a young athlete realizing his potential, or a mature adult who kept in shape by work and play. Pete was my first experience with a true physical specimen. He was a man who was more than fit, he was like a machine that was strong and limber at the same time.

His morning ritual was beyond me. I'd be in bed asleep. He'd wake up, start his ritual, and that would wake me up. I'd roll over and watch as he'd begin these gyrations. It surprised me that he never minded that I watched. Practitioners of modern physical therapy could give me the run down on what he was doing but as a kid this is what I saw.

This flexible fireplug would sit like a ramrod at the edge of his bed, feet planted flat on the floor and begin to stretch his neck. Side to side. Front to back. Up and down. Then he would crane his neck and move his head around, like the radar screens on the Navy ships scanning the sky of the Victory at Sea television program I had seen at Rosie and Lou's. Big giant circles.

Next, he would concentrate on his shoulders. In a circle forward. In a circle backwards. Pulling them up to his neck, pushing them down. Pulling them up, down, round, forward, and then some sort of movement side to side. I couldn't describe it but could see him take one arm and squeeze it across his face to stretch it to the side and then the other one in the other direction.

Then came gyrations where he would twist very hard and pull himself in different directions, as if he was trying to turn himself into a screw.

He didn't do push-ups, sit-ups, or exercises for his legs, but he did things with his feet that were hard for me to mimic. He seemed to be gripping the rubber backed throw rug with his toes in some kind of squeezing routine. Once the feet were done, he'd totally relax and stretch himself all different ways, like a scarecrow in a high wind.

This ritual took just twenty minutes and he followed it religiously every morning. One day after he left, I tried to do it just like he did. It was very hard to do, and I wasn't even doing it right.

When this first visit was over, I discovered there was something about his physical make-up bothering me. Not too much later I could explain it, I didn't believe he was a jockey. I didn't know squat about racehorses, but Pete was way too thick, broad, and muscular for a horse to carry in a race. So, what was the story?

I wasn't too happy with not believing him and tried to brush it off. Hey, maybe Yugoslavian racehorses are Clydesdales, I could see him on a Clydesdale. My brush was not doing the job.

Later still, I could feel deep inside that this chance to live with a physical man would be important to me. Having grown up with The Matriarch and The Reverend, I had more female than male perspective. In time, I came to realize my relationship with Pete gave my life some balance.

AIMLESSLY BULLSEYE

Not too many days into his first stay with us, Pete came looking for me and asked if I wanted to go for a ride. Sounded great. The Olds was big, surprisingly bigger than even our old Buick tank. As we pulled out of the drive, I asked where we were headed, and his answer knocked me over.

"Nowhere. Anywhere. Where you want to go?"

Now this was something new. I couldn't remember ever getting into a car without the 'where' clearly understood. Was he serious? How does this work? We just gonna ride around aimlessly? I was working on these thoughts and questions when I realized we were riding around aimlessly. I'd never been to this part of…where are we? Indiana. Wonderful.

Well, the scenery was interesting and the ride exciting. Pete liked to corner on the back roads and the Olds gave me the feeling I thought I'd get if I were ever on a boat. I found myself analyzing having no 'where'. It was not easy because I had no history of riding without reason, no experience of ignoring time, no exposure to having a choice of 'where'. Pete interrupted my analysis.

"I was watching you cut the grass and was impressed. What do you call that machine you were using?"

"Lawnmower. A push lawnmower."

"You are a big engine for that lawnmower. You are very powerful through the chest and legs."

Now this is something new again. Was that a compliment? What do I do with a compliment? I hadn't decided when he reinforced it. Now I felt I had to react. I explained walking to and from schools, the paper route, and tennis built up my legs while chores, the accordion, working for Uncle Charlie, and tennis built up my chest. Then I was off about how much I loved tennis before I got hold of myself and shut up.

He kept driving and took it all in. I kept wondering if he really was as interested as he acted. Then he wasn't acting as he looked at me as if in confession. "You know, I don't know how old you are."

I said I had just turned fourteen this past May. Then his questions about school began to flow. Kindergarten fascinated him; he just couldn't fathom "School before school." He easily understood six years of elementary, three of junior high, and three more in senior high. He seemed pleased that I was starting the tenth grade, although for the life of me I couldn't understand why.

And then, something new again. Unlike any of my other roommates, Pete talked about his youth. His school was different in details, but similar overall. As he talked, he seemed to be reminiscing. "I don't think I could have pushed your lawnmower when I was fourteen. No, I'm sure not. Especially on that little steep hill of your front yard. When I was your age, I was not powerful. I was like a reed."

I was surprised and interrupted, "You mean you were skinny?" He didn't have any trouble pronouncing it, but we had to spend some time till he could see what skinny looked like. Once he had the picture, he was very sure he was less than skinny.

He was also very sure that from his earliest memories he loved horses. Horses didn't need him to be powerful or not skinny, they were powerful and not skinny, and they were fast and once he started racing them as a jockey he was in love. The more he talked, the more I could see, horses to Pete were tennis to me.

"The nice thing is you'll be able to play tennis the rest of your life, whereas I had to stop racing horses. Once I started to develop, I seemed to grow like a plant and very soon no more jockey."

Aimlessly continued and then we were in front of the house. He dropped me off, he was meeting some people, and I went inside feeling incredibly good—or was it better?

***

Not too long after Pete's first visit, I was replaying our aimless ride. It was revealing to see him be so open and nice to learn a little bit about him. I recalled how when he dropped me off, I went inside feeling incredibly good—or was it better?

And then, I also replayed our first meeting. "I discovered there was something about him…bothering me…I didn't believe he was a jockey. I didn't know squat about racehorses, but Pete was way too thick, broad, and muscular for a horse to carry in a race. I wasn't too happy with not believing him and tried to brush it off. My brush wasn't working."

Now, it made sense. When he was young, he was jockey size. Then he started growing, not so much up but out. From what I could see, the muscles just layered until he became the powerful and agile specimen of a man who was my roommate. After our ride, I never questioned his being a jockey. I believed him about being a jockey and believed him about everything else. I felt both good and better.

* * *

Soon after came another frightening realization. He could read me. He saw on my face, that first day we met, that I couldn't accept him as a jockey. Heck, he knew I didn't believe him before I did, I just knew something was bothering me. Aimlessly my foot. The 'where' of our ride was to ensure our relationship had a solid foundation of trust. His target for our ride was to remove my not believing him as a jockey. With that target in mind, our aimless drive hit the bullseye.

* * *

Long after his first visit, I accepted the accuracy of my first impression of Pete, he was not another roommate. I decided I would depend on Uncle Brain and later, alone and in private, I would replay everything that went on between Pete and me. There was no way I was going to understand what was really going on as it was going on. There was a strong possibility I would never understand.

* * *

And just before his next visit, I'll be dang if there wasn't something else new. I replayed the questions about school. I had spent a lot of time and effort to learn and assimilate Americana. Now, I was helping someone else learn and assimilate Americana. Who'd of thought? Isn't this a strange turn of events?

DON SCHMIDT

Maybe it was the discussions with my Handler about my temporary roommates. Maybe it was the arrival of Pete. Whatever the cause, I was drawn to think about my relations with my peers.

The people I grew up with were people I watched. They played the roles of mentors and educated me in matters my background and family could not. Over the years I learned, digested, and assimilated Americana by watching those around me be themselves. During the eighth grade, I stopped my study and started practicing Americana. Now, in the tenth grade, I was comfortable with myself as an American, having a secret life, and keeping it from everyone. I was different and had no problem being so. Neither was it a problem that none of my peers understood my differences. They were all nice enough, but I honestly didn't care what they thought of me. So much for my relations with my peers. Intuitively, there was one exception.

He had dark red hair and a ruddy complexion. Beyond that he isn't so easy to describe. He was not cylindrical, although his chest was barreled and sat atop a round midsection. His head was round. Neither did his body have angles. He was taller than most, but seemed shorter because of his weight, but he wasn't fat.

His arms were big, but not muscular. The total was a kid whose promise was to be a large powerful man.

The first time we met was during the sixth grade when he came to our house and knocked on the front door. I opened the door, and he extended his hand and said, "Hi, I'm Don Schmidt." I stepped outside, shook his hand, and said, "Hi, I'm Ron Marksity." He continued. "Like I said, I'm Don Schmidt. We just moved here, five houses up the street, from Central Fairmount. You can call me Schmidty. You should know that lots of people have already called me Shitty Schmidty so you don't have to. I guess a lot of people have called you Markshitty?" Having said that, he looked at me with the face of a choirboy and was clearly expecting agreement.

In fact, no one had ever called me Markshitty, and I couldn't fathom how he reached that conclusion. However, most importantly, the sincere straightforwardness of his introduction could not be denied.

He said that as soon as they moved in, he had the notion we should be friends. I learned this was a typical Don conclusion. We were neighbors—we were going to attend the same school—we should be friends! He didn't know there was nothing in my background that related to his notion, but it wouldn't have mattered to Schmidty had he known. As we grew up, he consistently demonstrated his friendship, regardless. More often than not, I consistently didn't know how to reciprocate.

Often, he would be himself and I would learn something about myself. For example, as you know, I was uncomfortable going into anyone's house, that Serbian thing. Don made a point of not being outside when I would go to his house on our way to some activity. I would have to go to the front porch, or the back door, or the garage, which made me uncomfortable. Now and then members of his family would be there and that made me even more uncomfortable. One day I mentioned I was unhappy in these situations and Don barked, "That's because you never have anyone to your place. Even your yard isn't welcoming." Bingo! For the first time in my life, I recognized that my parents and Baba didn't want my associates in our house. Not one of my peers came in, ate supper, or slept over at the Marksity's. If you weren't Serbian or in need of help, there was no welcome mat at our front door. That insight was pure Don.

As the tenth grade started, Don introduced me to Hi-Y, where the experiences helped mold me. He said he joined Hi-Y because he didn't like fraternities while he liked the concept and mission of Hi-Y. An organization based on "Good Christian Fellowship" with the welfare and spiritual growth of the members and service to the community as priorities. I went with Don to have a look and not too many weeks later became a member with my formal initiation at the Westwood First Presbyterian Church. Hi-Y was linked to several churches and YMCA facilities, and by this time of year, we were playing basketball and holding our meetings at the Y across from Westwood School.

It soon became clear that the way he introduced himself was just a preview of his ability and tendency to completely take me by surprise. His Phantom Turn is one example.

He had an obvious mechanical dexterity and loved to tinker with engines and machines, especially his baby, a 1951 flathead V8 Ford. Drag racing was the heroin of the fifties, on the tracks, and more so on the streets. Want a rush, pull up at a stop, pump some testosterone, and see who can get to the next stop first. Even in everyday traffic, there were all kinds of drag races.

Now Don's Ford was competitive, but he wasn't interested in drag racing. For one thing he knew the toll it took on the car. For another, he was annoyed with drivers who presumed he wanted to drag. In time, he decided to annoy back in the following manner.

Guy pulls up next to Don. The flathead looks a wee bit small for the round driver. Guy guns his engine, the driver looks over at him with his choirboy face. Guy laughs. The light changes. Guy peels out and as he speed-shifts into second, he sees the Ford back at the stop. Guy waits for Don and when he pulls up the guy is bent out of shape, big time.

Guy peels out again and so does the Ford which keeps up with guy, and Guy begins to think flathead has been playing him. Speeds increase when Don looks at Guy and turns his steering wheel hard left. Guy yanks his wheel left to avoid being hit and ends up in the curb, ditch, yard, or any place other than the race. In the meantime, Don returns his steering wheel to the steering column and continues on his way. He was able to detach his steering wheel from the steering column anytime he wished. Once free, no matter how he turned the wheel, the steering column and the car kept going straight.

The first time I experienced The Phantom Turn, I didn't know whether to wet my pants for fear, stare in awe wondering how he thought of this, or grab him and kiss the big imp for the execution.

As it turned out, Don called me five days later. He felt I needed to know that, after thinking it over, he didn't really remember taking the steering wheel off. Then, five days later he called again because he remembered he was replacing his steering column. So, for a while his steering wheel wasn't attached, and he could have made a phantom turn. He wasn't positive that he did it, but he wasn't positive that he didn't do it. In this manner, he was comfortable with himself.

He was my ideal of the solid American, honest, loyal, decent, hard-working. He respected the world around him, was a good citizen, and a good neighbor. He was the first peer I trusted and his personal standards were validated.

He lived five houses up the street.

YOU DRIVE

It was a beautiful day. You know the kind, vast empty rich blue sky encompassing rather than looking down on the earth whose colors were radiant, vivid. We had been riding for over an hour when Pete pulled off the two-lane highway at a point overlooking a farm fantasy. Gently rolling hills, lush acreage, and off in the distance a red barn, silver silo, and huge trees ringing a white farm house. We stretched and just enjoyed the view.

Then it was time to go, and I took his cue. As we headed to the Olds, he caught my eye and immediately threw something my way. Instinctively I caught it and only then realized they were the keys to the car. Before I reacted, he said, "You drive."

"Me? Really?"

He didn't like the 'really' and gave me his look that meant, "Don't act like a kid." Ninny is probably closer to what he had in mind, but he didn't know the word. I pretended I hadn't noticed the look and headed for the driver's door, got in behind the wheel, put the key in the ignition, and felt the eyes.

"What?"

"What are you doing?"

"Fix'n to start the engine."

"Fix'n? Is that one of the words you're helping me learn for American? Fix'n?"

"Okay, I was going to start the car."

He was surprised, "Just like this?"

I said yes, and gave him my look that meant, if you're going to say something, please do. No response. That was it. Fine. I turned back to the key and started her up. I knew how to work things because I had watched him drive very closely. Once she was running, I released the emergency brake, looked over my left shoulder, and seeing nothing put her in Drive and started forward.

Dang, I sort'a didn't go exactly straight but managed to get her straight. Once on the highway, I seemed to drift left and right. It was a big front end and the thing felt like it was going to run away from me. It was slow going at first but soon we were moving along smartly. Then I thought I saw something from the right and hit the brakes. I hit my nose on the wheel and didn't look to see Pete's adventure but clearly heard his arm hit the dash to stop himself. Regrouping, I started off again. Traffic coming toward me was no problem and I gained confidence. Then I came upon a truck, and it got to be work.

During this entire time, no matter what I did, Pete didn't say a word or give me a clue of his feelings, he might as well have stayed back and watched the farm.

A car came up on me, passed and passed the truck. Well, if he could, I could. After giving it one try, I decided my thinking might have been somewhat of a stretch and settled in behind the truck. Finally, Pete was pointing to a spot for me to pull over. I did and shut her down. We sat and I waited.

He took his good time before asking, "You ever drive before?"

"No."

"Never?"

"Never. I just turned 15, I'm too young to have a license, even a temp."

And so, my driver's education began. In no time I saw that how he was teaching me was more important that what he was teaching me. His—there's no other way to put it—his handling of my education gave me a rendering of his thinking, a blueprint of his planning, and examples of his expectations, expectations he took for granted.

He started at the beginning. Get set to drive. Secure the door and position the seat for best visibility and control. Make sure your legs reach the pedals with total control and your arms are straight so you can swing them freely and control the wheel. Set the mirrors so you can see at least the shoulder on the right side, across the entire rear and at least the next lane on the left side. Check that the emergency brake is on, and the car is in Park before starting the engine. Now, let's practice.

I did it several times before he got out and walked around the car so I could see if my mirrors were positioned correctly. He made some adjustments to my seating position before continuing to the next level.

Getting going means check the situation of the road as you did before, but check both directions, not just over your shoulder. Then, again as you did, pull out and increase speed sequentially. The jack rabbit start is for jackasses and not so good for the car.

Convinced I had digested his latest serving, he looked at me and wondered, "What are you waiting for? Okay? Let's go." And off I went, that is after making sure the coast was clear from both sides.

As soon as I got on the highway, he motioned for me to get off. I learned to check the road and then decelerate, not like a jackass, "Don't slam on the brakes, pump, pump."

Once he was satisfied with my getting on and off the road, he wanted me driving and as I drove, he used my performance to make his lessons stick.

"Focus down the road, far ahead. That will give you the best control for positioning. As you saw, if you focus on the front of the car you see that big hood and before you know it, you're going left and right.

"Use the mirrors all the time. At any moment you should know exactly what's in front and what's behind. That comes from using the mirrors. You should know as much about what's behind and alongside you as you do about what's ahead.

"Do not tailgate and try to keep from being tailgated, that means pull over if you have to.

"No matter when you stop, make sure you have left enough distance to the car in front of you so that if the car behind you gets rear ended you have room to move forward and not be rear ended.

"Keep in mind how dangerous these iron missiles are. Be defensive all the time. You hit the brakes the wrong way but with the right reason, be defensive, even if it turns out there is nothing."

We practiced the rest of the day. I was an eager pupil. How he rated me was impossible to know and if I hinted at asking him how I did, he was back overlooking the fantasy farm. Finally, he must have been satisfied as he said, "Okay. Drive us home."

On the way he finished off with a general lecture on preparing for a trip. "Check the oil, battery, brake fluid, transmission fluid, windshield washer fluid, spare tire, tools, and jack. At least make sure the windows are clean as that makes it easier to see."

Before we got home, he had me pull over in an empty parking lot and taught me how to parallel park. From there he drove home as I convinced him other people should not know I was driving.

Later, our times together were to confirm that this entire experience was vintage Pete. He didn't care about my circumstances, for example if I had ever driven before. He wanted me to be able to drive so, "You drive."

Once he saw I needed help, he provided it. While doing so, he took the opportunity to reinforce our relationship. By giving me the keys, he clearly had faith in me. By referring to the things I had done after he gave me the keys, he demonstrated that he really did pay attention to me. By accepting my advice that others shouldn't know I had been driving, he confirmed our being equals.

Looking back, I'm not so sure about the day. It may not have been as idyllic as reported, but considering what I did that day, it should have been.

From this day on I drove frequently.

MY COUSIN DONALD

It was nice to get a call from my Aunt Viola, but I couldn't remember her ever calling me before. She and Uncle Nicky were living in London, Kentucky where Nicky was a Pastor at The Assembly of God Church. Their son, Don, was going to be driving down there to trade his '55 Chevy for a brand new Buick convertible, Nicky had gotten him some sort of deal. Aunt Viola was calling to suggest I ride down with Don to keep him company. She made a point of assuring me it was okay with him. It took me a moment to adjust to her proposal because I had never even had a chat with him before. I regrouped and said I was pleased to be invited.

The details were settled, we hung-up, and I thought about Don. What did I know about him? Nicky and Viola Golusin's only son. Donald. Five years younger than his sister Gloria. Five years older than me. What experiences have I had with him? None came to mind. None? None. I decided that agreeing to this trip was a good decision for two reasons. First, I loved to travel and had some history with riding in Buicks, although never a new one. Second, this was a chance to finally meet my cousin Donald.

During the few days before our trip, I made an effort to think about him. It came to me that when I was little, Don had two incredible outfits. One was a cowboy outfit of hat, shirt, bandanna, vest, holster rig, and chaps. The other was an Indian outfit of buckskin leggings and jacket, with an authentic headdress of real feathers. He could play cowboy and Indian by himself. One day Olga took me along when she went to visit Viola. When we got there, a man with a pony was taking pictures of Donald. First in one outfit and then the other. Donald, sitting on that pony, looked like the real things.

That was better, but no matter how I racked my brains I had no other memories of Don until he was in high school. I went to visit Aunt Viola and while looking for her found him lying face down on his bed while Aunt Rosie picked the pimples on his back. I was shocked and disgusted. I learned he wanted his door left open, he liked embarrassing others. As for the activity, he thought it was funny.

I was surprised that I had no memory of Donald at any family gathering. No matter how I tried, I couldn't see him in any picture of the family. I remember his parents making excuses for his absences, but I keep thinking he must have shown up sometimes. Finally, I accepted that if he had been there, I never noticed.

And then I did remember, clearly, the only encounter we shared. I was about seven and on went to visit Aunt Viola. She was downtown but Don and Uncle Nicky were home. At a certain moment, Don asked me for some help in getting things out of the closet next to the fireplace, what he had to get was way in the back. When I got deep into the closet, he locked me in and the two of them made a lot of noise as they left. I was there for a very long time. Finally, Aunt Viola came home and let me out. I remembered that I wasn't mad at Don because I was certain

Uncle Nicky put him up to it. The truth was that for some reason, I couldn't imagine Don having the creativity to think up such a thing.

Looking it over, all in all I didn't have much to go on regarding my cousin and therefore I was looking forward to the trip even more.

The morning came, we drove down, spent the night, made the trade the next morning and drove back. During the trip I learned the following. The guys at the gas station were right, the small block Chevy V8 was able to run. Nicky and Donald didn't get along. Nicky hadn't changed and I couldn't imagine him as a Pastor. Viola was someone I had never met before, docile and serving Nicky like an employee. The newly designed Buicks had new names and not the old comfort. That I didn't learn one thing about or from Donald, was a preview of the nothings he gave me the rest of his life.

He got married. His wife Char was from all angles, within and without, totally and sincerely nice. She worked the entire time they were married. They had no children.

Once I left home, I heard about Don in bits and pieces. He was some sort of metal worker, sheet metal I believe. He was active in the Union. He was accident prone. I doubt he worked more than half his employable life, the rest of the time he was on disability. He was a sports fan, but football was his passion. He liked to drink beer. A lot of beer.

When I returned to Cincinnati, I made a point to take him out for drinks. He had the same nothings to offer. He did not speak of friends. He said nothing that would help me know him. He had a lot to say about sports. During the times I took him drinking, I learned as much about him as I had on the trip to get the Buick.

I changed my approach and, on a few occasions, visited Don and Char together. They lived in his parents' house. He felt swindled because he had to pay them rent. He felt he should pay nothing because he took care of the house and paid for repairs and taxes, plus, his sister was receiving support of money and time from their parents and didn't have to pay anything. He didn't like his sister and referred to Gloria as a selfish, phony leach who took advantage of everyone and everything. He particularly hated the way she took money from Uncle Lou and Aunt Rosie. These, along with the hatreds typical of sports fans, were the only emotions I ever saw him display.

When my wife and I got settled, we invited Don and Char to our Christmas parties. They never attended. It was always Char who called the evening of the party to give their regrets. She made a career of covering for him.

When Nicky and Viola came back to Cincinnati, they moved into their home and Don and Char had to move out. It was odd, Don felt abused because he was having to move into a place of his own and honestly wondered why his parents couldn't move into some other place.

Nicky and Viola were both alive when he died in 1987. He was 52 and at the funeral I discovered his favorite watering hole was thirty-five minutes from his house and five minutes from mine. He had never called me from there.

Besides permitting Char to love him, support him, and take care of him, I don't know of anything my cousin Donald ever did for anybody. I've been told Char has remarried and lives a happy life in Florida. I hope so. She deserves to be happily ever after.

His life appeared to have had no purpose, accomplished nothing, contributed nothing. But I didn't know him. Maybe his life was supposed to teach me that everyone has purpose and value, even if I can't see it. Maybe.

He is here because he is on every version of the family tree. If he adds nothing, this picture is consistent with his life.

GONE

The trip with my cousin was not without benefit. The pitiful lack of any form of interaction with Donald gave me a new appreciation for my interactions with my Handler and Pete. With them my abilities in verbal, intuitive, body language, and other forms of communicating blossomed. Those relationships were evolving, as were my role-playing skills. Donald and his parents thought I had a great time looking up to my older cousin.

Not too long after that trip, Pete came for another sojourn, or that's what I assumed. In fact, just two days later he was gone. I couldn't understand him, he had appeared, settled into his half of my room and then, vanished. Everything of his was missing. There was nothing of President Tito's agent under his bed, in my closet, dresser, desk, the house or garage, not a trace. As it happened, the next day was a scheduled session with my Handler so I didn't call him, but I was looking forward to learning his take on Pete's disappearance.

The next afternoon my Handler started our session routinely with his summary of our current goals and then asked for my report. I gave him a brief of what had been going on and then mentioned Pete's disappearance. He seemed to catch his breath before asking me for details, all of them, in as much detail as possible, but only about Pete. I didn't understand why he wanted such detail on an obvious matter but didn't press him. Once I finished reviewing every conceivable detail, I saw he was deep in thought, maybe anxious. I was about to get jumpy over his behavior when he started.

"So, let me get this straight."

This was one of his favorite phrases and he used it several ways. To turn the conversation in the direction he wanted. To get me to repeat something for the umpteenth time without getting me so mad I'd clam-up. To check our mutual understanding. To show that he needed me because, without me, he might not have it straight. But today, he was using it to buy time.

"You say you came home from school, and nothing seemed out of the ordinary but, when you went upstairs you immediately knew he was gone."

We both knew that's what I said.

"Yes."

"So, based on what you saw you knew he had left?

"Exactly, gone."

"So, you saw no clothes, accessories, toiletries, shoes, nothing of Pete's in the house or garage, nothing."

He was definitely off his game. I felt my old faithful behavior would be best, I listened.

"And, you haven't got a clue as to where he might have gone."

I listened more.

"Not a clue? Could it be that he's visiting a horse farm and you just can't remember where he said he was going?"

Mum's the word from me, he had words.

"Come on, think about it, let your brain work, just a dropped hint, a passing word as to where he was headed. How about it?"

How about you're making me nervous? Let's move along. He did.

"You know, Ron, I'd a bet the farm on him letting you know something about what he was up to."

Well, he would have lost his farm. And then, more to himself than aloud I heard, "This is not good." So that was it, he had no clue where Pete was! He was embarrassed. He hadn't figured Pete to up and leave without giving us at least a clue as to his destination or intentions. My Handler felt he had mishandled the situation. Now I had plenty to say and I started from the beginning.

"Like I said the first time I laid eyes on him in our living room, I knew he was absolutely different from all the other DPs in absolutely every way. This is just proof of my read. He told us he wasn't looking for work or housing, he was looking for a base from which to satisfy President Tito's desires. All the others came, got situated, and left. Their leaving was like a graduation, with best wishes, thank-you's, and even some tears because they weren't coming back, Pete is. We don't know where he is, but I know he'll be back."

He wanted a guarantee. I told him to trust me.

Was that all I had to offer?

How often was that all he offered me?

Until our next session, that was that.

MRS. LEWIS

All my teachers were good, but I liked some more than others, just as I liked some subjects more than others. My favorite subject was World History, and my favorite teacher was Mrs. Lewis, the World History teacher. Some kids complained about the amount of homework she assigned, but I read more in the summer than I did during school and reading world history was just fun. Some complained about her being too tough while I thought chewing-out someone in class for ignoring her standards of behavior was too mild. On top of all that, I liked her teaching style. She was an enthusiastic speaker and presented organized outlines, complete directions, and attentive, detailed critiques.

On this day we were receiving our grades for a major assignment on the Roman Empire. After a typically comprehensive analysis of our work, she asked us to listen to the one report that got an A+ because it captured the historical reality. Wow, it was amazing, the kid had the facts right and had made them come to life.

When she finished reading, she asked who wrote the paper. I looked around but no hands were up. She asked again and again there were no hands. Then she asked individuals for their opinions, but none identified the author. When she turned to me, I said I wasn't sure, but I'd bet it was Ron Wiemann, and she replied, "It was Ron alright, Ron Marksity."

What? I was shocked and confused. I didn't consider myself a good student. I was diligent and took pride in doing the best I could, but the idea I had done this work was not in my self-image. The kids gave me some good-natured shots and a few way-to-go's and that was that. Not really.

Mrs. Lewis giving me the highest grade and reading my work in class had an effect on me which was compounded by the reactions of my classmates. Fortunately, she noticed and to my everlasting benefit she acted. She asked if I would like to discuss the paper after school. From that meeting forward, Mrs. Lewis became my academic mentor.

She helped me see that my image of myself as a student was based on my past experiences, which were mainly due to Serbian being my first language. She used the paper to demonstrate how this was inhibiting my recognizing and achieving my academic potential. She woke me to the reality that my classmates had no trouble accepting the paper as mine and by doing so she forced me to accept that the only student who questioned my academic ability was me. She sparked something inside me that enabled me to leave the problems of the past and gain confidence in my intellectual future.

But there was more to her mentoring than academics. In time, we discovered that we lived just four streets apart. This was particularly significant to me because it was just like Miss Knoechel, my third-grade mentor. The first time I went to visit Mrs. Lewis, there were several kids there and I was a bit uncomfortable. That didn't last as I learned the Lewis house was always open and all were welcome. This was a wonderful surprise because her home and the visitors gave me a view of a lifestyle I had never imagined. Further, the girls of the house and their friends gave me a completely new view of women. I witnessed ladies very different from The Matriarch or The Reverend. I watched sisters relate in ways I had trouble believing after only knowing my mom and aunts. Finally, I had a sort of incubator in which to practice being around girls.

In short, Mrs. Lewis contributed revelations, guidelines, examples, her time, and her undivided attention to my academic and social maturation that serve me to this day.

CHASNITZA

'CHAS-nit-za' is a three-inch-high pile of hand pulled and cut phyllo-dough sheets. As each sheet is stacked in a buttered pan, it receives sparingly and in random order, either a brush of honey or a dusting of confectioner's sugar mixed with cinnamon or a sprinkling of finely chopped walnuts or a ration of golden raisins. The top is slathered with honey. Chasnitza tastes even better than the ingredients sound.

Made only for celebrating New Year's Day, this delicacy was more than heavenly tastes and smells, it was an anticipated event as a year's worth of good luck went to the person who was served the piece containing a baked-in coin. Everything from its preparation to how it was eaten was full of long held sentiments and governed by traditions which were adhered to exactly.

Maybe I needed a mental break from the gas station and school. Maybe it was due to the development of my social side. I was attending football games, participating in the Hi-Y hayride and food drive, and enjoying the school performances for Thanksgiving and Christmas. Maybe it was because the Christmas vacation was so uplifting. Maybe it was because the chasnitza was to be made at our house. Whatever it was, something made me decide to spend this New Year's Eve Day watching the preparation of the chasnitza.

When I announced my intention to Olga, her reaction was, "Oh, you are, are you?" She followed this with enough sarcasm to fill the oven while she gave me what's what. "There's more to this than you think, sonny boy." A deep sigh, thoughtful, "You are welcome to watch, just make sure you keep quiet." An overly long pause and, "You are not welcome to help and you are not to participate." Then, dismissively, "And stay out of the way." I thought she was a little dramatic, I mean, they're baking dessert. I thought wrong. Olga would have been more help if she had said, stay out of the line of fire.

Beating a retreat, I reflected on what I knew about this tradition. The chasnitza was prepared New Year's Eve Day by the lady of the house hosting New Year's Day. This precluded any arguments over who would make the chasnitza, so they argued over who would host the celebration. This competitiveness of the Vukich sisters and brother was demonstrated in every aspect of the chastnitza tradition. For example, the sisters manipulated the tradition so that Charlie was not permitted to host New Year's Day. The reason for this amendment was always the same, he was not a baker. In fact, this was the sister's way of making sure his second wife never got her hands near the making of a chasnitza.

My thoughts were interrupted by the arrivals of my Aunts Viola and Rosie and I headed to the kitchen to say hello. By the time I got there, Olga had informed them of my intention. Wow! My aunts were not happy to see me. "You do know this is irregular, you being here to watch, so watch yourself?"

"And you do know to stay out of the way?"

These were directives not questions. I exited and found a place where I could see, hear, and feel safe, a place undercover. As for the three sisters, just like that I was forgotten. They focused on the ingredients.

"Too bad 'Mrs. American' couldn't make it."

"Oh, leave me alone. You never made a mistake?"

"Yes, lots of them but never one like this would have been. Olgie, Charlie almost had her here."

"You silly goose, what possessed you to make him feel she would be welcome? If I hadn't intervened, she might have shown up?"

"Good Lord, that 'black cloud' over our chasnitza."

"Well, she's not here and that's what counts. Can we get on with it?"

I learned the same recipe and pan were used each year, passing from host family to host family. I wondered how they could argue about who made the best chasnitza since they all used the same recipe and pan? The recipe started from scratch with the mixing of the ingredients to become the ball of dough. There was more banter, but I was distracted by the "ball". Why was it called a ball of dough? The entire time they worked it, it was never even close to round. Mostly it looked like something that had been dropped from way too high. No matter once mixed it was called a ball and had to be kneaded.

Who would knead? Using what method? Squeeze and roll. Good if you had strong fingers and big hands. Push and roll. Best for heavy people who could put their weight behind it. This took a lot of discussion, but eventually the kneading started.

"You're pushing too hard, you'll bruise it."

"If you're not strong enough to pull all of it together, let one of us take over."

"How long are you planning to torture that poor dough."

"What? Vi, do you really think you're done? I'd say half kneaded."

In time the dough was kneaded and ready to rest.

"Where did you learn to bake? Lazy you couldn't get rest there, much less the dough."

"Don't tell me you're actually thinking of using that to cover it?"

"Do you think it needs to rest as long as you do when there's work to be done?"

"This is fine. It's supposed to rest, not die."

Somehow the dough was put to rest and while it rested the table was prepared.

"Why must you always put in both leafs of this table? One is enough for pulling."

"Ruzitcha, we went through this last time. My house, my table. If I could, I'd make the table bigger. Wait, not just out from under the table, move all the chairs into the living room."

"Well, if it's too much for you to squeeze your big self between table and chairs against the wall, we'll move them, but you have to use a pad."

"I don't want the pad on the table, only the cloth."

"I agree with no pad. A pad doesn't give a hard enough surface for pulling."

Once the chairs were settled, the table was covered with a cloth. By this time the dough was plenty rested and needed to be cut.

"Don't saw at it, use some finesse."

"Rose Baker, it's dough! Stop hacking at it, you're not cutting a chicken's head off."

"Not like that, like this. Pull the dough gently and as it gives itself up cut along the veins exposed. And remember, the pieces have to be the right size for pulling on this table, not your table."

"That's the way to cut, but that first one is too big."

"No, it isn't; it will pull perfectly."

"If we have a tractor. Knead it back in and start again."

"Fine...finally that's the size, now all you have to do is make sure everyone that follows is the same."

"I know what has to be done."

"Knowing and doing aren't the same."

And on they went until the rested dough had been divided into smaller balls which were all about the same size and did look like balls. Now it was time to pull the dough. One of the balls was put in the center of the floured pulling-cloth.

"Put some more flour down, Olga, you aren't paying for it."

"She's right, we don't want the dough sticking to that thing you insist on using as a pulling-cloth."

"In the center for crying out loud."

A rolling pin was used to spread the dough until it was spread enough to be pulled by hand.

"Olga Marksity, this is the same stupid pin we had to fight last time. Why didn't you get a new one like we discussed?"

"It's a poor workman who blames her tools. Let me roll."

"That's enough. We can use our hands now."

"Oh, I'm sorry miss baker, but baker is your last name, not your skill. This needs more work with the roller."

Eventually, they began pulling the dough by hand across the table.

"You're pulling too hard."

"You're pulling too fast, let me keep up with you or go to another spot."

"You're pulling too big a section at a time."

"Can't you two pull any faster?"

Over and above everything else being said was a dictum, "For God's sake don't tear it."

They continued until it was paper thin and the tabletop was covered. The edges were trimmed off and the dough left to dry. The dough that was trimmed off became part of another ball.

"Okay, now we let it dry. You could have done a better job of trimming; didn't you work in a tailor shop?"

"I, unlike some people, have worked in many places and hard. If you don't like the way it's trimmed, trim it yourself, it's your house, your table, remember?"

Once dry, the tabletop of paper-thin dough was cut into sheets. The chasnitza pan was used as a template so each sheet was precisely the right size. Pulling and cutting took a long time due to waiting for the pulled dough to be completely dry before cutting. I was tired for some reason and decided this was a good time to take a break.

I visited the bathroom, went outside and played with Duke, and when I was sure they were out of the kitchen, made myself a sandwich and took it and a glass of milk up to my room. Soon after, I realized I was playing with my lunch, I wasn't enjoying it, I was…something. Slowly the something came into focus. I was tired because I had just witnessed a very private part of my Baba's daughters. I wasn't sure I was supposed to see what I saw. I was sure I didn't know what to do with the revelation.

At first, I had found their banter and chit chat fun. The way they poked at one another was entertaining. But at a certain point it was more than fun and teasing. I didn't want to admit it, it would show I was naive, but there was more going on than I was catching. Looking back, alone in my room, I admitted there was a lot going on just undercover. Their banter and chit chat had an undercurrent of meanness and, replaying the experience, I began to see patterns in the hurtfulness.

Olga, the youngest, was poor because she hadn't married well, and cheap, because she was poor. She was the baby and totally spoiled. A dreamer, flitting from notion to notion and frequently deciding not to distinguish fairyland from the world around her. She was playing at life, while they had to work hard to live.

Rosie, the oldest, was bossy in the worst sense, she was a bully. A bully with a wonderful smile on her "I really care for you" face. She didn't take anyone's wishes, opinions, feelings, or circumstances seriously and just went ahead and had her own way. So, everyone thought her kind and generous when she was actually selfish and presumptive. She was independent, stubborn, tough, and even got her way with Lou.

Viola, the middle daughter, had the image of being a diplomat negotiator, capable of smoothing things over while the reality was that she was sneaky. She had something to hide, and no one could find out what. Her motives and actions were suspicious and seemed governed by her desire to keep her secrets protected.

Botta, the youngest, was not involved. As a child, Uncle Charlie hadn't said a word till he was six and as an adult he might as well have remained speechless regarding chasnitza because his sisters totally excluded him. The only link between Charlie and chasnitza was that his second wife, the notorious shavbitza, Serb for German, but in her case the Vukich sisters meant Nazi, must never be permitted near the cake.

No wonder I was tired...and then I heard they were hard at it again, so I got back downstairs. The cast was already center stage as were the countless sheets of paper-thin pan sized phyllo. Assembly was about to begin.

"This is our home, and margarine is what we use."

"This is our New Year, it only comes once a year, coat the pan with butter."

"Is that all the honey you have?"

"Not only do I hope you have more, but I hope you have better, this is turning already. How old is it and where have you had it?"

"It's equal amounts of confectioner's sugar and cinnamon, not heavy on cinnamon because you like it."

"The recipe says finely chopped walnuts, not hunks of walnuts."

"Raisins are not raisins—this calls for golden raisins. The black ones turn out like clinkers from a coal furnace."

"Okay, right now, next time here, I'm bringing the rolling pin, honey, butter, walnuts, and raisins, golden raisins."

"This year it should be sheet, honey, sheet, sugar/cinnamon, sheet, walnuts, sheet, raisins, all the way up."

"No. It should be unpredictable, just like the year."

"Yes, where did pattern come from? There is no pattern, there never has been a pattern. Sometimes you're such a child."

"Most times she's a child who could benefit from a spanking."

"Put more honey on there."

About halfway up the pan it was time for the addition of the coin. Inserting the lucky coin was the honor of the hostess.

"This year, let's try to do it right. Stand with your back to the pan."

"You can stand any way you please put you can't look at the pan."

"Throw it over your left shoulder."

"I'm right-handed, it's better over my right shoulder."

"Don't throw it, you keep missing the pan."

"She's right, drop it over your shoulder."

"It doesn't matter how you stand, or if you throw it, drop it, or kick it in the pan, just get it in the pan or this won't be ready till Easter."

"No romance, none. Neither of you can take your time and enjoy the planting of this wonderful talisman."

"Fine, drop the coin. Talisman! Where do you get this stuff?"

"Wait! Don't look until we've got enough layers placed over the coin so you can't see where it is."

"Yeah, we don't want you tipping George off as to the location so he can manipulate the cutting."

"Can you say paranoid?"

They were actually considering that Olga might watch where the coin was and from that, have George manipulate the traditional cutting to insure a Marksity got the coin. I bet there were bank robberies undertaken with less analysis and debate.

They returned in earnest to coating and piling the sheets — in silence. It was strange. It didn't last.

"Did you make sure to wash that coin good?"

Hubbub and hoopla exploded concerning the asking of such a question and I was tired again. But I didn't quit. The sheets were disappearing into the pan and then there were only two left. These were placed on top and slathered with honey. This last touch ensured the top was golden bright when taken from the oven.

I got away while they were talking about the oven temperature and baking time. Duke and I went for a long walk, I needed the air and exercise. At one moment I stopped to pet him which was totally for me, I knew he had absolutely nothing hidden beneath his surface. What a day. When I went upstairs to prepare for supper, I found my half-eaten sandwich and untouched glass of milk.

The next morning was a different New Year's Day because all I was waiting for was the continuation of the saga of this chasnitza, the one I had followed from scattered ingredients. How would the sister's handle the tradition in the public of the family? Finally, the only things left on the table, which was returned to its normal function, but I recognized as the pulling platform, were coffee cups, spoons, dessert forks, and plates for the chasnitza. The sisters immediately demonstrated how they would handle the tradition in front of others, for them the others weren't there. It was their saga, and it would continue.

The chasnitza was brought to the table and placed before the head of the host family. It was his duty to spin the pan and thereby determine where the cutting would begin. From this starting corner, tradition dictated that chasnitza be cut into pieces and allocated using a specific formula.

The first piece went to the first person, who was not a member of the host family, to cross the host threshold on New Year's Day. This was the "pole-ou-snick". Uncle Charlie made a point of getting up early and visiting host houses first. One year, Uncle Stevie beat Charlie to the Baker's house and ruined Charlie's year. I found it wonderful as Stevie didn't know our tradition and was simply taking a New Year's gift to Lou and Rosie.

The second piece was for the house itself. The third for the head of the house. The fourth for the lady of the house. The fifth and more as needed for the children of the house. From there on the pieces were served on the basis of age and from this came the Vukich arguments about age. "I am 50." "You are 49." "Exactly, I have completed 49 and have taken my 50th!"

Our pan had clear grooves from being cut into sixteen pieces more than any other number. One sixteenth of chasnitza was over three inches high and more than three by three inches square, a big piece but never big enough. When there were more attendees each piece was smaller. Our family didn't like guests on New Year's Day. Our family didn't like all of our family on New Year's Day. Finally, the most important rule of the cutting, everyone present gets a piece and there are no unassigned pieces left. The cutting of this chasnitza took almost thirty minutes and enough verbal mayhem to embarrass Attila the Hun.

People had their own methods of eating chasnitza. Pick it up was the most honest and probably the best because this kept the layers from sliding on the honey. Others pulled apart the paper-thin dough looking for layers with specific ingredients. Novices and nitwits tried using the dessert forks. Everyone looked for the coin. But beware of these Serbs. The main reason everyone watched for the coin was to see if someone else had it and everyone had several others they didn't want to have it. The second reason everyone watched for the coin was to see if they had it. The last reason everyone watched for the coin, was to protect their teeth. Finally, about eating the delicacy, one rule, you can't take it with you, eat it here or leave it here.

For days after, whenever I thought about this experience, I was as unsatisfied with my understanding as I was that my piece was gone. Plus, George had given the "house" piece to Olga, and she wouldn't share a raisin. During the entire time I watched, everything about the tradition was critical. It was strange that dessert took this path. Everybody had a personal list of critical points which, taken together, made everything about chasnitza critical and here's the real insight, it was critical to be critical.

At the start of the process, I noticed that Baba wasn't participating and that she remained aloof throughout. It seemed a natural role for The Matriarch to head the tradition but after the experience, I believed Baba didn't want to see or hear her daughters as these characters. I asked her about it later and she was not forthcoming, she couldn't change what they were and wasn't the type to question herself by hindsight. I got her message nonetheless, I had been right, their interaction was past meanness and included vindictive behavior and bitter consequences.

Over the years, the consequences ranged from hurt feelings to periods when they wouldn't talk for months. Six or eight months of ignoring and avoiding is a lot of work in a family of only three sisters. Looking back, I began to recall times when explanations were offered as to why so-and-so couldn't make the occasion du-jour. Now I understood the real reasons.

Over time, I asked each sister privately how they felt that day had gone, their party line was, "Oh, that's just us." Unfortunately, they were right.

* * *

How our tradition was supposed to be, never changed. How it actually was, began to change before we even noticed. During the next years, Rosie Viola Olga Charlie and Lou acted like they honestly believed how it was supposed to be, was how it was. Nicky was noncommittal, George was Olga's parrot, Charlie's second wife was irrelevant, and Baba remained aloof. By New Year's Day 1961, the change was complete and saying that our celebration was how it was supposed to be was bogus. This is how it changed.

Chasnitza was made the day that was most convenient for the bakers, which was rarely New Year's Eve Day. It was not prepared by the lady of the house hosting the celebration but by any combination of the three sisters and at any house they picked for whatever reasons.

A chasnitza was always there on New Year's Day but chasnitzas began to show up on other days. One year a chasnitza showed up on Christmas. Then one showed up on Serbian Christmas. Not too long after that, we had chasnitza on Serbian New Year. In time, there was no telling how many chasnitzas any given year would bring.

As the years passed, the excitement of finding the coin only increased. Then, Rosie decided she would help the process. It bothered her that so many people were disappointed by not getting the coin, so she carefully put a second coin in the chasnitza. She liked that and next came several coins, multiple coins, and finally, a coin in each piece of chasnitza. There were differing reactions but mine was clear, she had taken the luck out of the tradition.

By the time I left home, we were so removed from how it was supposed to be that who made the chasnitza, regardless of who hosted the event, was as big a surprise as how many were made and what would be the denominations of the roll of coins Rosie added.

As I put the period to the paragraph above, I intuitively knew, like a mother knows the welfare of a son far away, that the ground in Arlington Cemetery finally stopped heaving as the Vukich's stopped spinning in their graves. Oh, I almost forgot, the chasnitza was fantastic! On this point agreement was unanimous and without reservations. May the Vukich's rest in peace.

RONALD E. MARKSITY

CANADA

1959 arrived, I went back to the tenth grade, and Pete came back to Daytona. Just as there had been no good-bye at his departure, there was no fanfare at his return. This became the routine for his actions and behavior. He came and went seamlessly, with no exits or entrances. When he stayed it was for differing lengths of time with no pattern. When he left, we got no report of where he went or who he saw, although sometimes he put in a bit about horses.

Okay, fine. I had enough on my plate with school, Hi-Y, weekends at the gas station, and my Handler. He and I were spending a lot of time on Pete. To be sure, I had no other temporary roommates since Pete showed up, but we weren't going into past personnel, or reviewing, or even fine tuning our work on others, we were focused on Mr. Johnson. Plus, I could tell my Handler was still sensitive about Pete's' disappearance before Christmas.

It was early February when he showed up and asked if I wanted to go to Canada with him. Before I could answer, Olga was all over it. "What an opportunity. Of course, he wants to go." That would be me that she was so sure wanted to go. I wondered what possessed her to give her opinion about my actions. Pete took my reaction to Olga as hesitation to go and was plain silly as he started selling me the trip. He explained he needed me to interpret…and keep him company…and we would be seeing some great sights…and there would be kids my age…

Hey, enough. I let him know I wanted to go. I didn't let him know that I wondered how my Handler would react. Turned out my Handler's reactions were the least of my worries because Pete and I left the next morning and until our departure I didn't have a second to myself, much less a way to alert my Handler.

As we got ready it was exciting. I tracked Pete as he prepared the '98 for the trip. The Olds was spotless, and he did exactly what he had lectured as he checked the oil, battery, transmission, brake and windshield fluids, spare tire, tools, and jack. I had a choice between Olga's' white Samsonite and George's' To-Europe suitcase, I took his monster. I didn't get much sleep but was wide awake as we pulled out of the driveway before sun-up.

Pete drove till the sun was full and then asked if I wanted to drive. Geez, let me think, I'm fifteen, don't even have a learner's permit but have the chance to air out an Olds '98 on the open road. It was wonderful. The big boat was in its element at 70 and just hunkered down eating road. I was so excited that it was some time before I realized Pete was dead asleep. Excitement was joined by a touch of pride, he had complete faith in my driving ability. He slept until I stopped for gas.

He took over after our break and I thought about him. I recalled that fine day in Indiana when he taught me how to drive and now, I understood. That was when. This was why. He needed a driver. There was more than one reason for almost everything he did, and I was learning his characteristics.

We took turns driving as we climbed north. When we hit the Canadian border, I was surprised by the security, lines, and formality. I had no idea what I was supposed to say or do or show or what. When our turn came, Pete showed his passport, and I just gave the man my wallet. I'm not sure but I like to think it was my library card that got me through.

Once in, I took over driving, turned right, and began cruising east. Then Pete took over and I focused on the scenery. I was amazed by the snow piled in huge mounds and had never even heard of posts to let you know where the road was. It was cold but no more than I had experienced before, good old Cincinnati and its four seasons. Then I took over and toward the end of my shift, now and then, we were able to see the drop off from cliff to water on the right edge of the highway. When Pete took over again the sun was low enough to be in the rearview mirror.

I liked it quiet when driving, but Pete preferred music and at this particular moment, "Smoke Gets in Your Eyes" was introduced by the DJ and I perked up, I really liked the song. Pete had her steady at speed but when we both noticed a jumble way up ahead, he took his foot off the gas. As we neared, we could see it was a pack of cars, trucks, a bus, and a police vehicle. Pete tapped the brake pedal and our lives changed.

The road was a sheet of ice, and we were in a spin. Nothing to do to get out of it. The '98 made two complete 360-degree rotations before I realized we were spinning in perfect choreography with "Smoke Gets in Your Eyes." To share our experience, play the song and whenever the phrase — da da da, da da da dada Da — is played, know that on that last upsounding Da — the Olds started another 360. Now, the comforting weight of the big '98 was potentially our executioner as we spun and continued toward the jumble until we hit something that stopped our spin and made us skid until something seemed to catch and turn us to the guard rail above the cliff and then we hit the rail and rode it for a bit which slowed us until a section gave way and we were on top of the crumbling rail, scraping on our frame and could feel the Olds grind the rail as it inched over the side. Then we were stopped, with the front wheels over the cliff and the last bars of "Smoke Gets In Your Eyes" ending the selection.

Very carefully, Pete switched off the radio. We were dead quiet.

My mind was crystal clear. I was standing before Camus' window; this was a privileged moment of my life. I was staring death in the face. If we moved the wrong way, we were going to plunge hundreds of feet onto the rocks below and die. It was that simple.

Also in this privileged moment, every fiber of my being knew I was surrounded by Peace, engulfed by Protection, ensconced in the security of Ultimate Strength, and this was God, under whose overwhelming auspices I was being taken care of, I had no fear, only faith.

We sat stone still.

There was noise, people approaching from our left. I couldn't stop myself and slowly turned my head to see. Pete had done the same thing. The noise got closer.

Now they were around us. "I'm Sergeant So-and-So of the Mounties. Are you okay?"

I don't think he heard our answers.

"Your frame's hung up pretty good but try not to move anyway. We'll get you out." Someone slipped on the ice and let out a yelp.

It was a Greyhound type tour bus, and they hooked a chain to our rear axle and the bus pulled us onto the road and free of the railing. As we were helped out, the crowd from the jumble had gathered and let out a great cheer.

Unbelievably the '98 had little visible damage, mainly the left front quarter panel and half of the grillwork. The mechanics in the gathering reported there was a lot of scratched metal underneath but no obvious problem, they agreed that anything wrong would come to light soon enough. I was very grateful, but don't remember saying anything. Then we were off again.

It was very late when we get to our destination, but the husband and wife were waiting for us. She offered a bit to eat but I couldn't, so she showed me to my room. As my head hit the pillow something that had been coming to my mind ever since the wreck hit me again. I couldn't forget it, I couldn't avoid it, I couldn't even ignore it. It would not leave me alone. The Canadian Mounted Police weren't wearing red jackets.

I was awakened by noise. I couldn't make it out. I went to the window to have a look. We were on some sort of farm. It was kids playing hockey after school on a pond behind the stable.

Pete and the lady of the house were in the kitchen when I got downstairs. They asked about my welfare as she fixed me a snack. We chatted for a bit and then she asked if I wanted to go outside and meet the kids. I preferred not to interrupt their hockey game and would meet them at supper.

At supper the kids were introduced. They were a little younger than me but very nice and invited me to join them tomorrow for some hockey. I thanked them but didn't mention I didn't know how to skate. They could learn that tomorrow.

After supper the kids went upstairs and a bit later some visitors arrived. Like everyone else, they spoke Serbian and the introductions were cordial. Not too much later I felt an awkwardness in the air. I looked at Pete for a sign and got it, I was holding things up. After nice-to-meet-you all around, I headed for the third floor. Before I got there, they were talking but I couldn't understand them. I slowed down but still couldn't make out what was being said and then I realized, I could hear them fine, but I couldn't understand the language they were using!

I slept past noon. Newly refreshed, I started working. Pete had not told me what I was supposed to do or how I was to act, but I knew exactly what my Handler would have wanted me to do. The lady fed me but had nothing of interest to share. She was not comfortable with my questions and as soon as I was done eating, she explained Pete and her husband were in the stable. On the way there I noticed the visitors had left. I listened to them talk in Serbian about horses and racing until the kids came home and learned I didn't skate and knew absolutely nothing about hockey. I urged them to go ahead and play and Pete stepped in and said he would give me a tour of the grounds, which gave the kids their game back.

After supper the previous night's visitors and several new gentlemen arrived. After some very sketchy introductions, I excused myself. I had trouble sleeping as I felt the cold and understood the windows in the dormers of my room, double panes with at least 14 inches between each and heavy drapes across the entire alcove. The lady had anticipated the frigid temperatures and showed up with a stack of blankets. Then she was gone, and I was asleep.

The next morning, after breakfast, Pete announced we were going to be gone for the day and the couple needn't wait up for us. The Olds seemed none the worse for wear as we drove through the fantastic winter wonderland of clear blue sky, green trees, and white piles, drifts, banks, and fields. We stopped at the house of a couple that spoke English. The visit, which included a fancy supper, was spent talking about horses. I learned more about horses, horse racing, breeding, buying, and selling than I could handle.

On the way back, a fog set in and in no time was so dense it was spooky. We had the windows down as we crept along so we could hear oncoming traffic but there was none to be heard or seen. We were about ten feet from him before we saw the waving lantern and closer before we saw the man waving it and on top of him before we could make out the bridge. Such fog was normal in this spot and the locals had a system for managing it. I was given a lantern by the bridge man and told to walk in front of the Olds waving it as he had been waving his. When I heard another car, I was to start a steady repetition of "h'low" and listen for a return. In this manner Pete and I went across the bridge and did pass a walker and vehicle going the other way. The experience was surreal and exhilarating, the sound, light, man, car, appeared from the nothingness and disappeared back into it. At the other end of the bridge was another volunteer who took my lantern and told us to be careful. I was thankful when I hit the farmhouse bed hours later.

The next morning, I got honest with myself, I was totally frustrated. I had learned nothing about what was going on and almost nothing about the people we were meeting. I certainly wasn't needed for interpreting, in fact, I needed an interpreter. My report to my Handler would consist of "Smoke Gets in Your Eyes" and fog. And then somehow the day had passed and people started to arrive, supper was served, and I was excused. I woke up twice during the night and they were still going at it.

Bright and early the next morning, Pete got me up and after a hearty breakfast we hit the road, being purposeful to not return the way we had come. We both appreciated that the ride was uneventful, but I was anxious. While we'd been gone, how was my Handler handling another Pete disappearance? How about my disappearance? How do I explain I had almost nothing to report after five days with our prime focus? What am I going to tell my teachers about my absence? Or, what have they been told by Olga? Why did Pete take me with him? I didn't interpret, run errands, sit and listen, nothing but drive. On that point, thank God for putting Pete and not me behind the wheel when we hit the ice. Geez, I totally forgot about Howard. Does he think I just decided not to show up for work over the weekend? How about...

...it can't be, that was Columbus. Since we left Canada, Pete and I had been lost in our thoughts and had hardly spoken except when changing drivers at gas and food stops. Now, our proximity to home got us working to cover details we both wanted to get straight before Cincinnati.

He thanked me for going along, couldn't have made the drives without me. He knew very well how hard it was for me to be the fifth leg, but it was the others, those he had been meeting with, who felt uneasy with a youngster sitting in. He hoped I'd be willing to go with him again.

I thanked him for taking me with him and suggested it was more an adventure than a trip. He agreed in a casual manner, so I started asking questions. He gave a virtuoso performance of talking without telling. When I asked what language they were using, he made it clear that was enough questions. We agreed there would be no mention of my driving or the fog or "Smoke Gets in Your Eyes" and then we were home. He thanked Olga and George for letting him borrow me and informed us it might be some time before he'd be back and then, he and the beat-up '98 were gone around the corner.

NORMAL IS A PLACE I'LL NEVER EVEN VISIT

That evening, the first chance I got I contacted my Handler. We agreed to meet the next afternoon.

At school the next day there was no record of my parents calling so I explained to my teachers that I had an opportunity to see Canada for free. As I detailed the trip, I didn't tell them about driving or "Smoke Gets in Your Eyes" but gave the fog a real tribute. It was nice as each let me know, with a wink or gesture, that they would have done the same thing, they just wished someone would have notified them of the situation.

Afterward, I kept reviewing these talks. I had established that there was a man I worked for and shared, as proof, what I had learned about the horse breeding business. Then I threw in the weather to purposefully manipulate the truth to fit my needs. Looking back, I had to admit I was comfortable with my actions. My opinions and attitude towards my teachers hadn't changed but the way I related to them was all changed, I was the one deciding what and how much they should know.

Late that afternoon, I headed to my Handler for our first

session since my disappearance. I was embarrassed and disappointed. Once I got there, surprise. His first questions were about me, my welfare. He had been worried about me. He knew we only had one phone on the first floor and figured I wasn't able to call. He didn't want either of us to feel so isolated again. He felt we needed to do something and asked if I had any ideas. I was frozen, unable to react, this was a serious change in his treatment of me. He gave me a minute and then wondered if I thought it would work if I told Pete I couldn't go with him on future trips without advance warning? What, I thought? Yeah, sure, I think it would work and, just like that, he made it our rule. Then he repeated that he was glad I was back and asked which dates were good for an extended debriefing. We agreed on a date and he said if it was okay by me, we could call it a day. Big surprise.

Saturday morning at the gas station I learned Howard had done my parent's work. When I failed to show up, he had called to ask how sick I was because he knew I had to be sick to miss work. He got the facts from Olga and when I showed up Saturday, he and all the others wanted the details of my trip. Over the course of the morning, they all got the same version. It was a golden opportunity to go to Canada, for free, just to keep a guy company and here's the route we travelled. That stimulated interest but no more. Later, to a much smaller group, I gave them the fog. They liked that but it wasn't a knockout. At the end of the day, to Howard and Whitey, I asked them to swear a pact of secrecy. They were glad to do so and understood my reason as I detailed driving the Olds. That lit them up but when I topped it off with "Smoke Gets in Your Eyes" ka-boom, knockout. The wreck remained our topic for months and our secret forever.

The day for our extended debriefing arrived and I was curious as to how things would go, would my Handler continue his new treatment of me or would he revert to his previous methods. As soon as we got started, these thoughts disappeared as I gave him my report and exposed just how little I had learned on the trip.

He was all pats-on-the-back and assured me that, as before, my work may seem puny, but Uncle Brain would have a lot to offer. He then proved his point over the next months as all our sessions focused on Pete and the trip. We created a timeline from departure to arrival. We completed a map of the entire trip with emphasis on the locations and details of the two houses and properties. We had the license plates and the locations where I had seen vehicles, to include some foreign cars and farm and horse equipment I had never seen before. We compiled a list of all the people I had seen and where I had seen them but had few complete names and no salient facts. He put me in front of pictures, but we got no results, and we never did determine the language they used.

Looking back at these sessions, I saw change. On the subject of Canada, he regularly gave me thumbs-up for deciding to go and for making the most of the experience. In general, he asked for my opinions, my reasoning, and even my recommendations concerning our topics and process. This change in the way he worked me became permanent and we became more like a team than like a handler and his implement. I told him I noticed and not too much later told him about "Smoke Gets in Your Eyes." Eventually, I told him that my confidence as an undercover operative was growing and becoming more of my self-image. He seemed pleased to hear that. Much later, I told him the Mounties didn't wear red coats.

But there was one thing I didn't tell him. How Pete affected him startled me. Pete was clearly an important part of his activities; however it was disturbing that he seemed to take personally some of Pete's actions. His behavior before Christmas, when he learned Pete had disappeared, was a perfect example. I got the feeling Pete was by far the biggest focus of his professional life. Based on these observations, I didn't tell my Handler that Pete was not the focus of my life.

Finally, I finished getting everything and everyone around me settled after the trip and settled into my routine. As time passed, every once in a while, I felt as if there were a shadow over me. More time passed and the shadow became a cloud. I may have thought I was settled in my routine, but that's not how I felt. Eventually, the cloud mushroomed into anxiety. This didn't happen overnight nor was it blatant, it was a subtle intrusion to my life.

I don't know if it was fortunate or unfortunate, but during this same period I had another sort of parallel experience. At random times, in no particular circumstances, I would see the specter of death looking up at me from the rocks at the bottom of the cliff in Canada. When this happened, I was surprised because my feelings were positive and I was totally free of anxiety and, as I was on the scene, I wasn't afraid. Rather than an oppressive threat, the specter seemed to be an inexpensive lesson in my mortality. In time I came to accept the specter's appearances as reminders of what could have been and confirmations of The Almighty taking care of me. Soon thereafter, the appearances stopped but, to this day, whenever I hear "Smoke Gets in Your Eyes" my stomach does a flip-flop.

As with the specter, again not blatantly but subtlety, I came to understand the shadow to cloud to anxiety. The trip to Canada had changed me, my insight was more focused, and I began to see elements of my life differently. What I needed to do to fit in with people and activities changed to what people and activities had to do to fit in with me. Prior to Canada, I was running as fast as I could to keep current with the times and events around me; these held my focus and I saw the start and end of things as dictums and evaluation points. No more. Now, when and if I ran, I ran as fast or as slow as appropriate for my view of things. Now, I knew I had to keep my faith in God and live all the elements of my life. Now, I had no doubt I'd master doing both and that spontaneous realization was the biggest change of all.

THE REST OF THE 10TH GRADE

Spring had sprung and my studies were running smoothly, weekends at the gas station were adding to my nest egg, working with my Handler was just another part of me, and even though I didn't drink smoke or date, there was plenty socializing. And, there was my passion, I was going to make the tennis team, the Varsity tennis team. Then, just as spring had done, up popped Pete.

Not too long after his return, I had a school holiday and we drove up to Whitewater State Park. He was something. This foreigner knew all about the lake and surroundings, while I had never heard of the Park.

On the way home, I was driving, and he congratulated me on how I used the rabbits. The rabbits? What was he talk...of course, now I get it. On our way to Canada, I watched him pick cars to follow. I noticed these cars were going faster than any others and that he followed them until they turned off or until another car, going even faster, went by and then he followed that car. My driving from Whitewater mimicked him and he explained he called the cars he followed rabbits. On the track the mechanical rabbit is the focus of the dogs and on the road, Pete expected his rabbits, not him, to be the focus of the police. I had taken on one of his characteristics without being conscious of doing so. I wondered if that was good or bad.

Pete left and the next meeting with my Handler was no fun. We both had hoped I would learn where Pete had been since Canada, what he had done, whom he had met, etcetera. In no time we had to admit the only things we learned were about Whitewater State Park.

* * *

On this day, when I got home from school, Mrs. Lakeman was visiting. She met Olga way back, when Olga was at The Assembly of God and they had remained friends. When Olga realized she was late for a meeting and had to leave, Mrs. Lakeman said Olga needn't drive her home, she'd walk. Olga suggested I accompany her. Turned out she lived a ten-minute walk away and she invited me in. I mentioned that I knew she was an artist and asked her if I might see her work. She saw I was sincere and gave me a tour.

Her oils were realistic and therefore right down my alley. During her tour I noticed a very nice piano and learned that she was an accomplished pianist and gave lessons. Well, isn't this just the oddest thing. In our living room was the upright piano from The Peniel Missionary Assembly, it had not been played since it left the church. Mrs. Lakeman and I agreed I'd start lessons the next week and they continued for over a year. I still have one of her oils and most of her piano instructions, but without practice, the music has atrophied. For some reason I feel the need to mention that, unlike the accordion, I never practiced the piano on the front porch.

UNDERCOVER

***

Several weeks later, Pete showed up and not too many days later asked me to go to Kentucky with him, just for a day or two. I thought of my Handler and the rule we had established after Canada. I gave Pete both barrels.

Just for a day or two? Did he have any concept of the trouble I had at school and the price it was still costing me for leaving like I did for Canada? Could he understand that my grades were being pinched due to what I missed, and did he realize this could affect my grades and my college and my career and my entire future? Could he appreciate Howard at the gas station, whose entire operation was in a strain the weekend we were away because he couldn't get anyone on Saturday morning to fill in for that Saturday, and of course he and his brother and sister had to delay their normal Sunday drive because he had to handle the station and I still feel guilty every Sunday as they leave. And what about the impact at Hi-Y where my explanation was appreciated but my reliability was questioned and...

Pete interrupted and apologized. He had the message. He was sympathetic. He had no idea. From then on, for any overnight trip, I had enough warning to be able to alert my Handler.

***

As you might imagine, I started looking for a car the day after Pete taught me to drive. I asked a lot of questions, read ads, kept my eyes open, and got an idea of prices. I learned about the steps to get a license and the costs, like insurance and upkeep, that I'd have to cover. When it was time, I asked George to teach me to drive. On my first lesson I did such a good job with his Chevy in the empty parking lot that he suggested I move on into traffic, where I motored here and there in such a manner that he was shocked. He decided I was a natural driver and when I parallel parked, he was convinced I had a gift. The first lesson was the last. He and Olga never had an inkling that I had been driving with Pete.

As my sixteenth birthday approached, I had found a car right around the block. The owner was a local radio personality who let me take the car so the guys at the station could check her out. They gave it an OK and we agreed on a fair price. I alerted the Westwood Homestead Savings and Loan Association, where I had my private account, that I would be taking out some money and learned I didn't have to do that. However, when I showed up and asked for $400 cash, they were taken aback. This was my first withdrawal from the account. In this way, just a few days after 3 May 1959, I was driving my 1957 Ford Custom.

For my cream with a black interior baby, Custom meant Basic. Small six-cylinder, three speed column shifter, four-door, vinyl seats with no radio, no mats, and no carpet. I could hose down the interior and cause no damage. It had not been garaged and the rocker panels were rusted out. That was when I got her.

I cut off the rusted sections of the rockers, filled the panels with steel wool and then painted everything with Rustoleum. I used imitation chrome sheathing to cover the rust inhibited rockers. Next came grease, oil, filter, and confirmation that the mechanicals were fine. I took off the fake chrome covers on the big round taillights so they glowed red and ready. Then she got the penultimate application of my waxing business expertise and looked like a new car with chrome rocker panel covers.

UNDERCOVER

* * *

I made the varsity tennis team. Second doubles. My partner and I won more matches than any other position on the team.

* * *

When the 10th grade ended in June, I was already following my personalized itinerary for summer vacation.

HAWTHORNE, WITHOUT THE SEVEN GABLES

My summer vacation itinerary started with tennis as the top priority. Everything else revolved around and adjusted to tennis. This included, in no particular order, working at the gas station, working my car waxing service, working for the FBI, reading and hanging out with the guys. Things went according to this grand scheme for about a week.

Coming home from the gas station, I saw that Pete was back, his Oldsmobile was in the driveway. That car was amazing, except for body work on the grill and left front end, nothing had to be done after our little dance along the cliff in Canada. Nothing mechanical had been affected, the frame had absorbed all the abuse from the ice, guard rails, and steel support posts.

Sure enough, he was inside with Olga and George. During the hellos I was surprised to learn that they had been waiting for me. Pete advised me to put my gear away and take a ride. When all four of us headed to the Olds, I knew something unprecedented was coming, Olga had joined us on a few of our little jaunts but George, never.

With George and Olga in the back, I rode shotgun and Pete took off. As he drove, he seemed headed toward Price Hill and the comments of the backseat drivers made me realize Pete was the only one who knew where we were going. Soon enough it was down Glenway to Price Hill. When he got to a light at Hawthorne Avenue, he turned right and part way up the block pulled into the driveway of a two story brick. He seemed right at home. I had never been in this part of town.

He had been silent during the drive but as he herded us out of the Olds, he began remarking on the neighborhood and other houses. Then, as if a tour guide, he maintained a running commentary as he led us along the driveway to and through the detached one car garage, around the house and yard, ending at the front porch. At this point he suggested we take a peek inside. We were off again, following our leader.

I couldn't imagine what he was up to, my best guess was that he had bought the place and wanted us to see it, but I wasn't sure. From the looks George and Olga exchanged, they didn't like their best guesses any better than I liked mine. Meanwhile, Pete the realtor was giving us the grand tour. We visited every nook and cranny and heard his version of the pluses and pluses of each. He didn't seem to notice any of the minuses.

Finally, back on the front porch, he finished his presentation with a look of satisfaction on his face. I couldn't reflect that look and didn't know what there was for him to be so satisfied about, while Olga and George were, at the least, confused. Pete was crestfallen as he saw we didn't get it. He let us see he was taken aback, shocked really, how could we not get it? Finally, he took up the challenge of helping us get it.

I was bracing for what was next when he asked me how I liked it. I told him fine, not really knowing what there was to like or not like. He said he was glad I liked it because it was mine.

"I'm sorry, what?'

"It's yours."

"WHAT?"

He didn't answer immediately because he was putting two sets of keys in my hand. He had to curl my fingers around the keys to prevent me dropping them.

"It's yours."

"WHAT?!" I had anticipated unprecedented. This was way past unprecedented.

He had no sympathy for my being discombobulated, I'd have to learn to live with it. Plus, we had things to do. He produced a valise and from it three copies of a bunch of papers. He handed us each a copy and stood there expecting us to read. Read, hell I was in shock, I could barely hold the pages. Olga and George were equally shocked but looked over the paperwork as if they knew what they were doing. Maybe they did but I couldn't even pretend to be reading, I could only look him in the eye and say I trusted him. Made sense to him because he handed me a pen and showed me the various places where I was to sign.

As I signed, he went on to explain I should rent the house for income. He'd noticed my work schedule and habits; he knew I needed money. More importantly, he had never forgotten my welcoming him to share my room and since then I had been of help to him on a regular basis, like in Canada. He was just treating me like I treated him.

When George and Olga were finished looking over their copies, they started signing and in no time all three of us had signed all three copies in all the right places. With the signing complete, he explained that now I was legally the owner of the house. He pointed out the copy we should keep and suggested we might want a third party to evaluate or inspect the details, that was just good business.

Once he saw we were overwhelmed, he allowed himself a reprise of his look of satisfaction as he suggested I close my house. My house! When I finished, he got us back in the Olds and drove us home, all the way he was the only one talking.

Back on Daytona we were all thank you's and embarrassment, we weren't sure how to act in the face of such generosity. Pete shrugged us off and left for a previous engagement, with that look of satisfaction spread from ear to ear. Still not able to understand, George, Olga, and yours truly went our separate ways.

My separate way was to the garage and my six banger. I needed a drive to think things over. It's hard to believe but, somehow my drive ended in the driveway of the house on Hawthorne Avenue. I just sat there and looked at the place. I didn't know what to think or feel in the driveway of "that house." Nowhere in my makeup was there a place where "my house" had been sequestered waiting to get out. It would take a long, long time for this to be "my house." Night fell and I couldn't see any house anymore, so I headed home.

SUMMER 1959 AND BEYOND

The next morning confirmed that "my house" on Hawthorne was not a dream and that my summer itinerary was invalid. Over time Hawthorne impacted me in such a way that I came to see my life as made up of the constants—tennis, my education, the gas station, the FBI, car waxing, and Hawthorne. These constants were my responsibilities irrespective of the date, school year, or other experiences that came my way.

When I told my Handler about Hawthorne, he merely shook his head. He asked some questions and a few sessions later informed me that, "Yep, it looks like your friend bought the house and gave it to you." We never went beyond that. To my amazement we didn't see Pete for the rest of the summer. With him gone, our efforts concentrated on others while we waited to see when he would resurface.

As for Hawthorne, I anticipated the yard, the part that everyone could see, should get first attention. However, as soon as I turned in the driveway, I noticed the front porch. Funny, during my first visits I hadn't noticed the junk, or the smells, coming from under the porch. On closer inspection I was reminded that I didn't like snakes and discovered that I didn't like mice or rats.

Once I was satisfied with my evaluation of the world underneath the porch, I turned my attention to my original objective, the yard. The yard was like under the porch, without the porch to cover it. In a few weeks, the area under the porch was nothing but raked dirt and the yard as good as any in the neighborhood.

Not too much later, the place was rented and through the summer, one project a at time, Hawthorne became a home. I covered the exposed area under the porch with lattice work, sanded, primed, and painted the porch floor and sanded and varnished the tongue in groove porch ceiling. That varnish job was the last project. If you haven't done varnish, don't. From here on I cut the grass and then in the fall raked the leaves. It was up to the tenants to shovel snow while I supplied salt for the walkways.

I have to emphasize that none of this could have been accomplished without the help of Sally and Milt Schneider, Howard's brother and sister who ran the hardware store. They helped with this two-story just like they had helped with my first bookcase. I made sure they knew how much I appreciated their guidance and patience. I learned it's good if a homeowner has connections in the hardware business.

During this same time, my other responsibilities were filling my days. I worked at the station 8 to 8 every Saturday and alone on Sundays, 9 to 3. Howard was completely supportive and gave me as many other hours as I could handle. I adjusted my waxing service by only taking jobs for previous clients or people referred by previous clients.

Of course, tennis remained my first priority; I gave it my all. No matter when or where, if there was an opportunity to play, I was there. This was not obsessive, this was necessity. There were no indoor tennis courts in the 1950s, so we had to play whenever the weather cooperated.

All was well, my life was grand, full, and moving along in a smooth rhythm. So, I should have anticipated that a completely new experience was waiting around the corner, waiting to turn my life upside down.

Actually, not around the corner, around the West Hi courts. Of course, I didn't notice them when I was playing. I'd learned not to notice people last year at the State Jaycees Tournament. But I did notice them when I wasn't playing.

First, I noticed them at the courts. Then I noticed them on the courts but couldn't understand what they were doing, they had two balls and two racquets but they sure weren't playing tennis. Then I noticed they were there a lot, even though they were doing nothing to learn how to play tennis. Then I noticed they were there almost every time I was there. Then I noticed they were at the drinking fountain whenever I got a drink. Joyce with raven black hair. Nellie, a blonde. Joyce was the instigator of what developed while Nellie was along for her friend. In fact, I was glad Nellie was involved because she seemed to understand that I knew less about girls than they knew about tennis. At times, Nellie had to tell me what Joyce's actions and words meant. I may have spoken Serbian, American, and Biblican but I didn't comprehend one syllable of Dateician.

So, we met and over time they educated me. They taught me not to be nervous around them because they were girls. They taught me that it was okay that they liked me and that they had orchestrated our meetings. They taught me that girls and guys talk on the phone, a lot. They taught me that it was okay for a boy to visit a girl at her house and one day when Joyce said I should drop by, I said I would. As she was giving me directions to her house—we discovered that she lived at the top of Daytona—our houses were 300 yards apart! There was no way I could not accept this as a sign and from that revelation on, Nellie stepped into the background and Joyce and I spent time together.

It was Joyce who taught me it was normal to talk on the phone forever and hang-up feeling it had not been long enough. Joyce taught me to hold hands, hug, kiss, and talk till her father sent me home from the porch swing or living room couch. Joyce taught me not to be ashamed when Olga asked about the red stuff on my collars. But most importantly, Joyce taught me about romance. Why she liked me, I would never know. That she liked me, she made sure I knew.

However, there was one thing she couldn't explain. After our first time alone, my responsibilities that had so demanded my time, weren't so demanding. More to the point and worse, I always had time for her. I had time for Joyce when I didn't have time for tennis! See what I mean, my life was upside down.

THE MATRIARCH: IN HER GARDEN

I was looking for something in my room when I happened to glance out the window and saw Baba in her garden. I stopped to watch her and as I did so, a smile came across my spirit.

As she tended her tomato plants, I didn't see an elderly grandmother in her tiny garden. Instead, I saw the young Maria with dark complexion, full lips, high cheek bones, significant nose, wide set large eyes, and silky dark hair. Not unattractive, she was average height, coordinated, extremely strong, and blessed with uncommon physical and mental stamina, two attributes she sorely needed for the life she faced.

Watching her doggedly administer to her other vegetables, she seemed safe, happy, and at home. What a difference from her home in Serbia and a life as hard and cruel as the mountainous setting where they lived off their land. She was careful that they not be described as farmers, rather, they were a family that pooled their talents and the natural resources around them to survive. Watching her in her garden, I could only hope she was truly safe, happy, and at home, because she never admitted being anything less.

When she turned away from her garden and appeared to survey the yard, I thought of her surveying the world of the early twentieth century. As a young, widowed mother of four, with almost no formal education, she anticipated World War I and determined to get her kids to America. When she was prevented from doing so for lack of a special form and its seal, she took matters in her own hands. She found someone who could provide the forms but not the seal. She filled out the forms and then killed a chicken. While the chicken bled, she broke dry corncobs in half and dipped the broken ends into the blood in an attempt to make the seal. When she was satisfied with the results, she used a cob in the blood to make the seals and brought her children to America.

In the yard, it seemed the grapevines, apple, pear, and other trees, flowers, and shrubs were gathered around waiting to learn who she would visit next. It was to be the grapes. The scene took be back years to McMicken Avenue, where the iceman and a group from the neighborhood gathered and waited for her decision. Baba was all decorum as she evaluated the iceman's offerings. She looked them over, hesitated, just long enough, and then gave a slight nod of approval toward her selection. As with the vegetation in our yard, The Matriarch gave those gathered her decision.

Maria Vukich making decisions and following through was nothing new. I was reminded of her at the table in the room behind the church where, as The Matriarch, she was judge and jury to the man who beat his wife. She advised the man to stop, and when he wouldn't, his knees were broken so he couldn't.

Back in the yard, she had finished with the grapevines. The fruit trees were next. As she moved toward them, there was no question her mobility was inhibited, yet no question she would get to where she wanted to go. She moved slowly, steadily, knowing when to rest and demonstrating what she had lately taught me. She was getting old, becoming what we all are supposed to become. She did not want adjustment of this natural progression. She had faced life as it had come to her and that was the way she wanted to act through the very end.

It was her character in focus that, as she physically deteriorated, she increasingly refused assistance. Since we did not routinely use doctors, Baba was not carted back and forth to physicians, nor would she accept house calls. No cane or medicines, no doctor strategies, no support group. She had no circle of friends. All her friends were long since dead. No, all she needed were her will and toughness. She had those and more than tenacity, she was loaded with plain stubbornness. For example, she loved America unabashedly, but chose never to speak American.

Down in the yard, she was struggling to prune a stubborn pear limb and eventually disciplined the tree by completing the cut. I was reminded of her kids whose behavior frequently merited discipline, yet she only interfered one time that I witnessed. The entire family was gathered with Baba at the head of our dining room table and her son, my uncle Charlie, on her right-hand side. I still don't know what he did or said, but she backhanded him and his chair into the kitchen. He landed against a kitchen table leg, while the chair came to rest on his thigh.

Unlike the puny pear limb, Baba's stubbornness was iconic and included a mean streak that evolved during a life of surviving. She thought survival, and identifying enemies and danger were essential to her perspective. Once identified, no matter the enemy, destruction had to follow. The lowly fly was an example. From my earliest memory she caught them with a swipe of her right hand but never killed them. Rather, she removed their legs, so they crashed on landing, or removed their wings so they had to walk about or removed one wing to watch then fly in circles. Even at her current advanced age she displayed this sleight of hand which recalled a glimmer of her coordination. It also was a glimpse of how, as The Matriarch and years before as the Serbian immigrant, she administered her responsibilities.

I knew I truly had no concept how tough this woman was. I realized that though she had reared me, I really didn't know what her life had been like, the pain, the challenges. I knew she had reared four children by herself, I also knew I would never fathom what it felt like, what it cost her, how she had done it. But, just by growing up under her wing, I learned to recognize and experience the depth of sorrow and height of exaltation that are the outer edges for living life.

She was on the move again and I was surprised that she was headed back to the garden, she seemed satisfied with the work she'd done before. Once there, she moved among the vegetables and beneath a plant located a saucepan, the white enamel type with red rim and handle. She moved to the foundation, supported herself against the wall and relieved herself in the pan. When she was finished, she went to the water spigot, added water to the pan and spread the contents across the grass. She repeated this twice more before ambling back to the garden and returning the pan to its hiding place. From there, she was careful to avoid the canvas yard chair put there for her use and made her way to the concrete back steps where she sat down, leaned against the metal railing, and surveyed the scene.

Surprisingly, I was not embarrassed. Instead, I felt a heightened awareness.

What I had witnessed was merely another proof of her failing health and confirmation of her fundamental pragmatism. To use a bathroom, she would have to go up two flights of stairs or up one flight and down another. In either case the exertion would have to be repeated for the trip back. She could better expend her limited energy on the living things around her than on hiking up and down stairs. It was also clear that there was no way she was going to sit in a comfy canvas chair, that was foreign to her roots. Rock and stone were the chairs of her youth in Serbia, and she recalled her youth better on concrete and iron.

As she continued to gaze about, I realized she wasn't looking at the various vegetation, she was looking at the bounty they represented and rejoicing in the bounty of her life, she was at worship. Daily reading of the Bible was her life blood, and this was evidenced in many ways. Her faith was her health insurance. But my new awareness highlighted a fact; in her entire life, no matter what went on around her, she was connected to one lifeline, total trust in God and His judgment.

Finally, and most wonderfully, I saw that it was the righteous truth that Maria Vukich was safe, happy, and at home.

I never knew how much I loved her until this incident.

MR. FINDLAY

I blinked, summer was over, and it was September 1959. School started, Hi-Y got cranked up and I continued to work on tennis, knowing I'd be on the varsity but not knowing where. My 11th Grade class schedule had only good and better subjects and a mechanical drawing teacher who was new to West Hi, a Mr. Findlay.

Five-five or six, he was extremely fit, but his receding hair line made him look bookish rather than muscular. In fact, he was a specimen. One day, to demonstrate a point about leverage, he pulled up his pant leg and demonstrated the point with his calf. It was incredible. The two muscles of the calf seemed to be having a tug of war beneath his skin. He credited the muscles and his entire physical condition to having played minor league baseball, which was his true love.

Perhaps a lesser love, but none the less true, was his love for teaching. He gave me a lasting appreciation for mechanical drawing, drafting, and architectural drawing. He taught me about perspectives and three dimensions. How he taught was unforgettable, his sincerity for you to learn was motivated by his wanting to witness you experience the pleasure of knowing. You could feel his interest in his topics and his students. His lessons and critiques were as intense as the concentration of a professional athlete.

I was in his classes during my 11th and 12th grades. During those years, and the ones before and after, Mr. Findlay gave each of his students the same assignment. No ordinary assignment, it included an agreement between each of us and Mr. Findlay stating that, if our assignment proved successful, the two of us would share the bounty equally. The assignment was to design a wheelchair that could go up and down stairs.

At the time of this writing, it is February 2002, the current issue of U.S. News and World Report has an article concerning Science and Technology and lone inventors, titled American Ingenuity. It mentions an inventor, Dean Camens, and his colleagues who won the patent last year for, you guessed it, a stair climbing wheelchair.

More than forty years ago the need for this device was recognized by a balding, fit, ex-minor leaguer who taught me how graphite could make ideas come to life. Forty-two years later, Mr. Larry Findlay's assignment was finally completed. I know he was happy the device was invented and not unhappy that he wasn't sharing the bounty.

THE FLAMENCO TATTOO

Almost as soon as school resumed, Pete resurfaced. I hadn't seen him since he made Hawthorne "my house" and I was a little skittish wondering what he would do next. Seemed he wanted to go to a movie and thought I might like to go along. I did. From this point on, Pete was never gone very long and when he showed up, either as my roommate or just in passing, we regularly did things together.

On this night we were in the Olds, headed home after a double feature at a drive-in. I thought back to the first time we went to a drive-in. On the way he stopped at a grocery store and I wondered why. He explained that we had to be properly equipped and he was getting the goods. Some guys at school drank in the drive-ins but that didn't figure with us because I didn't drink, and I only saw him drink in Canada. When he returned, he gave me the bag with the goods, a Sara Lee sour cream-topped cheesecake, two napkins, and two plastic forks. We never went to a drive-in without the goods.

We hadn't exchanged a word since the movie ended when Pete remarked that a car was following us. I looked and so it was.

It caught up with us and began tailgating. Then it passed and as it did, I could count six occupants, six big occupants. They pulled in front of us and started slowing down. They let us pass and resumed tailgating. Then passed, cut in front of us and hit their brakes. This pattern of pass, cut us off, and slow down, let us pass and tailgate, continued until I felt we were in a forced dance. A dance accompanied by obscenities and wild gestures. They were big, loud, and angry.

This continued for more than ten lights and intersections, during which Pete didn't say a word. He drove along as if nothing were going on. When they passed, forwards or backwards, he appeared not to hear the noise or see the gestures. Finally, and by this time I had no clue how long finally was, but it appeared finally was forever, Pete's demeanor changed.

They were in the passing lane waiting for us at a red-light. When we pulled alongside and stopped, all six cranked up the yelling and gestures. Pete looked at them as if seeing them for the first time and then opened his door enough so that the interior lights came on. He unbuttoned his coat and took out what appeared to be a holster. I was unaware he was armed and froze. Casually, and ever so slowly, as if placing a rock on an egg, he put the holster in the glove compartment. This was clear to me and equally clear to those in the car next to us.

Once the holster was in place, in one fluid motion he closed the glove compartment, ejected himself from our car, sprang unto their hood and began making dents in it with his metal tapped heels. They were dumbfounded. I was catatonic.

Pete continued his flamenco tattoo from the hood to the top of the car, where the damage was more severe. While I remained a zombie, he danced down to the trunk and left his marks. Then he stepped off the trunk and started to the nearest door. The driver did not wait for the light to change but did his imitation of a drag racer. We never saw the car again.

Pete got back in our car, closed the door, leaned over and opened the glove compartment, took out his holster and only then did I realize it was not a holster with a gun. It was his wallet! He closed the glove compartment and as he leaned back into the driver's seat, gave me his look that said, "What?" put the wallet in his coat and waited for the light to turn green.

As we drove, my senses came back to me. Finally, I was composed enough to start to ask a question, but before I could get it out, he said in Serbian, "It is important to wait until you are sure what you want to do. Then, when you act it will be without fear. It is best if they think you are crazy. You want to get something to eat?"

* * *

A few days later we left in the morning and drove a good while before we stopped somewhere and walked a good while until we arrived somewhere and sat for a good while. Then, we played it all backwards and got home in the night. That's all I can recall of the day, as for what was said all day, I feel I remember every word.

"You know that was quite an experience, that night with the six guys in the car."

No reaction.

"I've been thinking about it a lot and there's something I can't figure. I don't remember feeling scared. I must have been, but I can't remember. I don't know."

He was busy driving.

"Well, I do know you were unbelievable. I couldn't imagine

what you were doing. I felt like I was there watching but not really there."

Still nothing.

"Look, this was a major thing for me, and I need to talk about it. Those guys wanted to fight. I know what can happen in a fight, I've seen it up too close in a playground on East McMicken. But I don't know about fighting, I've got almost zero personal experience. You can help me. What do I need to know?"

His deep breath was not because he was yawning. He was deciding between me as his pest, or he as my helper. I'd wait…he could stop a clock…finally…

"Well, there is a lot to know about fighting."

He said this in American, not Serbian, with a voice that sounded like I imagined the Supreme Court sounded. For the next many hours, the Court's opinions were handed down to me.

"Whenever possible, don't fight.

"A fight is a proof that you are weak and stupid. Too stupid to avoid getting into a fight and too weak to run away when the fight can't be avoided. You're not weak or stupid so don't act like you are.

"Never fight in public, you can't cover up what happens in public.

"Never let someone else get you into a fight. Use your brains and get out of it.

"Fighting accomplishes nothing. Think about fighting for vengeance. You want to avenge something. You fight. You win and people want to avenge the loser. You lose and other people want to avenge your loss. It never ends. You know any Sicilians?

"In the same way, issues of pride, honor, territory, love, hate, all have no solution by fighting.

"Don't fight because, win or lose, there will be physical results like scraped knuckles or busted bones. These become advertisements of you as a fighter and people will answer those advertisements. Winning a fight makes you a target of those who want to prove themselves. Losing a fight makes you a target for the bullies."

Court took a recess. He could see I needed time to think. The Court's opinions were totally opposite the opinions I had developed growing up. To me, Indians taking coup and cowboys facing off in the sun, were fighting with courage and honor for right and wrong that was as plain as black and white. After more than a good while, Court reconvened.

He taught me that by using wits, deceit, humor, brains, guile, it was possible to defuse most situations. Once defused, it was an easy matter to slide away from the scene.

I learned that in situations that could not be diffused, for example where the other guy just loves to fight, I was to beg, grovel and...

"If you can't get out of it, run away from it. You understand run away?

"Whether by brains or feet, once you get away, wait. Wait and think. Think until you know exactly what it is you really want."

His sideways glance and the length of time until he continued, announced I better be ready for the rest of the Court's opinions. I waited.

"The only reason for fighting is to kill."

My mind raced back to Sneaky Mean and Favorite in the playground. Favorite was fighting because he wouldn't run away from Sneaky and disappoint his admirers. Sneaky was fighting to kill Favorite, and he almost did.

"If you are not fighting to kill, don't fight."

When I considered a fight from this perspective, that it can only have one result, I'm going to kill someone, there was a lot less to fight about. Do I really want to kill the man who cut me off in traffic? Do I really want to kill the guy who made fun of Joyce and Nellie and made me the laughing stock of study hall?

"If you are to kill, wait, plan, and prepare to eliminate the target. There is no right and wrong, there is only you live, he dies. Nothing honest or fair. Not no second chance, no first chance. Sneak, ambush, not courage. Living coward, dead target. If you do it right, it will not be a fight, it will be an attack and only you will do any fighting, the target is there only to die. And all of this in private. No one should know it was you, not even the target. For everyone else, you are the one who ran away from the fight.

"This is where strong and smart pass weak and stupid. This is the tough part. This is where one must be hard. In public, grovel, beg, look the coward, and run, because for you the only reason for fighting is to kill. No one must know this. Most will think poorly of you."

He paused and gave me a sideways glance that looked like an angry dog sounds.

"You have understood that surviving is all that matters?"

His pause became a hesitation and for the first time since we met, Pete looked at me with questioning eyes, he wasn't sure I understood. He said, "Survival, above all else." and then nothing but silence.

In the silence a sense of comfort came over me. I felt I had found a truth I sorely needed. The truth for me was that the Court's opinions were perfect in their simplicity and intent, perfect for my life. From this day forward, I weighed getting satisfaction, saving face, fixing a wrong, standing up for myself, revenge, and a lot of other things to fight about, against killing someone. From this day forward, the Court's opinions were my laws.

It was quiet for a long time before I realized Court had adjourned. I didn't know what was on his mind, but I wasn't about to break the silence. Finally, Pete broke the silence with a mix of Serbian and American and the voice of a teacher who has a needy pupil.

"So, the other night with the car was quite an experience. You couldn't imagine what I was doing. It was simple."

And on he went to review the night of the flamenco tattoo. The guys in the car were not accepting that he was ignoring them. They were not accepting that he was not participating. They were not accepting that he was trying to get away from them. In effect, they were not permitting him to either defuse or escape the situation.

I asked why he didn't try to outrun them. He explained that he wasn't sure he could and if he tried to run away and failed, we would be facing six big, loud, angry, and newly confident fellows.

Whether they wanted the car or money or what, he had no clue, but they were becoming more brazen the more he tried to defuse them. His experience told him the longer they went unchecked, the more convinced they would become that we were a hapless target and they could get whatever they wanted. It was at this point that he felt he had no choice and began forming his plan.

Finally, at the red light, he put his plan in action. Opening the door so the interior lights came on stopped the cycle of them in control, they went quiet as they tried to see what he was doing. He made sure they could see what he was doing, thereby extending the time when they were no longer in control. Then, when he removed his wallet so that it looked like a gun and put it in the glove compartment, he changed the momentum, now he was in control.

He wanted to make sure I understood he was sacrificing nothing. He didn't have a gun so giving it up was for show. The six in the car were shocked that he had a weapon and more shocked that he was putting that weapon away. They had to think, what kind of an idiot doesn't need a gun when he's facing six of us. It was a ruse that happened to work. It wouldn't have made a difference to his plan if the ruse hadn't worked.

Jumping out of his car and physically attacking their car made each of them feel they were being attacked. This put them back on their heels. Even I could see the brains in this, everyone knows most Americans think of their car as an extension of themselves. This crazy man was attacking each of them and all of them by damaging their car. What logically followed was, if he is doing this to our car what is he going to do to me. His plan ended with him getting off their car as they ran off, and that's exactly what happened.

He acted as if he had just tied a ribbon on a present and fell silent. The silence was for my benefit and included an invitation to ask questions. I was sure I'd have questions but, at the moment, I needed time to digest what he'd said. Sitting and thinking led to accepting that I had a suspicion there was something else. There was something he wasn't telling me. I took my time and decided I needed to look at the incident again and to concentrate on him more closely.

He wasn't afraid. Surely not. He wasn't ruffled. Right. He wasn't nervous. Nope, not even excited. Well, what was he, angry? I don't think so, I've seen him angry. Did he have any emotion? Of course, there was something, I just couldn't see it. Well, I was going to stick to this until I could see it.

So, what happened…a car full was following us…tailgating…passing and slowing down in front of us…letting us pass and then cutting in front and hitting the brakes...all accompanied by a constant roar of obscenities...they were big, loud, and angry...he appeared not to be aware they were there...finally, his demeanor changed...we came to a red light...he opened his door enough so that the interior lights came on...the gun...in one fluid motion...ejected himself from our car onto their hood and began making dents in it...the flamenco from the hood to the top...the trunk...he stepped off....the driver did his imitation of a drag racer and...and then I knew how to see what he was keeping from me, how to understand the incident completely.

I started with Pete stepping off the trunk and heading for the nearest door, everything as it was except, this time, the driver doesn't drive off. From that instant, this is what I saw.

The driver and the passenger behind the driver begin to get out. As they do, Pete steps to the opening back door. He grabs the door at the edge to gain maximum leverage and using his entire body slams that door into the front door which is being opened by the driver. This effectively disables both doors and acts as a trap so the driver can't get out except through the window.

This leaves Pete with the rear seat passenger who is in the process of getting out. Pete is standing, with his full range of motion available to him while the passenger is half seated, half raised, half in, half out, off balance, with a very limited range of motion. At this moment, the front of the exiting passenger's head, meets Pete's knee and the back of the no longer exiting passenger's head, meets the door frame, repeatedly. The completely immobilized passenger becomes an obstacle for any other passengers trying to get out of that back door. But wait, I forgot the cavalry, the other four of the big loud and angry six.

There is no cavalry coming to participate. The cavalry is still trying to get out of the stable. Now I saw the beauty of his plan as I recalled where he had stopped the Olds. He had stopped the Olds at an angle up against the side of the other car, smack against the back door, very close to the front door and over a foot from the front windshield. Parked this way, the Olds made it impossible for anyone to get out that side, even by trying to use a window. From this perspective, I saw Pete waiting beside their car, a warden watching over the prison he had created for the big, loud, and angry.

Now it was easy for me to replay the way he had ejected himself from the driver's seat and onto the other car's hood. In fact, he hadn't opened his door any more than was needed for him to step on his seat, squeeze his torso up and out sideways until he stepped on the ledge of his window and then their hood. His feet never touched the ground.

From the time he mentioned we were being followed he wasn't afraid, ruffled, nervous, excited, or angry, he was busy. Busy developing a plan. A plan that anticipated all the possible contingencies and the best reaction to each. Then, at the next light, he put his plan into action. Pete was in complete control of the situation, but busy with his plan.

Now I broke the silence. I assured him I understood survival was the only option. Then, I gave him my deductions.

He gave me his patented reaction in situations when I presented something and wanted his reaction, evaluation, critique, or just an at-a-boy. I got a long pause accompanied by a sideways stare. Then, no sound but a nod of his head and the slightest smile that could be interpreted a thousand ways. Not this time. This time, his patented reaction had only one meaning, my deductions saw right through him. And, even more, he accepted I understood survival was the only option.

***

The flamenco tattoo experience was a live, real world application of the Court's opinions, opinions which have guided me from that day forward. I did understand survival was the only thing, but by this experience I came to understand it was my survival. I needed to be careful, to question myself, to ensure I was living, not playing, my undercover role. In a blink I could get in over my head.

One more thing, no question. If they wanted to fight, if they hadn't driven off, he would not have fought, he would have begun killing. He was in survival mode.

HANDLER

Over the next several sessions I danced the flamenco tattoo for my Handler. It always felt good to have him know my secrets, I'd concluded this was what Confessionals were all about.

As we worked on the specifics of this incident, my Handler confirmed what I had been noticing, there was a pattern in his reactions to my reports about Pete. He would listen intently, gradually roll his shoulders forward, and inevitably just shake his head. Then, he'd start the cycle again as he listened intently. During the tattoo debriefings, his head was shaking like he was a dashboard doll.

I remembered the make and model of the car as well as most of the license. It turned out the angry six had nothing to do with our efforts, they were just in the wrong place at the wrong time. I said it was more a matter of with the wrong guy as I confessed that I had seen a side of Pete that was ominous. My Handler agreed. Further, he introduced more training to develop my proficiency and confidence in operations.

During the course of the tattoo debriefings, I felt a change in how we worked together. Later, I saw that things had indeed changed.

He began opening up. Turned out he accepted and wholeheartedly endorsed The Court's opinions and was honestly impressed with both what and how Pete delivered those rulings. In fact, he added some of his personal doctrine to reinforce the Court's judgments in my mind.

He let me see that from the beginning he had been closely watching my development. He had taught me how to determine if I were being followed and I took great pride in being completely aware of who was around me at all times. The first time I was headed to a session and felt I was being followed I gave him a full report. I was on my bike and two people in an ugly Ford were behind me way too long. When they followed me as I turned on a new street, I picked a house at random and stopped. I got off my bike and saw they had pulled to the curb half a block back. As soon as they stopped, I got back on my bike and pumped directly toward them to get the license plate and see what they looked like. The couple were puzzled as I stared at them and looking back, I watched them go into the house. I had forgotten the incident, but he remembered even my first attempt to keep our sessions secret.

He began to react to my questions. He might tell me I had no need to know. He might give me an answer. He might explain why he couldn't answer. He might explain why I shouldn't want to know. No matter which, the questions no longer hung in the air as if they were never asked.

He had always been complimentary and encouraging, that was good technique, keep the workers happy. But more and more he routinely began to fill in blanks about our work and about himself. He was an intuitive, intelligent, sensitive man, and truly nothing like the first two suits the Bureau foisted on me.

He had paid attention when we talked about my belief in

God, my faith, and how I felt taken care of since day one. He respected my faith. This may have been an even bigger hook than the one he used to successfully pull me into this job to begin with, the hook that I could help him, The FBI, and The USA. He never let me know if he believed, but he made it very plain, he believed that I believed.

He made me understand what I needed to do in order to be what I needed to be. I never missed an appointment, briefing, or debriefing, but with equal certainty I never missed an activity that made up my other life. He completely supported that I be at school, tennis, extracurricular activities, or on my jobs. In this way, he explained that we were making sure I looked, to anybody watching, as a totally normal student, athlete, participant, employee. Normal, boring, unremarkable was what he was after from my image and behaviors.

He became comfortable with my abilities and trusting of my efforts. His debriefings became much more activities between two equals, each having completely different backgrounds and purposes for participating in our relationship, and each realizing that the success of our activities depended on our mutual efforts.

He let me see when he had no idea, or little, or wasn't going to let me know if he had any idea, about what Pete was doing. But, when I gave him the facts as to what I had been doing, what I had observed, experienced, he was meticulous in gathering, recording, editing, and refining our exchanges until he knew what had happened as if he were there with Pete and me.

And finally, a little at a time, he let me see the picture. The Bureau knew an espionage ring was operating in the area. The ring's primary focus was The Cincinnati Milling Machine Company. The ring's primary targets were The Mill's world-famous technical expertise. There was a good probability that there were other targets and other rings, and or differing levels of both. It had been confirmed that a few of my temporary roommates were subordinate operatives from Eastern Bloc regimes. The Bureau was using intelligence from other sources to correlate the identities of personnel from overseas with personnel here. Most enlightening were the facts that much of what was being uncovered pointed to Pete as the leader of everything going on in this geographic area. The idea that Pete was using the horse buying bit as his cover was no longer an idea.

In time, our work evolved into a pattern of keeping track of past personnel and operations, scrutinizing newcomers and their operations, keeping Pete my top priority, and searching for knowledge. Knowledge about any type changes in any operations. Facts about anything anywhere that related or linked anything anywhere. Similarities, differences, no change, changes, concentration, and periphery were key to our collection. In this setting I felt I was in the right place doing the right thing. After all, I was in up to my neck because of my parents, and my parents were going to be exonerated and someone was going to make a very big apology.

However, most importantly, during this part of my working for the FBI, my Handler humanized our relationship. It was still business, and he was the clear-cut leader, there were no questions on those points. But we were no longer a Handler and his implement, we had become a team.

MEANWHILE

Joyce and I cooled into friendship, Nellie reentered the equation, and by the fall I was dating Nellie.

***

Hi-Y was a wonderful surprise. Our meetings, sports, and civic activities provided Christian fellowship and time to ponder the eternal verities. In public, I determined our solar system was one molecule, in a doorknob, on the inside of a little used closet door, in a house without an address. In private, I determined that a feeling had been growing in me and I needed to find out what it was.

This feeling started when my first temporary roommate said goodbye. I didn't remember his name, but the feeling was real and steadily increased as more DPs passed through. In time, I sensed that DPs were not the root of this feeling. When I went to work for the FBI, the feeling seemed to blossom and I thought it related to the Bureau, but that was not the case. Now, in the middle of my junior year, I felt I understood the feeling. It was not about something other than me; it was about me. It was about my destiny.

Focusing on how to identify my destiny, I learned I had a debt. My debt was the American Dream in reverse. Baba Maria was a matriarch of grand proportions, who included in my upbringing an unassailable conviction that America was the greatest place on earth. Her children, my parents, aunts, and uncles, as well as those in her sphere of influence and those in our church, merely reinforced this conviction. For most of these people, the American Dream was to get to America. For me, the American Dream was to pay the tab for already being here.

Added to this feeling were personal experiences that reinforced my owing a debt. When we got a house and I had a bedroom of my own, it had two beds so I could share my room with a flow of temporary roommates, recently arrived DPs from Czechoslovakia, Hungary, and other countries, but mostly Yugoslavia. From the third grade on, I frequently went to bed listening to the realities of life in Eastern Europe, during and after World War II, as relived by those in the bed on the other side of my room. All too often, I was awakened by their nightmares. I saw that for each of these people, everything they had, they owed to America. How could their debt be repaid?

The people and experiences around me identified my feeling. I had to repay my debt, the debt I owed for having been born here, and I had to make restitution for the debt owed by all the others. Of course, I accepted this, it encompassed all the values I had learned since birth. In short order I learned Baba and members of the family had assumed that is what I would do, and I found it heady that, "Ronnie has to do this something special. Not because he is special, but because it has to be done, for us." I felt it was an honor. I felt it was my destiny. Now, how to fulfill it? That would require a lot more pondering.

UNDERCOVER

***

Academically, my junior year was a success. Work at the station was consistent. In the spring, I was back as gardener-handyman at "that house" on Hawthorne. And there were some unexpected events as well.

***

I was coming home from school and as I turned into our driveway, I almost had a cow. I had only read about them, I had never seen one and now, one was parked in our driveway. I left my Custom blocking the sidewalk and gaped at the rich cream-colored beauty. Four doors, chrome trim everywhere that added a touch of elegance, whitewalls with full chrome wheel covers, and plaques that confirmed it as a 1957 Lincoln Premiere. This was the super deluxe, big engine, automatic transmission, top of the line model, and then some. An interior of red leather and black fabric trim, steering wheel that matched the cream paint, arm rests, ashtrays, overhead lights, reading lights, makeup lights, chrome appointments, power windows, and air conditioning! It would be an advantage if the driver was an organist because the high beams, passing gear, sound system options and self-greasing feature were all foot operated. You read it; this Lincoln greased itself! It was early 1960, but if this Premiere wasn't brand new, the previous owner must have only driven it indoors.

When I caught my breath I remembered how, when Olga and George refused his offer to pay them for their help, Pete's reaction gave me an intuitive feeling that he would make it up to them one way or another. My intuition had been correct. The

Lincoln was a gift from Pete to George and Olga. They made sure I knew they had paid him $500. Like I said, a gift.

*　*　*

I was curious what the hubbub was as I headed to my locker between classes. Once there I learned someone had put a prophylactic on the doorknob of the girl's restroom which was across the hall. It seemed a bit of a yawn, but kids were having a good laugh.

Later in the day, I was summoned to The Principal's Office where I learned I had been identified as the person putting the prophylactic on the doorknob. I calmly assured the principal it had to be a mistake. I had never had or handled a rubber. The closest I had ever been to seeing one was when guys took out their wallets to show how the rubber they carried made an indentation. Definitely a mistake, let's get whoever identified me and talk this over.

Rather than accepting my truth, he was accusatory. There would be no reasoning, my parents had been called, and were on the way so the punishment could be agreed upon. He had already decided to suspend me, the only issue was for how long. This lit me up and when I finished waking him up, he had given me the name of who identified me and understood he and my parents could do whatever they wanted, I was leaving.

Her name was Mrs. Walters, she was the Advanced Math teacher and there is nothing in this narrative that I didn't tell her to her face. I headed straight to her classroom and barged into the middle of the class. I slammed the door and as I headed for her desk where she was seated, I confronted her as a liar and demanded to know why she was falsely accusing me. She froze, as did the class members. I leaned over her desk and demanded she tell me to my face that she had seen me place the rubber. She remained frozen and I could see right through her, she was lying and knew that I knew she was lying. That was good enough for me. I left her door open as I returned to the Principal's Office.

In fact, George and Olga were there and I couldn't help myself. What irony, this was the first time either of them had set foot on the West Hi property. The principal's demeanor had changed. He was not ready for The Reverends and learned that he didn't know diddle about them or their son. The three of them agreed I would be suspended, not for placing the prophylactic but for busting into her classroom in front of all the students. More importantly to me, the suspension would not be put on my record. That was fine, I knew the truth. They also accepted that I would not apologize to anyone and, until I graduated, every time I ran into Mrs. Walters, I'd look her straight in the eyes and grunt "liar" when she couldn't maintain eye contact.

Over time I came to recognize how profound an affect this incident had on me, but at the moment, I just knew I was flat mad. This incident was all about injustice. There was no attempt to find the truth, there was only prejudice and privilege. This was just like my experience with the judge who refused to hold his friend's son responsible for the wreck with the mother and kids. As I thought of that injustice, my anger grew into an unexpected ferociousness. I needed to get a grip on myself. I was weighing the Court's opinion and, I wasn't sure I didn't want to kill Walters.

**

It was during this period that my definition of honor evolved. To this point I felt that honor was linked directly to others. Baba was honorable as a mother. My parents were honorable for leaving the Assembly of God and for both the purpose and results of the Peniel Missionary Assembly. In both examples, their honor was earned by affecting others in observable tangible ways.

I also thought that honor did not have to be seen. Working for the FBI, I was doing something that needed to be done. I believed could make a difference. However, what I was doing undercover was, by definition, unrelated to others and the fewer who even suspected what I was doing, the more successful the accomplishment. Further, I hoped how I was affecting others would never be observable or tangible. It didn't matter what others could see. It didn't matter what anyone else knew, thought, or felt.

From this came my definitions and beliefs regarding honor. Honor is not linked directly to others. Honor is not a shield. Honor is not something to display on the field of life. Honor is the subsoil upon which the field could be cultivated and made bountiful. Honor is a foundation. Honor is personal and solitary.

From this I determined to identify an honorable career. But, how to do so? How to find a career that would satisfy my definition of honor? I decided to ask questions, listen, and watch everyone around me, especially family, those at school, and the parents of my associates. This group could provide data for my decision. This line of pondering pushed my anger aside and my search for an honorable career lasted almost all the way through high school.

* * *

The school year ended. Our tennis team had a winning record. Once again, this time as first doubles, my partner and I had more wins than any other position on the team.

THE BREAKTHROUGH

Most of my experiences came packaged. There was a setting, events leading up to the experience, the experience, and the conclusion. This experience was not packaged. This had such an overwhelming impact on me that except for the conclusion there is little I remember clearly. Everything else is vague, out of focus, incomplete.

I don't know who was working with me at the station, but there were more than two of us. I don't know the summer day when it happened, but it wasn't a weekend. I don't know the time, but it had to be afternoon because that's when I worked. I don't know what I was doing, but I was inside.

Suddenly, there was the crunching metal sound of a serious accident. I don't know who else did what, but I ran outside. I don't remember the other car, but Pete's Oldsmobile was one of two cars that had rammed together and come to a stop on Montana, where it dead ends into Glenmore.

I don't know how it happened, but it appeared one car was turning right from Glenmore to Montana and the other car, coming the opposite way, was turning left from Glenmore to

Montana. They got to the same point on Montana at the same time. They got there very fast.

Pete was lying on the ground by the open driver's door of his Oldsmobile. He was bleeding but I can't recall why or how badly.

I can't recall the other person or persons involved in the wreck. I don't know who else ran to the scene or anything else that was going on around me, but there must have been a lot of activity if for no other reason than this was a very busy intersection.

I ran over to Pete, worrying about his wounds. That was not on his agenda. Neither was it on his agenda to have anyone else approach him, tend to him, or talk to him. He was on the ground bleeding but wanted to talk to me. No one else, me. As usual, Pete's agenda was the one followed, regardless the personnel involved. As others backed away, he pulled me close and directed me, in Serbian, "You've got to get the stuff out of the glove compartment and keep it with yourself. Now."

I followed his orders and went to the glove compartment. There were two packets of papers and the Owner's Manual. I took the two packets, closed the compartment, and returned to him. He looked at what I held in my hand and nodded. I had what he wanted me to retrieve.

"Now, get into the trunk and behind the spare tire is a valise. Get it out, put those things in it and get out of here." With that, he grabbed my hand and the two packets I was holding, motioned with a toss of his head for me to move, and pushed me away.

I don't know how I got the trunk open, but when I did, there behind the spare was what he called a valise. I yanked it away from the spare and out of the trunk, opened it, put the two packets inside, closed it and returned to Pete.

At that moment I saw Howard, Milt, Sally, several guys from

the gas station and other passersby looking at me. It hit me that Pete and I had been speaking Serbian and these people had never heard me speak Serbian. Someone asked me, "You know this guy?" I don't know what I said, but it must have been something that satisfied everyone, as Pete and I were alone again, talking Serbian.

"Are you okay?"

"Don't waste time. I told you to put the packets in the valise and get out of here. And keep those packets away from anyone. Anyone."

I don't know when the police and ambulance arrived, but they were approaching Pete who was still lying on the ground bleeding.

I don't know how I got home, but I was going to the back door as fast as I could without running. Under my arm, in a death grip, was the valise with the two packets. I don't know how much time passed to this moment, but now comes the part I remember as clearly as if it were going on today.

The house was empty. I headed upstairs. Three steps from the top was a landing and a window. I opened the window so I could hear anyone approach and then continued up the steps and across the hall into my room. I sat on the floor leaning against my bed and put the valise on the floor leaning against the bed opposite me. We sat for a while. I could feel my pulse.

As I stared at the valise, I noticed it was small, black, and made of what looked like fine leather. I debated whether it was a guest or something to be responsible for. We sat for a while more. Rather than becoming settled, I was becoming agitated.

After a time, I admitted that no matter how long we sat, the reality of the moment would not go away. The valise was neither a guest nor a charge. It was a golden opportunity for collecting information. In the valise could be the key to unlock the workings and workers of the network my Handler described. This was what every intelligence operation prayed for. This was a breakthrough.

I recognized that the cause of my anxiety was twofold. First, I might not capture all that had been put before me in this golden moment. Second, I might not be able to handle what I learned. I had to think this through and plan my approach. I had to be calm before entering this world of potential. Most importantly, I had to make sure whatever I did maintained my cover. A cover so effective that a known agent, when lying in the street bleeding, trusted me with hard copies of his secrets.

So, the questions began. Is this a secure enough place to be doing this? What will I do if I hear anyone approach? Cover what I'm working on? Hide it under a bed? Put it in the closet? Should I answer the phone? How should I handle pictures? Objects? How much is in there? Will I have enough time to do the job? What is his condition? When might he show up? Will I have enough time to do the entire job? The entire job, right? I will only give the valise to Pete, so what will I do if someone comes for it? If this is truly sensitive material, can anyone just open it up and get the contents out? Is there something inside that will prove the contents have been tampered with? Was there any click or lock when I opened it to put the packets in?

Wait! The questions are not helping. Let's try a different approach. Fine. What approach?

Listen to his words. "You've got to get the stuff out of the glove compartment and keep it with yourself. Now."

Listen. "Don't waste time. I told you to put the packets in the valise and get out of here. And keep those packets away from anyone. Anyone."

There's the approach. It's the packets. He was more worried about the packets than lying there bleeding. The valise is just a bonus. It's got to be the packets.

Slow down. One thing at a time. I'm already linked to the packets. I'm linked to them outside the valise because I got them from the glove compartment. I'm linked to them inside the valise because I put them there. I'll start with the packets and use what I learn going through them when I get to the valise.

I went to the linen closet and took out the oldest sheet. Returning to my room I placed the sheet on the floor between the beds. I would do everything on this sheet. I tucked my bedspread up under the mattress and made certain there was nothing under the bed except my tennis gear, which I moved from under the bed to a position between the two beds.

If I were interrupted, my plan was to put the packets back together and jam them between my spring and mattress. But, if I were interrupted and unable to put the packets back together, I'd use one side of the sheet to cover the other, slide the sheet under the bed, put the tennis gear in front and drop the bedspread. I practiced sliding the empty sheet to insure there was nothing on the hardwood floor that would make the sheet stall on its way under the bed. It worked but would do better when it had some weight on it. The tennis gear hid the sheet nicely and the bedspread covered the tennis gear. Okay.

More to relieve the tension than for security, I walked around the second floor looking out the windows at the yards and street.

I returned to my room, arranged the sheet, bedspread, and tennis gear, and resumed my position across from the valise. Taking a deep breath, I leaned over, picked it up and placed it on the sheet in front of me. I believed I understood just how important this valise and its contents could be. I hoped I would do this job well.

If there was a lock or click when I opened it in Pete's trunk, there certainly was neither now. The clasp worked perfectly and felt expensive. The valise opened smoothly; its hinges silent. Inside, the two packets seemed vulnerable rather than ominous. I reached in, took them out and placed them between the spring and mattress of my bed. I turned back to the valise and closed it. Again, the workings of the mechanisms impressed me. I stood up, picked up the valise and headed for my closet. This was not the best hiding place but at least it separated the valise from the packets. I rummaged around in the farthest back corner and covered it with the typical closet floor inventory. To find the valise, someone would have to spend uncomfortable time in the back of the closet on hands and knees.

Before returning to the bed, I made another circle of the upstairs windows. Nothing I could see had changed. Of course, I couldn't see me. Had I been able to, I would have seen change. I would have recognized fear.

I was afraid. What was I going to uncover? What was in the packets? Who might be exposed? What if someone I cared about and trusted turned out to be part of this espionage group? What if Baba was involved? What if Olga and George were involved? I was afraid of the answers to these questions. Perhaps my taking so long preparing to look at my find was not a sign of thoroughness but a proof of my fears.

I was cold and clammy as I got back to my room, removed the packets from between the spring and mattress, and sat down on the sheet. I placed the packets in front of me. From the beginning I thought they were the same size. Now, with closer inspection, it was clear they were the same width but the left one was longer and thicker. In lifting them, the left one was clearly heavier. I decided to open the right one first and jammed the left one between the spring and mattress, making sure the bed looked natural. Now, if I were interrupted, I would have the least amount to do to look like I was doing nothing.

I turned to the packet on the sheet beneath me and pulled the flap out and reaching inside felt paper wrapped around something else. I probed further; the paper was wrapped around a stack of pictures.

Still afraid of what was inside, I removed the paper while the pictures remained in the packet. The paper was somewhat crumpled and not white. From this angle nothing was visible, so I spread the paper on the sheet and tried to smooth it out. Once satisfied, I turned the paper over. There was nothing on it. I held it up to the light, nothing. I looked for indentations, nothing. No matter how I looked or how many times I turned it over, there was nothing. It was time to look at the pictures.

I removed the stack from the packet and placed it on the sheet. The pictures were upside down. I turned the first one over. What I saw hit me with an impact I still feel today.

This couldn't be. Something was wrong.

I looked again. The information had not changed. There's some mistake.

I turned the second one over. Same intelligence. This was impossible.

The first and second were followed by the third, and fourth, and fifth, and sixth, and so it went, through all twenty-four. This was not happening. I raced through the stack again. It was happening. There was no mistake.

Had someone driven in the driveway and honked the horn I doubt I would have noticed. Dazed and not in control, I reached between the spring and mattress, pulled out the other packet, flipped it open and poured the contents on the sheet. This was the last thing I could have imagined. No, I couldn't have imagined this. My history had no frame of reference for this. Being exposed this way, under these circumstances, in this setting, by this agent, overwhelmed me. I leaned back against the bed and waited.

After a time, I reached down and shuffled the pictures into one big stack and went through them again. There was no mistake. It was painfully clear. The intelligence scoop of the operation, the key to the workings and workers, the proof needed to clear everything up, remove the stigma from my parents and silence the FBI threats, the golden potential of the breakthrough, turned out to be fifty-two different views of he and some woman in pornographic gymnastics.

I was not an undercover operative as I headed to my Handler, I was a limp noodle, beaten by the distance between my assumption that a breakthrough was in my hands and two packs of dirty pictures. That my Handler didn't see it that way didn't help. He thought Pete's trust in me was evidenced. He liked my mechanical processing of the incident. He agreed that it was too big a risk for me to have brought him the valise and based on the contents, we only missed the chance of identifying the woman. Now he wanted me focused on who would come for the valise and when. He ended with another attempt at encouragement, the look at the big picture pitch.

A few weeks later, Pete came to get his valise. His health was fine. He was getting a new car, the mighty Olds was truly dead. He was looking forward to us getting together and was very appreciative of my taking care of his things. Only when he was gone, did I realize I had never looked at what else was in that valise!

How would I ever face my Handler? He may not have thought I was a putz, but when he learned this 'tidbit', he would agree with me.

Three days later, as I left the session where I shared the 'tidbit', my Handler tried his best to convince me to hold my head up and carry on. I'm sure when I was out of earshot he added, "You putz."

THE REVEREND E. J. BRUTON

It had been five years since I decided to stop attending The Peniel Missionary Assembly, but I couldn't think of a better place to begin my search for an honorable career than The Reverend Olga and her associates. Things had changed. Her role as Handmaiden for The Lord had gradually evolved and no longer included her healing ministry. In the meantime, at The Assembly, the number of DPs and those in need dwindled until the congregation consisted primarily of ministers, missionaries, theologians, and evangelists. So, a few years ago, 64 East McMicken was closed and services that were more like meetings were held in The Gibson Hotel. For my purposes these changes were wonderful, the new congregation had to be a jackpot of people who loved their honorable careers.

It was at the Gibson that I met The Reverend E. J. Bruton. He was a prophet in his 70s when I saw him towering over those around him in the meeting room. He was over six feet tall, but it was not his height that made him unforgettable, it was his aura. He noticed me, smiled, and let me know he'd make his way to me. My eyes were glued to him until he was there, offering his hand. He said my parents had told him about me and he was glad to meet me. As for me, I was staring at the incarnation of dignity.

From our first meeting until he died, E. J. Bruton benefited me. Our relationship was bonded by our mutual love of God, but it was strictly one-sided, him promoting my future. Every moment spent with him advanced my spiritual, intellectual, social, or physical development. The following random pictures show how he affected me while I learned who he was and how he lived.

He was an adult, American as apple pie male, who didn't have a drop of Slavic blood. He couldn't have been farther from our East McMicken background, the congregation of Peniel, or my temporary roommates. E. J. Bruton was educated, well-read, cosmopolitan, spiritual, worldly, confident, generous with both his time and resources, and seemed to fit in every venue as though it were tailored to him.

He was over 70, yet had plans well into the future and seemed to have no aches or pains. Every adult I knew had countless aches and pains and their future was next month, maybe. My father had one foot in the grave from the time I was six.

He lived in The Essex House, an upscale hotel in Indianapolis. I never imagined a person living in a hotel. Even though I witnessed his comfort there, I was uncomfortable, with the place, not with him. With him I was truly at ease, not having to be alert and aware all the time was uncharted territory for me.

He was a widower with children and grandchildren and loved them all. Imagine, an imposing man openly sharing that he loved his kids! Another thing he shared was his method of disciplining those kids. He never punished them when they were bad, instead he would wait until the emotions of the issue had passed and then have a discussion of cause and effect, ending in understanding of the punishment. This was how George had disciplined me and with Reverend Bruton's endorsement of this method, I decided it would be mine.

He had been successful in business before entering the ministry and shepherding the flock of his church where, over time, he emerged as a Prophet.

He had a professional knowledge of antiques and was fond of fine things, nice cars, good food, and living well. However, his pride and joy was an immaculate silver Winnebago Travel Trailer. After his retirement from his church, he used the Essex as a staging point and drove the Winnebago on lengthy, country wide tours, preaching, teaching, and ministering.

From the time we left the car until we returned to it, we were not in a crowd, we were in a frenzy. Brother Bruton had seats high at center court for the NCAA playoffs. He knew basketball and the ushers knew him.

He was a gifted listener and helped me in my undercover work by demonstrating techniques for taking in both what was being said and what wasn't being said. As a speaker he always seemed to speak the language of his audience and I saw this led his listeners to respect him and pay attention.

He ate three meals a day and diet meant managing his food, not losing weight. Not so long ago having something to eat was my issue, so paying attention to what I ate was a new concept. I soon saw and felt the difference in my physical self that his regimen created. Once I felt the benefits of paying attention to my body, I saw the wisdom in his naps and recognized that rest was a powerful ally, however I could not develop any of the relaxation methods he employed.

George and I had made a deal, I would give the Lincoln a

wax job and he would let me use it for a date. During the date, Nellie and I found ourselves parked off the road at the bottom of a hill in Mt. Airy Forest. At a certain moment we heard a car going way too fast on the road at the top of the hill, then it skidded, then the engine revved, then it ran off the road and started down the hill. As it crashed through the foliage it gathered speed and we could see the headlights headed straight for us, then it hit a boulder, which slowed it down and then it hit a tree, which temporarily stopped it until it heaved and slid into our right side. No one was hurt.

The next morning, I was explaining what happened to George, Olga, the insurance man, and The Reverend E. J. Bruton who had come to visit. Everything was sensible until the insurance man said we had to go to the scene. I knotted up; do we really have to go? Yes. My only chance was to limit the gawkers. No chance, the entire ensemble just had to go and were piling into the insurance man's car. When we got to the entrance to our parking spot, unless you had walked it, it was impossible to see. The ensemble offered guilt, grimaces, moral failures this scene suggested, and a lot of harumphs, except for Brother Bruton. He merely smiled and thought it wonderful to be young. I think we stayed at the scene for a week.

The very next time he visited, he had a brand new big V8 Ford Fairlane convertible. We spent the afternoon together and he was sorry I had a previous engagement and had to leave. When I explained it was with Nellie, he said, "Wonderful. This is an opportunity to see what she can do. Give her a spin." I wasn't sure what he was saying...until I saw the keys to the Fairlane flying through the air toward me.

From my search for an honorable career to countless other life topics, his attention and counsel gave me wisdom beyond my years and answers that exceeded my most optimistic expectations. He was a mentor to mankind and made me feel proud to be with him. E. J. Bruton's incorporating the spiritual and the carnal, remains a life style I try to emulate.

BY THE WAY

The morning Pete called it had been months since he totaled the Olds. He asked if I wanted to go for a ride. I didn't have anything else going on and we agreed he'd pick me up at noon. Before he hung up, he offhandedly mentioned he had a new car. Offhanded my behind, he knew he had just made noon seem months away for me.

He loved cars. To him, taking care of them was more than the sensible maintenance of an asset. More than a habit and more than a hobby. For Pete, it was an obsession. An obsession that had an immediate and lasting effect on me as I embraced his attitude. He was the inspiration for my car waxing business where I tried to mimic him, tried.

He set the standard. The goal was perfection. Mechanical and cosmetic perfection. Only the best mechanics worked on keeping the mechanicals perfect. Only Pete worked on keeping the cosmetics perfect, which meant cleaning the mats, rugs, and interior and then treating the leather. Cleaning the trunk and engine compartment, to include the insulation he had attached to the underside of all his car's hoods. Washing the car, wheels, and whitening the whitewalls. Pre-waxing and then waxing the car, polishing the chrome, and cleaning the windows and mirrors.

He had two tests for evaluating his work on the cosmetics. The first test was when he was finished waxing. He would back away from the automobile, walk around and then arbitrarily throw a towel on the hood, trunk, or top. If that towel didn't slide right off the car, his wax job was not done. I had seen him apply this test many times and he always did so with success.

The other test required a lot of patience to administer. I had never seen it satisfied but didn't share that fact with Pete. Whether it was ever accomplished or not, having it was enough. For this test, he would wait until a fly flew by and attempted to land on the car. The surface had to be so slick that upon landing the fly would skid and break its neck. I loved every minute of him trying to apply this test.

Noon finally arrived and coming up the street I saw the brand-new Lincoln that was replacing the Olds. Sort of an off green with a cream-colored leather interior, this four-door hard top was gorgeous and ran like a Rolls. The style was special as the four doors opened from the middle like French Doors opening to a formal room. The leather seats were sumptuous, the appointments fantastic, and it did not require my imagination to pretend I was riding as the rich did, because I was riding as the rich did. I had history with the Olds, but I didn't miss it. This new Lincoln was in a class by itself.

We had been riding for over an hour and hadn't said a word since leaving the house. That, coupled with our lack of direction, convinced me this was just another road trip.

A little later my attention shifted, from the car to the day. It was truly unremarkable. Not sunny but not cloudy. Not bright, not dark, not hot, not cold. No matter. I was enjoying the countryside, luxuriating in the cushioned leather seating, and riding like the rich.

As the ride continued, I noticed Pete seemed characteristically relaxed. This was ordinary during these rides. But today he was more than relaxed, he was like the day, unremarkable. In fact, as I watched him maneuver the big Lincoln along the two-lane country road, I got the impression he was almost bored. I never got bored. But if I did, this could be the time and place.

Ordinary, yes that was it, everything about this ride, from Pete's car being spotless and running like a top to the fact we weren't going anywhere particular, was ordinary. We were comfortable in each other's company and didn't feel pressure to make conversation. It was ordinary for us to be together in silence. I leaned back in the deep cushioned leather and watched the trees go by. This was great, riding along like the rich, perfect. I let myself sink into the wonder of the day.

Another hour passed and the day changed. It was brilliant and the Indiana countryside rolled across the Lincoln's windows creating hundreds of postcards that would never be sent.

As if he were in the same state of mind, Pete, like a person who just woke up, began casually stretching his neck. He turned his head slowly as if to be sure it was still attached. In time, he seemed to focus on something down the road but didn't say anything.

Eventually, I looked over and saw Pete watching the curving road and at that moment he yawned and said to the windshield, "By the way, the woman in the pictures is my wife. Well, she was my wife. We aren't married any more. She was something. I like to keep the pictures as a souvenir."

KABOOM! Ordinary time was over. I steeled myself and didn't react. This was good because it helped contain my insides which had turned to mush. I had been careful to put those pictures back exactly as I found them. The exact sequence in each stack. I had wrapped the papers around the stacks, and I had closed the packets precisely. I laid the packets in the valise exactly as they were laying when I opened it over the sheet. No one else could have been involved because I put the valise back in the closet and covered it up. It sat there until I gave it to him. I never touched it after the initial opening. I had worked very hard to get it all straight. I had done a good job.

I was an idiot. I had never before seen a pornographic picture and then suddenly there was a stack of them in front of me. As if I were outside myself, I asked me, "Do you remember how composed you were at the time? Fifty-two different poses of the man that's been living with you and influencing you, and sure Ron, you definitely remembered the sequence of the pictures and how they fit together. Remember that you threw the contents of the second packet on the sheet? How did you know the sequence in that packet?

About putting the packets in the valise exactly as they were laying when you opened it over the sheet, he didn't know how they looked. He hadn't seen how you had put them in there in the first place. He was lying in the street bleeding, remember? What an idiot.

He never talked to me about being married and he talked to me about a lot of things. Nice of him to pop that fact on me right now. Why had he not told me before? Why at this moment?

I'll tell you why...because he's working you, me, us!

He didn't ask me if I had looked in the packet and looked at the pictures. That would have alerted me to the topic. He didn't try to trick me by asking me what I thought of the pictures or what I thought of the woman in the poses. I didn't have to lie, try to wiggle, avoid, pretend I didn't hear, act shocked. I didn't have to do anything except listen to his explanations that they were pictures of his ex-wife and he liked to have them around. Then, if I hadn't looked at the pictures, the only thing I could have possibly done was reflexively react, "What? What are you talking about?" That was the only response that I could have had if I had not seen the pictures and that response would have been instantaneous. What an idiot.

Regardless the time it took for my mind to cover the thoughts above, it was too much time. It was time during which I said nothing. That I was unable to say anything was enough said. By my lack of response, he knew everything he needed or wanted to know.

As for me, I knew I was an idiot and the time for response was long gone. The best thing to do, the only thing to do, was more of the same, nothing.

Pete didn't seem to care one bit that I had looked in the packets, which was nice of him. But, during the last several years of working with my Handler, I had learned to think in differing fashions. In this case I was thinking suspiciously. His reaction was nice but there was something telling me that this was an experience I would revisit one day, and it would not be one of my better days.

We continued the drive in silence. I was no longer comfortable in each other's company. I felt pressure in the silence of this ride together. The ordinary and neat had changed to unique and tense. By the way, I was an idiot.

* * *

"I'm an idiot. Let me make this clear right off and don't try to make things better with a dose of pump-me-up chatter. You'll see, you'll agree, I'm an idiot. What we're going to do about it is up to you, but I'm the biggest damn idiot ever."

We hadn't finished shaking hands when I started. His first reaction was to stop me, but he let me rant. I went through the ride with Pete in detail and once I was vented, we sat in silence. As I gave my report, his shoulders hadn't rolled forward and he didn't shake his head. Then, when he started, he handled me as he had never done before, he gave me his opinions.

My 'I'm an idiot' line, my kind of perfectionism and my judgment of myself, were childish and nonproductive. The reality was that I was like everybody else, I made mistakes and I would continue to make them. I had developed nicely in my role but who did I think I was, imagining that I could deal with Pete as something like an equal. Did I have a clue how good this guy was? Just his cover, direct report to The President of Yugoslavia, was so far over my high school head I couldn't even hear it whizzing by. He was dropping bombs and I deserved them, but I was glad when he was done.

For me, from this session on our relationship was more complete. I felt that by sharing his opinions, my Handler added a personal dimension to our efforts. As time passed, our work settled into a routine consisting of reporting new personnel and developments, reviewing the past and analysis of both. My training continued intermittently but everything was superseded whenever Pete came around.

***

Before summer started, I announced I would no longer be detailing cars and started working open hours at the pharmacy across

Montana from the station. Unlike car waxing, the pharmacy gave me earning hours year-round.

During the summer, tennis ruled my schedule while the station, Hawthorne, and the pharmacy filled in any spare minutes.

Once school started, classes and Hi-Y were added to the mix.

THE MATRIARCH: THE BURDEN

The times she and I were spending together were becoming more and more intense and more and more full of reminiscences. Recollections not of her past, but of our past. Did I remember this? She remembered us doing that. She seemed to have something on her mind, but I had no idea what. When I asked her what, she didn't answer.

In the last week she had a couple of difficult nights, unable to sleep and in some discomfort. We didn't know if it was pain because she would not admit pain. During those few days, I was glad that members of the family came and went with a frequency not seen before.

I believe intuitively I knew she was dying. Intellectually, I understood this was the natural order of life. Emotionally, I would have none of it.

It was late afternoon the 10th of October 1960 and we were alone in the house on Daytona. She called me and as I entered the room, I felt a conclusion approaching.

I sat on the chair beside her bed and held her hand. I had no inclination to cry. I had a clear understanding that soon, I was going to experience the true meaning of the word loss. I recognized this was to be a defining moment in my life. For that, and for knowing that she would not have to suffer, I was thankful. It was fitting that The Matriarch was teaching me what was an inevitable part of God's plan. She was ready for her reality.

But something was out of order. It was as if she was preoccupied. I could understand that, but was she really preoccupied? I didn't think so. The few things she said included no feelings of regret, no sadness, no remorse, but there was something. She had no fear, I knew fear and there was absolutely no fear in Maria Vukich. It was no use; I couldn't tell what she felt inside or what was going through her mind.

In time, she began with observations. Nothing of her parents or childhood. Nothing of her and Ponta or even what happened to him. She saw herself as a mother and her life consumed, as it should have been, with rearing four children. She reflected on her children. Their characters and behaviors as children. The paths they had chosen to follow or been led down. Their characters and behaviors as adults. The people they married, the resulting relationships, and the characters and behaviors of their children. She was clear, with the exception of me, she had no grandchildren, even though her children had children. She reviewed the key "Words to live by" that she taught me so long ago and then, she was quiet. The one matter on which she had no observation, not even a comment, was love.

After some time, I got up and helped her raise herself by arranging her pillows. I took my position on the chair and again held her hand. We didn't speak but I could feel the bond between us stronger than usual. Now, I could also feel she had something on her chest.

We sat for quite a time when she motioned that she wanted me to get her a glass of water. When I returned to the bed with the water, she had shifted herself into a very upright position. She took the glass, looked at the water as if she knew the source from which it came, and took a long drink. While giving me back the glass, she told me to sit down on the bed next to her. Closer. Whatever it was that was on her mind was about to be shared.

She was sorry, in a way, that I had to be the one to take this burden. She had planned to take this burden with her, but in the recent past, she realized she could not. She had to rid herself of the burden before she could move on.

She had been struggling with whom to give this burden to, but no matter how hard she tried for a different direction, she was always directed to me. Finally, now, she accepted that it had to be me, and she was sorry for that, but she could not change the situation. I was going to have to take this burden off her chest.

I felt humbled that she trusted me in this matter. I had no inkling what the burden was or what responsibilities would come with knowing it, but I was glad to be there for her. I was thankful to be of use to the person who reared me. The person I loved above all others. A person I respected and liked. I waited for her to continue and give me her burden.

Instead, she clammed up. Baba Maria was not a person who could be talked out of her positions or decisions. I knew and respected this, so I sat and waited.

Time passed and I could sense she was wavering. I kept quiet.

Finally, she started again. In no time she was having physical difficulty continuing, but she persisted and focused on Lou and Rosie. Whether it was Lou who loved Rose while she did not love him, or the other way round, I'm still not certain...but it is certain that the marriage had been arranged. Arranged by The Matriarch. Lou and Rose had worked hard, had a fine home, the respect of their peers, and financial success. They were charitable with their blessings, supporting family members, the church, and those less fortunate. They had one son, Ronnie.

At this point she stopped. She was clearly fighting an inner battle and it wasn't all physical. I kept quiet and tried not to squeeze her hand any harder. More time slipped by and then she went on.

The infant Ronnie was not well and suffered a lot. When his ailments hit, they caused constant discomfort and made life hard for Ronnie and everyone around. When sick, he seemed to sleep between fits of lurid crying and his pain tore at the senses. He was sick often.

She stopped again. Considerable time passed. Enough time to make me wonder. Was I named after their Ronnie? Was I their Ronnie, taken by or given to George and Olga? I cleared my mind and waited.

Then, as only she could, not making a drama, she composed herself as I had seen her do so many times before, turned her head, looked me in the eyes and said, "Zorana..." and continued with a flat even tone. There was no accusation, judgment, remorse, or guilt. Life was as it was. The motive for what had been done was sincere and full of caring. One was supposed to understand and make the most of life. My grandmother was completely dispassionate as she gave me the burden as fact. Lou killed Ronnie.

Once free of the burden she had been carrying for so many years, she became physically and spiritually lighter. Some color returned to her face and her breathing was less labored. Her eyes regained some of their sparkle and her voice was full of peace. Now that she was finished, she was clearly content and was no longer preoccupied. There were still no feelings of regret. There was still no sign of fear. She seemed to be relaxing after getting rid of the terrible burden. A burden known only to her, Lou, Rose, and now, me.

We sat together in silence, and she seemed to be comfortable in her rest.

Then, at a certain moment she began to tremble as if cold. I bent forward, encircled her in my arms and brought her to my chest. She didn't smile but rather gazed at me with a look of softness. A tear formed on the far edge of her left eye, she took a strained breath, shuddered, and died.

As the breath left her, I felt I was surrounded by peace, the peace was engulfed by protection, and the protection was ensconced in the security of ultimate strength. Once more, the sense of Something Bigger, which remained beyond my comprehension, was pacifying, nurturing, and guiding. It was okay to see her die under the overwhelming auspices of God. As always, God seemed to be there just for me.

The time from when I entered her room, to when she left her room, was more than four hours.

I sat holding her and eventually George and Olga came home and into the room. It was only then that I released her and laid her back down on the bed. Olga had a very difficult time and, of course, would not accept George's attempts to console her. Charlie showed up next and as he entered her room I got up and left the house. Knowing I was in no condition to drive, I walked. The time from when she left her room, to when I left her room, was more than an hour.

Hours later I returned and saw from the cars on the street and the lights in the house that all were gathered for the next phase.

As I walked up the steps to the front door, I looked at the swing on the porch where she used to sit in the summer and catch flies in midair while asking me how I was, what was I doing, and what was going on in my life. It had been good. It was good. I was ready for the next phase. I thought I was ready.

When I entered the house, things became a blur and the timeline obscured, but certain images are unforgettable.

Rosie, Viola, and Olga were devastated and adrift. Hulls, without mast sails, rudder, or anchor, they were empty and suddenly, as if surprised, aware they had lost their most precious cargo.

George, as always, was only concerned with Olga. How to help her. How to ease her situation. Consequently, he had no reaction that could be called his own.

Charlie was strangely and fittingly inarticulate. He was never good at expressing himself verbally and now he was pathetic in his inability to express himself emotionally. I wondered if he had any emotions or thoughts in his oversized head.

Lou was clearly devastated and oddly insecure. It was clear how he felt, but he was unable to decide what to do or say.

Nicky was respectfully sad. He made me think he was merely assuming the role any good minister assumes at the death bed of a parishioner. Any parishioner, even one little known by the minister. I was never sure of Uncle Nicky's spirituality, but was once again witnessing his mastery of playing pastor.

Uncle Steve was beside himself with grief. I found this amazing because of the way Baba had ignored him while permitting her children to mistreat him. But Toza Klajic had that love about him that made him able to amaze. Uncle Steve's pain was palpable.

Margaret was there because she had to be.

The family had history with The Gump Funeral Home and their people arrived promptly and took the body. It was not a surprise to witness honest feelings of sadness for the loss of Maria

Vukich on the part of the undertakers. Her natural propriety had always engendered respect, even from people who didn't have firsthand knowledge of her background or roles as a mother and The Matriarch.

Over the next days, the family members maintained the internal feelings observed the night she died. Externally, they exhibited the anguish of grief and loss mingled with a disciplined approach to the hubbub and demands of funeral arrangements. The overall result was that Maria Vukich was put to rest by a contingent of loving, bereaved, respectful, and admirable family.

The Vukich's were supported and encouraged through the entire ordeal by friends, acquaintances, neighbors, and even those with only passing exposure to Maria Vukich. Everyone paid their respects with utmost sincerity and the cumulative effect was that Baba was buried and celebrated with the dignity befitting her life.

As for me, I sobbed uncontrollably as we put her coffin in the hearse and continued until we reached the gravesite. Once there, I stopped crying. It was to be a very long time before I ever cried again.

One aspect of the proceedings epitomized the whole. The traditional Serbian Slava, a celebration for the soul held immediately after the gravesite at the home of the eldest child, was held at Rose and Lou Baker's. The celebration was generous not opulent, caring not perfunctory, elicited the genuine feelings of everyone who attended and created the environment necessary for the grieving process to flourish, wither, and be naturally satisfied.

Without a doubt, everything was done correctly and first class, which was both appropriate and to be expected. It was the signature of the Vukich Clan that when there was an outside audience and they found themselves on stage with the spotlights on, their performance was impeccable.

Then it was over. Baba Maria Vukich, The Matriarch, was dead and buried. The curtain came down, the lights went off, the show was over, and the audience went home. Now, as was also typical, the family took on a different character.

In record time they managed to reach the depths of ugliness. They argued over her estate. Estate? Baba had nothing. No jewelry, money, stock, bonds, property, not even a life insurance policy. Her Bible, glasses, clothes, and memories were all I could tally. After that, nothing. But someone coming upon the scene without this knowledge would think the deceased had left the Rockefeller fortune.

Perhaps there was some therapeutic benefit from their behavior, a catharsis among siblings. Perhaps they needed this for closure. Perhaps the pettiness was the hallmark of their relationships. Perhaps this is what happens when you're Serbian and you never forget. Watching them, I knew I didn't understand, but also knew I found it grotesque.

Not too long after I reached this conclusion, I interrupted them and expressed my feelings to the bickering Rosie, Viola, Olga, and Charlie. I ended my comments by asking how they thought their mother would have felt watching them. Silence was their answer as I left, but before I was out of earshot, they were at each other again. Oddly, their behaviors didn't hurt me. Instead, they exorcised any lingering doubts about my feelings toward each family member. I distanced myself even further from the family and was comfortable doing so. Then it was over.

No. There was still the matter of the burden. She had such a difficult time giving it to me, I wondered if there was a message I was missing. I reviewed the entire experience. When she shared it, it didn't seem of any consequence. Days later, her burden still hadn't made it to the forefront of my thoughts. Now, when everything that had to do with her burial and memory was complete, I realized I hadn't even thought about what she said. No matter how I tried, I had no reaction and could find no message.

Armed with this understanding, I went to her grave. I told her not to worry about me carrying her burden, it had been heavy for her but wasn't for me. I made sure she knew her secret was safe with me, said goodbye, went back to my car, and headed home. She carried the burden almost thirty years before giving it to me. I carried it another forty plus and now it's no longer a burden or a secret, it's history. May they all rest in peace.

PRESIDENT, MAYOR, GOVERNOR

My senior schedule of classes was packed with electives I wanted to experience. I didn't expect one of the experiences to be getting elected. The membership of Hi-Y was a fine group of Christian guys and I was humbled and proud when I learned they had elected me President.

I knew I would need help as President and knew I would get it from our faculty advisor, Mr. Paul Nohr. Coach Nohr is a baseball legend at Western Hills who coached future professionals including Don Zimmer, Art Mahaffey, Russ Nixon, Jim Fry, Pete Rose, and Eddie Brinkman. His method of coaching me eventually proved to be the way to get the most out of me. I had to explain what I had in mind and how I planned to accomplish it, while he asked questions until we agreed. Then, he'd leave me alone unless I asked for help. I respected his willingness to let us try new things.

We focused on setting new standards for contributions and service to the community. Our paper drive funded our endeavors, and our Thanksgiving food drive was the best of any previous

Hi-Y, for both volume and quality. At The Peniel Missionary Assembly I had learned a thing or two about older people, so at Christmas we visited, provided refreshments, sang, and most importantly, we spent time with the elderly. We also provided comic relief when I unwrapped my accordion to accompany the carols. The guys tried their best to sing over my mistakes, but I was the comic, and the relief was when I finished. Finally, it was a mark of our group that each of us felt our holidays were enriched by what we were able to share.

* * *

As mentioned, I had determined to identify an honorable career that would enable me to pay "the debt" and fulfill my destiny. Since that decision I had been asking questions, listening, and watching everyone and anyone in the hope they could help me find the answer. So far, I had learned from people of varying jobs, careers, and professions. People with all types of personalities, backgrounds, capabilities, and character. Many were recognized as successful in all manner of different endeavors, while many more were unsung, unrecognized.

I was surprised by what I uncovered. Few of this large group were doing what they wanted. Even less were doing what they believed. Many didn't even know what they believed. I was deflated when I had to admit almost no one related what they did to honor. Few had ever considered such a relationship, in general they felt they went to work, had jobs, and put in their time. My search was another proof that not everybody shared my view of life.

Well, it was one thing that most people didn't find earning their daily bread had anything to do with honor, that was their lives. It was something else that I couldn't find ways to link any of the jobs, careers, or professions to my definition of honor. As I evaluated each, it seemed something was always missing. No matter how hard I tried to see honor in what others were doing, I couldn't and, I couldn't explain why I couldn't. What was missing? I didn't know, but I did know I could see the end of high school and I had not identified my honorable career. I had to intensify my search.

* * *

Nellie, Gertrude Nellie Jusintha Sidenstick to be exact. The blonde half of "Joyce-Nellie

Inc.", the raven haired-blonde partnership who taught me everything I was to know about girls while remaining a virgin. The partner who stepped aside while Joyce administered basic training from handling initial meetings to guiltless enjoyment of necking. The more cerebral partner who took over for my advanced training while Joyce and I settled into friendship. Nellie's curriculum covered an overwhelming number of facts about girls that ran the gamut from "Standards of Behavior in Catholic Girls Schools" to the physical characteristics of the opposite sex. My co-pilot in the Lincoln, the night a boulder and tree saved everything but embarrassment. The articulate intellectual who stayed up all night as we pondered the dilemmas and exhilarations of life. Her lessons could have continued, but my days were out of minutes. After about a year, Nellie and I stopped dating.

The preceding could easily qualify Nellie as unforgettable, but there was more. The objectivity of her thinking that enabled her to see reality and make it clear to others. Her ability to see the truth, soft pedal it for some, while sticking it to those who deserved it. The ease with which she could close herself down and become isolated from the unimportant or negative. I imagined all these special qualities were somehow related to the large unsightly scar around her left eye. She didn't think much of my imagination and preferred not to share how it came to be. No matter, unless someone mentioned it, I never really saw it. Even when someone mentioned it, Nellie didn't flinch, she was all about character and the future.

* * *

My undercover life was never far from my thoughts, but the following was the first time it was intermingled with another of my lives, high school student. There was a car full of us on Central Avenue near the bus station. A group of locals were walking along, and someone threw the first insult and it escalated at a rate only possible with the hormones of teenage boys. And then…Surprise! The blah blah had turned into a show down between me and one of the locals. My buddies were promoting the fight and his buddies were doing the same. Everybody but me was wild and ready.

Then the scene froze. I thought, "Oh my God, I'm about to do something because of these guys. I'm letting them influence how I act, what I do. Who are they that I would let them make me do anything, not to mention to fight this stranger? How'd I come to this?" The scene returned to normal, and I immediately defused the situation by saying that I was not going to fight, period. The locals called me chicken and my buddies wanted to agree. Then we moved on.

I didn't wonder if they thought I was a chicken, or who they would tell what to. I didn't care what other people thought or felt or saw or interpreted. I was shaken. I heard Pete's voice as The Court and my Handler's voice as his echo. This was a wake-up call. I had a relationship with The Almighty, only He could influence me. But I had seen that it was possible for me to want to be part of a group, and from that, it was possible for me to be influenced by others. How dangerous was that? My Handler's words fit the moment, "Who do you think you are?"

* * *

When Mr. Nhor announced that Hi-Ys and other organizations related to The YMCA sponsored a youth government program, we unanimously wanted to participate. We had to read and discuss outlined topics, determine our individual beliefs about government, and then hold a mock election, campaigning for what we believed. We had several compelling candidates, but when the dust settled, somehow, I had captured the nomination. We all agreed this was fun and an eye-opening experience.

Only then did Mr. Nhor announce phase two, a city-wide election of a Youth Mayor. I wanted no part of this, but the membership had other ideas and I found myself on the campaign trail with the winners from each of the other local organizations, people who really wanted to be elected. The entire process was a microcosm of electing a mayor and it was exciting to share my beliefs in front of a packed Council Chamber. It was rewarding and a surprise to be Youth Mayor.

Mr. Nhor had another surprise. I was now obligated to be Cincinnati's candidate at the regional election. I panicked when he told me this would be held at Wilmington College. I had been to Wilmington before, on the tennis courts, where I had my head handed to me. If this election was like that tournament, I'd be tarred, feathered, and on a pole headed out of town. My brothers wouldn't let me drift. Preparation followed with people from all over offering advice and encouragement. Again, the opportunity to say my piece was exciting and the reception my platform received was awesome. Here was a crowd of people who saw life as I did. I won the election and was going to Columbus as one of four candidates for Youth Governor.

I must confess I didn't do any work to come up with my platform. Everything I said was merely sharing my life's experiences. That all should be welcome in our city. It was more congregation, DPs, and temporary roommates than Statue of Liberty. That we are not equal but are guaranteed equal opportunity was as much The Peniel Missionary Assembly as The Bill of Rights. My support of schools and libraries was just homage to places that were my childhood friends and mentors. My commitment to law enforcement, justice, and capital punishment, merely Baba and Uncle Lou. Finally, my faith in God and optimism for America, from founding fathers that were English or Serbian or yet to come.

Columbus was the big time. It started with all types of hoops to jump through. The first phase ended with a runoff for the two final candidates. I was one, and then there was my opponent. My road to Columbus consisted of giving three speeches that reflected my beliefs and applying those beliefs to all the questions put to me. My opponent's road to Columbus began two years ago when he and his staff started working toward this event. Their efforts paid off. In and around the Capital were banners and posters with his picture, volunteers handing out flyers with his platform, volunteers carrying placards, and more volunteers running phone solicitations. Behind the scenes, his staff kept things humming and worked to get votes for their man. He was running a political machine and it was headed straight for me, I could only hope it had good brakes.

In the end it came down to our speeches, and the most volatile topic of the time, capital punishment. I was for, he was against. He won. It was easy to congratulate him, he was meant for this moment, he was an honestly nice person. His campaign was professional and like him, his supporters were gracious. Several people commented that the election was very, very close. It didn't matter, I had no negative feelings, the entire experience was great and evidenced Hi-Y's aim of good Christian fellowship. However, when someone told me that I had lost the election by one vote, I ignored the comment as apocryphal. It is not apocryphal that I voted for the winner.

That night at the formal celebration banquet, he demonstrated why I cast my vote correctly. He was a natural politician. I knew I didn't have the social skills to handle the banquet while he was as comfortable socially as he was competent politically. While I managed to not embarrass myself when he asked me to say a few words, he managed the social event as he had managed the election, confidently, competently and with just the right amount of dignity. On top of all this, he didn't take himself too seriously. I really liked the guy.

* * *

I had intensified my search to identify an honorable career but had uncovered nothing new. Worse, I still couldn't find a way to link any of the things others were doing to my definition of honor, my destiny or, how to pay "the debt."

It might have been having to make the decisions regarding college, I'm not sure, but one day it all fell into place. I knew the military was the career for me. I could see clearly that a military career included, albeit only as a possibility, my missing ingredient. By choosing the military, I was accepting the possibility that someday I would have to put my life on the line for what I said I believed. If this possibility materialized, I would find out the true strength of my foundation, the real depth of my faith in God, and the actual degree of my personal commitment to my country. No one else would know. No one else would see. It would all be inside of me, personal, solitary, honorable. A military career would put "paid" to the "debt" my temporary roommates, my family, and I owed America.

With the Military as the career for me, I had to identify which service in the Military. The Marines were eliminated because they had no Service Academy, and I wanted an education along with a commission. I could give no real consideration to the Navy as I had no affinity with water, I mean taking baths in a galvanized tub and cranking the washing machine rollers was hardly resume material. My first choice was the Air Force because the Academy was just being built and it seemed fitting that my career and the school share inaugurations.

My rejection for physical limitations made three impressions on my seventeen-year-old mind. First, it was polite not negative. Second, it was based on criteria that made sense, my right eye was not correctable beyond 20/400 and the standard was correctable to 20/20. Third and most important was the reassurance I found in the fact there were many more qualified applicants than myself. A person with my background should not have been one of the country's best candidates. Perhaps my children would be, but not me. The Air Force's rejection made application to West Point pointless as it had the same physical criteria.

This entire process made it clear that the Army was my

service and Army ROTC, Reserve Officers Training Corps, was the vehicle to join that service. So, I declined a tennis scholarship elsewhere and enrolled in Army ROTC at the University of Cincinnati. I picked UC for specific reasons. It had an Army ROTC Program. I could continue my undercover work. Tuition was inexpensive. I could live at home. I could continue to work at my part time jobs.

Now that I had found my career, reality clamped its jaws around my head. I was not about to become wealthy as a Military Officer and no matter how professional my performance, I would never receive social status. Few people accepted the military as a career. American society prided itself on being peace-loving and its military personnel were shadows that few acknowledged, less recognized, most ignored, and none invited to the country club. So be it. I was never keen on fitting in and was very comfortable being alone. Yep, I had my career that could enable my destiny and a school and program that were necessary to begin my journey.

* * *

I played number one singles on the tennis team and won more matches than any other position. After the season, Coach Otten called me in and asked what I wanted to do about the upcoming State Championships. I wanted to win; he wasn't surprised. Then he did something that I still cherish. He said there was a guy in Cincinnati and one in Cleveland that were in a class of their own and my chances of beating either were slim to none. The fact he considered me a man, capable of hearing the truth and discussing it unemotionally was, for my value system, the highest praise. He suggested that if my old doubles partner, who played second singles, and I entered the tournament as a doubles team, we could win the whole kit and caboodle. I agreed and we won the City, District, and Regional, but lost at State. Incidentally, the guy from Cleveland was Clark Graebner who ended up on the pro circuit.

During the All Sports Banquet at the end of the school year, every athlete or coach who spoke tried to be agreeable and said the same thing, thank you and thank you and you and you…Tennis was near the end of the event, our record may have been the best of any of the sports and, we had gone to State. I took a different approach.

"We were barely beaten by Walnut Hills, just edged out by Indian Hills, upset at the very last second by Sycamore and the victims of a bad call at Hamilton. We annihilated Withrow, ravaged Taft, stomped Woodward, destroyed Hughes, obliterated Central, humiliated…, erased…, crushed…, wiped out…, demolished…, disgraced…, plundered…, embarrassed…, ransacked…, shamed…, overpowered…, and beat Elder into a pitiful unrecognizable mush." Halfway through, the audience was trying to guess the next adjective.

* * *

I graduated Western Hills High School in June 1961. Much ado was made, and rightfully so, about the date. 1961 reads the same way right side up, upside down, forwards or backwards. Another example of this peculiarity is 1001 but in all of history there are only a few such dates.

No ado could be made regarding me at the time because I could be accurately described as, no girl, no drink, no smoke, no time, no show. I was making progress on my way to anonymity, a good place to be if you're undercover.

PARTNER – TUTOR

It was the summer after the fifth grade and the day I went to the 'Y' to workout with my tennis partner, the place with the big green board with the white horizontal stripe. When I got there, someone was already playing with my partner. He saw me but pretended that he didn't. I didn't get it at first but then I did, he was waiting to insure I knew he was in charge of the board.

Eventually, he acted as if he had just noticed me and asked if I wanted to hit. I had seen that he could play and agreed. When we finished, we exchanged phone numbers and our relationship was born.

From that first meeting until we graduated West Hi, Bill Petrick and I spent a lot of time together in school and extracurricular activities. But more than anything else, we worked at tennis. Anyone who knew us during those years could describe us as tennis addicts, partnered by the game, and most would have said that we were friends.

Nothing was farther from the truth. With his pretending not to see me, Petrick became my tutor and until this writing no one ever knew it, especially not Bill. As described in CONGREGATION, the kids I grew up with tutored me in my transition from

Serb to Yank and helped me assimilate Americana. They did this by being themselves. What makes Petrick unique from all the others was who he was when he was being himself.

On my way home that first day, I had some disturbing feelings I couldn't explain. Later, I still didn't know what the feelings were, but I did know two things. One, I had a new tennis partner, he moved on the court, wasn't green, and had no white stripe. Two, I didn't trust him.

Bill was average height but looked taller because he was thin and angular which, when coupled with his long-pointed nose and chin, too bashful to be seen, made him look like a caricature Silas Mariner. However, his most pronounced physical characteristic was his complexion, which suffered the challenge of acne. He was a drummer and played in all the school's musical groups. Smart and clever, he excelled in math and science and was a regular participant in extracurricular and social activities.

One example of Bill's tutoring was our sixth grade English class when our teacher introduced a contest, whoever read the most books over the year would win a nice award. I read the most books. Bill read the second most. I won. Those were the facts that Bill could never accept. "You read more books because you had your appendix taken out and couldn't go out and play. I won the contest." The first time the class heard him we laughed. The second, third and more times, the class laughed, and I laughed a little less. Finally, I asked him who kept him from reading more, who forced him to go outside. He had no answer, and everyone got a good laugh, except me. I saw that he still believed he won, it wasn't that he couldn't accept the truth, he consciously wouldn't accept it. He lied to himself, even in public, and it didn't faze him. I was shocked by what I saw and knew he had a lot to teach me.

And teach me he did, by demonstration and repetition. His basic perspective was to look down on others, embarrass them, make them feel bad, use them, and denigrate everyone and everything in order to promote himself. One of his basic tactics was to excuse whatever he did by claiming he was just being funny. Clever and sneaky, he was purposely disrespectful of adults and a virtuoso smart ass. He had to be in charge and if he wasn't actually in charge, he would act as if he was.

He had an uncanny ability to get away with things and treated honest and dishonest as the same thing. Deceitful, he made a habit of blaming others for his failures and taking credit for their successes. It wasn't that he couldn't accept the facts, he wouldn't accept anything that wasn't in his best interest, regardless the cost to others. Another of his tactics was to intimidate by referring to his academic talent. He believed that life owed him and he was determined to collect. He was overconfident and I was unable to determine on what basis he rated himself confident, much less overconfident.

As an example, he took pride in making fun of physical aspects of others while his appearance was a magnet for ridicule. His attitudes triggered his behaviors and together they exposed his philosophy. Petrick was a practicing elitist, self-absorbed, self-aggrandizing, and bigoted toward anything that struck his fancy at the moment.

In time, his family gave me insight into Bill, not exoneration, just some insight. He and his parents, older brother, and younger sister, lived in a first-class ranch in a fairly new subdivision. During our years of tennis, we met regularly at his house, which was between my house and West Hi. Over that entire period, I never had a conversation with his brother, getting hello out of him was like conducting an interrogation. I have no recollection of even seeing his sister. Mrs. Petrick said hello when Bill introduced me and spent the rest of her days trying to avoid being seen. So help me, she walked backwards until out of sight whenever she happened upon me. The first time I met his father I said, "Hello sir." Mr. Petrick didn't say a word, he just got up and walked out of the room. Thereafter I spent all my time waiting for Bill outside the house.

However, I was thankful they treated me as they did because it made it easier for me to study them. I felt that taken in the context of his family, Bill was just doing what they all did, he wasn't even original. I'm not sure what to call them beyond prejudiced bigots, but they made my skin crawl. I was very careful around them because at times I felt the root of their behaviors was not too far around the corner from evil.

On the other hand, in our tennis relationship, we were a perfect match. We had the same objective and commitment, we wanted to excel and were willing to pay the price to do so. Our endless hours of practice were mutually beneficial, and we enjoyed success in summer tournaments and at school, both in singles and as doubles partners.

However, Petrick was instrumental to my success in a much more significant way. I didn't like him or his treatment of others on the courts any more than I liked him or his behavior off the courts. This gave me a powerful motivation. I determined I would never let him beat me in any match that mattered. And he never did. Not in the round robins at the 'Y'. Not at Gamble. Not in the Jaycee's Tournament. And last and most satisfying, not at West High in our senior year where he played 2, while I was Number 1.

It is a fact that Petrick is one of the unforgettable characters in the population of my life. I am thankful for what he taught me about the darker side of human nature and for developing my tennis game. But given the chance, I'd just as soon forget him.

* * *

Several years later, Coach Otten and I were playing, and he asked me the following question. "Did you know that Mrs. Walters is Bill Petrick's aunt?" No, I didn't.

LIFE WITH PETE

To this point, sharing my day-to-day experiences with Pete has been limited. Unlike the events related to my being undercover, which were easy to put in their proper chronology, I can't establish the chronology of the normal events of our relationship. So, rather than fabricate when an event occurred, the following are snapshots of things that happened sometime during the years of our relationship. Taken together, they, and not the undercover activities, are what my life with Pete was like.

***

The first impression Pete made, "…I saw him and immediately knew he was absolutely different from all the other DPs in absolutely every way." never changed, only became more vivid. His clothes always looked new and were tailored of the best materials in a traditional style George, 'the tailor of Dior' appreciated. His cars either looked new or were new. He was faithful to his belief that horseshoes were the bedrock of success for a horse trader and always wore a horseshoe shaped ring, with diamonds filling the horseshoe of white gold which was supported by a band of yellow gold. His watches were magnificent, each with a horseshoe pendant hanging from it, most with diamonds placed about. He always had money and I never saw him skimp on anything.

* * *

He loved to drive, and I loved to ride, and we spent a lot of time in the car. Our rides lasted anytime from a couple of hours to all day long, in Ohio, Northern Kentucky, and his favorite, Indiana. I would not be surprised to learn that we had been on every two-lane road in all of Hoosierdom. These spontaneous trips never had a destination or purpose other than to relax and drink in the sights. During our rides it was not uncommon for "Hello." and "See ya later." to be the only words spoken. Neither was it uncommon for us to spend a day together and talk so much that taking a breath was merely providing an opportunity to be interrupted.

* * *

I wish I had a better picture of where he was from, something more about his background. But all I have are the tidbits that he offered, most of which were linked to his cover as President Tito's horse buyer. They may have been tidbits but they, along with his command presence, impact on other people, and treatment of me, were the fabric with which he encircled me and drew me tight. He treated me as an equal from first to last, even though that equation was beyond Einstein to calculate. Make no mistake, he had more influence on me than anyone had ever had before, and much of which I didn't recognize until years later.

UNDERCOVER

* * *

Whitewater State Park in Indiana was a favorite destination and the place we visited more than any other. He said he loved to swim and preferred the lake to a pool. Once I saw him in the water, I realized how seriously he swam, there was more to him and water than exercise.

From our first trip there I fooled him, by my excuses not to swim, into believing I knew how to swim. Then, by using his philosophy about lying and going along in rowboats and canoes, I managed to avoid swimming. Finally, he discovered I couldn't swim and threw me in the lake from a rowboat. He was unhappy that I had been boating while unable to swim while I was proud that I had fooled him for a comparatively long time.

It was Pete who taught me to swim and whenever I do the sidestroke, I remember how it was his favorite because, "When you do it correct, you can move through the water without a sound or ripple. Sometimes in life, being able to move unnoticed is good." I never did learn what it was about him and water.

* * *

I was never afraid of Pete, rather, from the first day I laid eyes on him I felt comfortable with him. Of course, this reflected my total faith in God but, I felt a part of the reason for my feelings was that he seemed comfortable with me. Whatever the reason, we soon discovered that we were at ease in each other's company. Early on I understood that physically he could do anything he wanted to do to me. But that was after we already had some history of being comfortable together and I didn't give the matter a second thought.

* * *

It was just another, "Hey, you wanna go with me Saturday night?" By this time, I had stopped asking where, what, how long, or any other questions. When he asked, it was either go or don't go and so, let's go. Very soon after we left Daytona I was lost. He wasn't. I think it was the Cincinnati Gardens but wasn't sure because I had never been there before. He had. "So, what are we going to see?" "Pro Wrestling." "What?"

To that moment he had never talked about, casually mentioned, or even said the words pro wrestling, yet he knew everything and everyone, the language, the scenarios, and the gimmicks. He'd lean over and shout, you had to shout to be heard because the place was a madhouse, "Now, get ready, he's going to …" and by golly he would do exactly what Pete predicted. And, as if to top this all off, he was a fan of Dick the Bruiser.

This set off a flood of questions. How did he find out about this stuff? Did he think it was a sport? Did he really like it? Why Dick the Bruiser? etcetera … I had not yet learned to stop asking all the questions begged by being with Pete.

On the way home it took us some time to stop yelling at each other as we talked, our ears had to adjust. During the ride he explained his attitude. He was positive it was all fake and that's what he loved about it. As he saw Pro Wrestling, it was making fun of violence, which he considered an inspired idea.

* * *

He insisted on having cut to fit pieces of asbestos insulation attached to the underside of the hoods of his cars. He claimed this muffled the engine noise and kept the engine temperature in a smaller range of highs and lows. It was only later that I considered the insulation might have been for something else altogether. Perhaps as a place to hide and transport items, who in the world would have thought to look under the asbestos under the hood?

* * *

In the beginning, he presented himself as needing help speaking American and wondered if I would provide it. I wasn't sure. He was charismatic and didn't need help getting people to understand him. Further, he spoke noticeably better than any of the DPs I ever met and all my temporary roommates. But it was flattering that he thought I could help him, so I said I would try. Looking back, I'm not sure whether he was learning American, or I was being evaluated relative to a relationship with him.

To start, we spoke American almost exclusively. In the next phase, we talked American or Serbian with no particular pattern or reason. Then a pattern emerged as we spoke the language that would either fit or not fit the people we were with. Finally, came the driving lesson, after which I realized he changed to Serbian at the end of the lesson to purposely change the mood and get me settled down before going home. Once this example of using language to influence a situation sank in, we spoke whatever suited our purposes, such as letting others think Pete needed an interpreter.

* * *

He and Uncle Steve were the only ones of all my temporary roommates who returned for a stay after leaving, and Pete came and went like a yo-yo. But he was the only one who left some of his things behind in my room. There was no pattern to his comings and goings and no explanation for what he left or where he left it in my room. I wondered if he did this to reinforce that it was useless to try and understand him.

* * *

The futility of trying to figure him out hit a zenith during the following episode. Out of nowhere, he suggested to George and Olga that we install a shower in the basement for he and I. It would be easy, he had it all measured. Using the double-tub faucets, he could run pipe to a position over the floor drain, affix a shower head and mount a 360-degree shower curtain fixture. It made sense and we all agreed four of us using the same bathtub was awkward. We did it and it was good.

Olga, the drama queen, was always relating her image of this or that back home in Serbia and pig roasts led her list. She did this with heartfelt longing, but I had to practice the accordion on the front porch because of one of her longings and tuned her out. Pete tuned her in. The next time she took to reminiscing, he said he would hold a pig roast, he had it all measured. He knew where he could get a pig and another place where he could get a cooker and now that we had the basement shower over the drain, he had the place to butcher the pig and hang it to bleed out. Afterwards, I was convinced he built that shower for pig roasts, even though we had only one.

* * *

He loved his cars. His care and maintenance routines have been reported, but there was more. Pete used sprays, brushes, and the hose on the engine and engine compartment, to keep them as clean as the body work. This was the one aspect of his routine that I did not include in my car waxing business.

* * *

"No, I don't know anything about soccer…oh, yes, sorry, football. No, I have no interest in learning about it. Look, this isn't Yugoslavia or Europe or the rest of the world, this is here, and soccer-football isn't part of Americana. Now, if you want Americana…"

He got the idea of baseball quickly and by the fifth inning felt satisfied he didn't like it. It took him a little longer with football, the pads of the players and measuring by the officials kept distracting him, but he couldn't understand why anyone would want to play it and was indignant that it presumed to be called football.

"Fine, at least you tried, plus, your taste probably is better suited to pro wrestling; and you have history with the sport of kings." He ignored the wrestling shot but got serious informing me that horse racing was not a sport, it was a passion.

These incidents relating to sports were examples of my playing the role for Pete that my peers had played for me. I was helping him speak American and assimilate Americana. This was complicated for me as I couldn't grasp how such a turn of events happened and questioned my qualification to play this role.

* * *

I would be in my bed, in the dark, my eyes and ears open, staring at the ceiling, waiting. And then, in a voice stripped of any emotion, he would talk to the dark. He would talk about the mundane, relate things of his past that paralleled my situation at the time, and review something we had done together to give me different views of things. He would explain, recall, make me laugh, make me bite my tongue, challenge me, and encourage me. The topics he covered were at the same time spontaneous and calculated, intricate and simple, bold and subtle, his experiences and my coming opportunities.

He shared his growing up weak and underdeveloped, being a jockey, the Army, the latest movie, his relationship with President Tito, his taste in women, combat experiences, his cars, the importance of being fit, what he was doing here for President Tito, etcetera. The only change to these talks in the dark came when he learned I had chosen the Army as my career, after which he focused on his military career and particularly survival under fire. The voice that came from the dark told of the life he had lived and how I could better live mine.

* * *

In all our time together, I never saw him smoke, never saw him with a woman, and only saw him drink in Canada. He was generous with everyone, the Lincoln Premiere for George and Olga is one example, and as for me, during all the years we were together my money was no good whenever he was present.

* * *

While he was learning American, he was teaching cussing. Prior to him, Aunt Rosie calling drivers jackasses in Serbian, Uncle

UNDERCOVER

Lou and his pinochle buddies turning the air blue over the cards, and the usual school yard expletives were my exposure to cussing. Pete taught me an entire language, its nuances, subtleties, and vulgarities that I never heard matched again, until the Army.

* * *

Pete liked the movies and frequently took me along for company. His knowledge of things in our culture and vicinity no longer surprised me, so when he knew what was playing where, the stars and the premises, I acted like my Handler and simply shook my head. But the first time I asked him about Drive-Ins he wasn't ahead of the topic and brushed me off. He knew I saw the tightening of his lips and I knew he'd get back to me. He did.

It was the typical invitation to see a movie but as soon as I saw him, I knew there was more, he had his look of satisfaction. Seems he had looked into this Drive-In thing...there was a lot to be said for it...he had gone a few times...he felt he knew how to maximize the experience...What the hell was he jabbering about? Why was he stopping at a grocery store? What was in the grocery bag?

At the Drive-In, he drove to the spot he wanted, adjusted the speaker and his seat, reached in the bag and pulled out a Sara Lee Cheesecake, two napkins, and two plastic spoons. He was right, polishing off an entire Sara Lee New York Style maximized the Drive-In experience. We never went to the Drive-In without Sara Lee.

* * *

I couldn't figure out what the thin flat short piece of metal, screwed on one end into the door jab next to the door light switch, was doing in the Olds. He demonstrated, he pushed in the switch and then moved the metal piece until it held the switch down and, beam of pride across his face, the door was open, and the light was off. It was only later that I figured out, actually it was Joyce and Nellie who taught me why you would want the lights off with the door open.

* * *

Two lane roads make their own demands on a driver, for example patience and especially when passing. Pete had long since mastered these demands, but on this trip to Whitewater something was up. At first, I wasn't sure the driver ahead was baiting him but there was no question that every time an opportunity to pass presented itself, he speeded up so Pete couldn't get by. In time it was clear that the driver was sticking it to Pete. What focused my attention was that Pete was letting the guy get to him.

The guy must have been a local because he knew the road and exactly what to do to keep Pete behind. Pete could see this as well, which added to his frustration, frustration I could see. Finally, we powered past the guy and as we passed, Pete looked at him and pointed his index finger to his forehead. In its most civilized interpretation this was the international sign for "You dumb ass." The driver just smiled. I was sure it was because he didn't understand the gesture. Pete however was already weighted down practicing patience, and this pushed him over the edge.

He was livid and as he completed passing, he flung his left hand toward the ground in a gesture to humiliate the driver. I had never seen him in such a state and got worried when he slammed on the brakes and ripped the Olds onto the shoulder.

The baiting driver didn't need any translation and hugged the opposite shoulder as he high tailed it by. Meanwhile, Pete had charged out of the Olds and was out of control. It took a few moments until he told me that his diamond horseshoe ring had flown off with the force of his second gesture. We spent hours searching for that ring, to no avail.

It took weeks for me to understand everything I saw that day. First, it was the first time I had seen him angry. I didn't want to see that again. Second, he was not angry with the other driver, he was angry with himself, he had let the guy get to him, he had let his emotions escalate, he had lost control. Third, he had done all this in front of me. That I had witnessed the entire episode consumed him with anger, even loathing for himself. There was nothing I could do to help the situation and nothing about the situation I ever forgot. The next time I saw him he had a new diamond horseshoe ring. It had more diamonds and they seemed bigger.

* * *

When he taught me how to lie, it was like a math class. Here is the equation: If you want to tell a lie, tell the truth. Everything except the lie must be the absolute complete truth. A lie is usually about one thing but there are always a lot of things leading up to and following a lie. Don't change any aspect, not even the tiniest detail, of the truth before and after the lie. The more truth, the more detailed truth, the more peripheral truth, the easier it is to remember the truth. You don't have to make up and remember a story or memorize a script. The only thing you have to remember is the lie. Plus, except for the lie, everything you say can be verified, because after all, it's the truth.

* * *

He told me about his hate. Hate for the Germans and their idiot idea they were superior. Hate for the Nazi occupiers who fouled his country. Hate for the soldiers he and his Partisan brothers fought. Hate for the sadistic animals in the SS. As he covered each hate, his anger increased so that by the time he was discussing the SS, he was vicious.

But his descriptions of what he hated weren't the point. He wanted me to be sure I knew what I hated at any given time and to what extent. Only then would I be able to use my hate. Once he was satisfied I understood the point, he continually gave me examples of how to use my hate for focus, strength, speed, stamina, survival.

Years later with my young sons in our back yard, they watched me split logs and become so tired I could hardly lift the maul. This was a routine event and they always wondered how I could keep swinging. One day they blurted, "Dad, you really truly hate the wood you're splitting." I didn't tell them that I didn't hate the wood at all, I just needed hate for energy, and I didn't tell them who taught me how to use it.

* * *

On this day Pete and I had rented a rowboat and were paddling all over Whitewater Lake. We'd row to inspect a section of lake, float to take a breather, row to another exploration, and every once in a while, he'd use the boat as a diving board. How he left the boat I could mimic but I didn't even understand his technique for getting back in and certainly couldn't reprise it, somehow he'd use one leg to catch the prow edge and the other leg to carry him over the side.

There he went again, making an athletic dive on his way for a swim. I waited to hear him surface and wondered how far he would go before doing his magic reentry. It was a beautiful day, and I was totally relaxed and then I wasn't…my sensors said something was wrong…holy shit…I hadn't heard him surface. I stood up to have a look and the boat felt funny, as if something was underneath it. I dove overboard and he was under the rowboat, his left hand stuck to the boat's bottom. Up close I saw that a piece of metal sticking out from the hull was jammed through his horseshoe ring and because of the angle of his arm he wasn't able to pull himself free. Using both hands, I was able to bend the piece of metal and finally broke it off, freeing him. Back in the rowboat, he wiggled the metal from under the ring and suffered only a minor cut and some scratches to his finger. He always felt that I saved his life. I couldn't see it that way.

***

He taught me simple was better than complicated. Following is one example of his point.

At first I was hurt, he obviously thought I was totally stupid as he did things right out in the open, right in front of everyone, particularly me. I learned I shouldn't be hurt. This was his Method of Operation, and it reflected his experiences. The more things you do in the open, the more people assume you couldn't be doing anything irregular, everyone knows it would be insane to do something irregular right out in the open. Acting in the open makes others less suspicious and the less suspicion you arouse, the more apt you are to be ignored.

***

I was excited that he was taking me along. First, because he said he needed me to act as his interpreter. The gentleman he was meeting had a sort of accent and Pete didn't want any misunderstandings, this man might be a source of the horses Pete was seeking. Second, except for the trip to Canada, I had no exposure to his horse buying activities, this was a golden opportunity for me to learn. Third, the man was Dave Frisch. That's right, my buddy from across the ocean was taking me to see a friend of his whose restaurants, Frisch's Big Boys, were the hangout of all the other kids as we were growing up.

Mr. Frisch was an extremely nice person, but I don't have anything remarkable to add. His place was across the river in Kentucky, but I'm not exactly sure where. It was impressive as we drove up, huge inside, and had a view of the river, but I'm not certain which river, the Ohio or Great Miami. The accent that worried Pete was just a touch of southern and my input was hardly needed. The discussions about horses didn't open doors of understanding regarding how things worked, but my memory is sketchy. Okay, okay, the fact is, there is only one thing about this entire experience that is clear, and that thing was in the middle of the large room where we met, a cowhide covered grand piano.

Good-bye and thank you all around as we parted and nothing more until we had been in the car awhile. Then, the voice of a track announcer came from the driver's seat. "And the results of today's Focus Your Concentration Race are: Marksity—Place; Piano—Win."

UNDERCOVER

* * *

I wondered why I woke up in the middle of the night. I felt a sort of something but... then I realized it was him. I could tell that he wasn't anxious and didn't have a story to tell me, he was just awake and his being awake was so vibrant that it woke me up.

In the dark, lying on my back, I could tell that he was lying on his back in the bed across the room, smiling. A sincere smile of recognition that his being awake had awakened me. He didn't need confirmation that I was awake. He didn't need validation that I had been awakened by his presence, he knew.

The frightening thing about this, there was nothing frightening about this. It was unbelievably expansive that I knew what was going on. I knew what had happened and I knew he knew I knew.

* * *

Pete was the second adult male to talk to me about sex and just like my neighbor Mike, he found sex normal and natural. Looking back, maybe the pictures of his sexual gymnastics wasn't a normal beginning, but when it came to women and sexual matters, Pete was a full-service tutor. He taught me techniques in specific detail and trust me, his instructions relating to ice, positions, baker's chocolate, not sweet mind you, what to look for, how to look for it and more, were characteristically thorough. His experiences and personal guidelines took me to a completely new world of sexual awareness.

However, when I should enter that new world was not part of his instruction. He knew my background and respected my matriarchal upbringing and Old Testament foundation. He never asked about my experience and, this is critical to understanding him, he never tried to put me with a woman. Although he acted like he wasn't sure, he knew I was a virgin, but he was not the older buddy who helps his younger buddy lose his cherry. Pete would never offend our relationship by such a presumption. He'd answer my questions and offer his opinions but what I did with that knowledge, that was strictly up to me.

* * *

The issue was to survive artillery. When under an artillery barrage, survival was simply to jump into the crater made by the last shell. Artillery shells never, ever, hit in the same spot consecutively. So, no matter how many shells were falling for how long, the crater produced by the last exploding shell was the piece of earth you wanted to be in when the next shell exploded, and then you wanted to be in that crater, and so on and so on, just simple straight forward technique.

He was across the little room talking to the dark as he relived anticipating the attack and where the first round might hit, then leaping into that crater and crouching, sprinting to the next most recent crater, anticipating, running, jumping, crouching, manipulating his body into the last crater, crouching, running, flinging himself sideways...and so on during the entire barrage until the firing stopped and he could lay there...until his legs would support him...until he could walk...

* * *

The first times I saw him watch horses on tv and at the movies, I was impressed. He would study their performance, be it a horse race, tv western, or big screen cattle drive, and then explain how the horses were handled and trained. That he could make me visualize and understand what he was explaining impressed me more. But what impressed me most was that he made it easy for anyone to understand him.

However, as time passed, his reacting to horse races on TV went way past impressive and right to awesome. He could tell what was going to happen in a horse race while we were watching it on TV. He would watch intently and by the first quarter pole would predict who was going to win and, he was never wrong! When I asked how he did this, he would answer that it was all a matter of recognizing how the jockeys related to their horses, their body positions, knees, use of the whip, how the pair, horse and rider, worked together. This is no fantasy. This is my first-hand experience and to this day, I have not met anyone who can pick the winner at the first quarter pole. Pete did every time and come to think of it, it was way past awesome.

* * *

The dispassionate way he talked about his experiences in general and then combat in
particular demonstrated that he saw death as capricious and each of his experiences merely another part of his life. Unlike all my other temporary roommates who talked of combat and fighting, Pete also talked of killing. Killing the enemy enriched his life.

* * *

In time, I came to see that Pete was not hobbled by his past self-determined failures and limitations. He was excited about life. He honestly looked forward to the future with optimism. So, if it happened that he screwed up and lost his ring, he'd just get a better one.

* * *

I never had a satisfactory idea of his age.

FRESHMAN YEAR

Driving home from my High School graduation ceremony, I left the festivities and that part of my life behind. By the time I pulled in the driveway, I was a college student with three months before classes started and an agenda packed with undercover activities for the Bureau, life with Pete, and work at the gas station, pharmacy, and Hawthorne.

Three months later, I had the same agenda and was in class as a psychology major with a minor in European history. Registration at The University of Cincinnati College of Arts and Sciences and a stop at the bookstore, were rude wake-up calls. I needed a lot more money to finance my future than my 'nose to the grindstone' all summer had produced. I needed a serious job and help finding it, so I went where I always went for help, I prayed.

The answer to my prayer was three houses down the street. The Fromme's had the best house in the neighborhood, the only pool other than the Y's and three kids, Martha, Bob, and Neva. I had a crush on Martha which established my preference for girls with voluptuous figures. Mr. Fromme was respected for his business success and was very nice, but I had no contact with him and felt awkward about talking to a high-level executive who dressed in suits all the time. But he was where my prayer led me, so I asked him for a moment. He was easy to talk with and listened closely, asked a few questions, and said he'd get back to me. I thanked him but didn't have the nerve to ask what that meant.

Turned out Mr. Fromme was a very high-level executive at the Formica Plant on Spring Grove Avenue and when he got back to me, he gave me a full-time job as a press feeder on the third shift. This was perfect. Starting work at 11pm and finishing at 7am fit with classes starting at 8am and finishing at 3pm. I bought a window air conditioner for my room and was set to go.

The first day on the job I thought of my prayer as I met my teammate "Preacher," a Reverend who worked to fund his ministry. The two-man team required to feed each press could get free time if they worked together, and hard. The challenge was to unload the pressed product and load the product to be pressed, in less time than the oven required to press the current load. Preacher wanted time to study his Bible and I wanted time to study my lessons. In no time, we were able to do both. Our press room became known as 'the library.'

Preacher's experience working third shift helped me understand the way I felt every 3am and, how sleeping in the daytime isn't like a good night's rest. He taught me that the nose bleeds I was having were normal reactions to the chemicals in the press rooms and that almost everyone had their nose cauterized. I was flat against that option so he taught me to use gauze for packing and how to insert it so it wasn't visible. But I was most thankful that he spared me the initiation suffered by most new press feeders, as he explained how to minimize the intense electrical shocks we could get while unloading.

About two months into the job, we had unloaded and loaded with plenty time left for our studies and I decided I would tidy up 'the library' floor. I found a broom and was sweeping up around the press when holy shit!!!...a monster grabbed me from behind, yanked me off my feet and put me face first hard against the wall while growling in my ear...what the hell was I doing...how the fuck dumb was I...did I think he was gonna let me waltz in here and take the food from his family...Preacher got him off me and monster settled down before the ruckus reached the foreman's ears. A group had gathered but I saw it was not to see the incident, it was to prevent the wrong people seeing the incident. No matter, I was just glad to be back down on the floor, he had to be a head taller than me.

"Look mister, I don't know why you're pissed off at me and don't understand any of what you were saying."

He found me ridiculous. Didn't I remember filling in the union forms, getting my card, becoming a member? Wasn't I paying dues? Sweeping the floor was HIS job and if anyone else did it, it could be interpreted as proof that he couldn't or wouldn't do his job and he could get written up and from that first step it was a slippery slide to...It took a long time for him to finish venting and some more time for him to accept that I had no idea what unions were all about. Finally, he left with a warning, "Watch your step."

In the days that followed, he made a point of checking on me, watching me work or study.

When he was in my vicinity, I kept a lot of space between us. Unfortunately, this only seemed to encourage him. In time, it became clear other workers were thinking of joining the fun of picking on the college boy. Preacher's advice was pure Christian, turn the other cheek, this too will pass. I remembered the advice of Pete and the Court.

It was what I called the 'hour of the vacuum', around 3am

when the third shift world seems vacuous to anyone in it. I had learned that Monster had a habit of getting through this period by going to the rear of the parking lot and catching a few winks. On this day I was there waiting for him.

He was very surprised to see me but tried to cover it, "I thought I told you to watch your step. You lookin' for trouble?"

"No sir, I'm looking for you and, for the record, I figured you'd be surprised I found your secret place."

"So, you found me. Now beat it before…" He was shocked as I interrupted him.

"Before what? We both know I can easily run away from you." He was off balance, and I continued. "I had no trouble finding this workplace bedroom of yours, or where you live, or the route you take from here to there. I will have no trouble waiting for you to be preoccupied with your life, and then I will surprise you just as I've done tonight. I will attack as a coward, without warning I will stab you in the back, not in the front, and if I do it right you won't even be sure it was me. I'm learning how to fit in, so stop harassing me." I turned and was gone without hearing a sound.

A few days later, days free of any evidence of his watching my step, he was passing 'the library' when he stopped, clearly to listen, and then apparently satisfied with what he heard, joined us. I was ready with an escape route but didn't need it, he was wondering if he could interrupt. Then the monster, the union floor sweeper, proceeded to teach me, the college student, the correct pronunciation of both Renaissance and bourgeoisie.

From that incident a relationship developed between the two of us and "The Sweeper" became my tutor regarding organized labor in general and labor relations on the Formica floor, in particular. Not incidentally, in time he wanted me to know that, about my little chat with him in the parking lot, he had given it a lot of thought and decided I would have done him. Considering my entire freshman year, what he taught me at Formica was more useful in my life than everything I learned on campus.

That was UC's campus where, concurrently with my life as a third shift laborer, I was living an entirely separate life as a college student, working for an education to gain a commission, and follow my destiny. My learning began the first day of registration when I found parking was impossible. I started looking for a solution and ran into Russ Smith who played tennis at Hughes while I played at West Hi. Hughes was next to the UC campus as was Russ' mother's apartment. The apartment had a garage, but Mrs. Smith didn't have a car and Russ and his red 1961 Corvette convertible were up at Dennison, so Russ suggested I use her garage. And just like that I parked inside, two blocks from the walkway to McMicken Hall where almost all my classes were held. I never had a hard time remembering that Someone was looking after me and this was just another example.

Unfortunately, I had a hard time forgetting two "Words To Live By" from my youth. First, never ask for help: receiving help makes you indebted, it is not under your control how, or when, such a debt will be recalled. Second, be independent: it is better to have nothing but your independence, than to have everything and be dependent.

Regarding the garage, I had asked for help, and I was dependent. I couldn't handle my feeling of indebtedness to the Smith's. I tried paying Mrs. Smith and offered to do things for her but she would have none of it. Finally, when I sent her flowers, she called Russ and asked him to, "Knock some sense into his stubborn head Russ, the use of the garage is free." Russ tried, but in the end, I just couldn't take the generosity and before the school year ended I made excuses to explain why I couldn't park there any longer. More in my end, my inability to break from my past not only left me without a parking space but prevented me parking in the area where Mrs. Smith might see my car and know, that in addition to stubborn, I was an idiot.

College parking aside, there was my 21-credit hour schedule. My favorite class was philosophy and Professor Workman remains my favorite UC instructor. During the first day of class, a student flicked his cigarette ash out the window. Professor Workman demanded the kid stand up and once he did, Workman exploded, "You incredible boor, you have the impudence to use the world as your ashtray?" Then he sent the kid downstairs to clean up the ash. You had to love it; the kid left to do so. From up-East, slight and very fit, Professor Workman had a gift for teaching. Our interaction was fueled by his intuition that there was more to me than college boy and his desire to figure out what. He had lived in New York City and was street smart, but never got under my cover. Off and on, during and well after my freshman year, we ran together. He helped me understand and adjust to the realities of college life.

A highlight of my freshman year was Spartacus Crabtree. The impersonal lecture halls of the first semester, prompted me to recruit some ROTC guys to enroll Spartacus Crabtree in all our auditorium-sized classes. The entire second semester, Spartacus always answered here but his voice seemed to vary class to class. Spartacus never turned in a paper and did poorly on his tests, but he appeared on the final grade sheets with a bunch of incompletes.

About my major, psychology. Before college, I took all the tests and meetings with advisors I could find and, in all cases, the results screamed that I was a natural psych major. During my first year as a natural psychology major, I found the "profession" full of pretentious bull-shitters, and their activities devoid of any observable results. I mean even those in the medical profession had the common decency to admit theirs was "the practice of medicine." but the yo-yos in psychology had limitless gall and argued that their failure to produce was proof that their work was needed. To me, the proof that psychology was a load of crap was that psychologists had put together the tests and interviews that said I should go into psychology. Well, I corrected their error, Modern European History became my major, with a minor in The Balkans.

The way things were going for me, I was not surprised to find a way to pursue my passion for physical fitness in the middle of campus. Tennis had become an infrequently satisfied desire, I couldn't even try out for the team because of my work for the Bureau, but in the Fieldhouse, by the basketball court, I found a new partner, a wall that looked like a relative of my old, green with white stripe partner. This tennis, calisthenics, and running, made up the routine I followed Monday, Wednesday, Friday and more if classes permitted. I would bang the board next to the Bearcat's court while they would work out under Coach Jucker. One day as they took off to do their laps they yelled, "Hey, Mr. Tennis guy, come on and do some real work." From then on, every day I was there, I'd do laps with the team. I don't recall having a conversation with any of them, but it was great to run with a group, even though it took a lot more steps for me to get from A to B than it took those a foot taller. Oh yes, that UC men's basketball team, The Bearcats, they were the reigning National Champions.

Physical health was one thing, but my spiritual health was the foundation of my life and my top priority. For this I needed alone time and eight hours of people all night, followed by eight hours of people at school put a strain on me. I took advantage of the proximity of my car and at lunch I'd drive to the Frisch's on Central Parkway, park in the spot farthest from the building, which was in the shade all afternoon, and eat my lunch in the car, alone and quiet.

My third life, as a worker bee for the FBI, carried on unseen. In fact, this work was only exciting when Pete surfaced, otherwise it was the same steady routine, watch, listen, report, plan, and do it again. At Formica it was counter-tops, at UC it was term papers, and at work with my Handler it was nothing anyone had a need to know.

When my freshmen year ended, I made a point of thanking Mr. Fromme who truly was the answer to my prayer. In less than a year on third shift, I had earned enough to pay for all four year's tuition, books, and fees. I left Formica feeling I had reached my goal and returned to the gas station, drug store, Hawthorne, tennis, and reading what I wanted to read. And, for the first time in my life, the money I made was not slotted to fill a need.

CONTINUING EDUCATION

One day in early June, Olga wanted to talk and urged me not to ask questions but just take advantage of an opportunity coming my way. Uncle Steve wanted me to buy his not even a year old, metallic blue with gray, white and blue special naugahyde interior, Wide Trac V8 Pontiac Ventura, for next to nothing. He knew how I treated my car and knew his Ponytrack would be in loving hands. I had no questions, I was too busy falling all over myself saying yes, great, thanks, wow! I got almost as much for my Ford as I paid for it and using my war chest was able to pay Uncle Steve cash. What Olga wanted hidden from questions was that Uncle Steve had a drinking problem and since he couldn't give that up, he had to give up driving. What no one knew, was that he remembered how I accepted him as a roommate and how much I cared for him, no matter his circumstances. Now, he was thanking me but preferred I didn't share this fact, he didn't want to look soft.

It was midsummer when I got a call from Pete who was, "…glad to hear your voice because it has been too long since last I saw you. What day would be good for a get together and don't you reshuffle your schedule, this has to be at your convenience."

I didn't know what to make of his language or his cheerfulness. It hadn't been that long since he was in town but, it was Pete, so, fine.

We agreed to a date and time, and he showed up in his Lincoln all smiles and fit as a fiddle. Soon after we left, I could tell we were headed to Hawthorne but couldn't guess why. Pulling into the drive, he began remarking on all the things he knew I had done to improve the place. He was particularly impressed with the porch. Still in the car, as he pulled papers from his valise, he assured me my efforts had made the place ready to sell and pointed to where I should sign. I signed. He returned the papers to the valise, gave me an envelope of money, backed out of the drive and, cheerful as could be, dropped me off at home.

During the meeting with my Handler that followed this transaction, my head was shaking more than his. I was not oblivious to my naivete in some matters being as significant as my discernment in others, but I was at a loss for understanding any of this development. I had never given a thought to the sale of Hawthorne, much less anticipated it would occur as it did. Tis Pete, was a long walk past enigma for me and my confidence was strained. I mean I had no clue of the who and when, never mind the what. No clue, and this was the guy I was 'working'. The seriousness of our work and how much more I needed to learn was highlighted by this incident, and my Handler and I hunkered down. He intensified my training on techniques of the craft and I intensified my fitness efforts. But no amount of running could make me ignore how dramatically Pete could impact me. How dramatically, to this day I have no memory of how much money was in the envelope and, at times, I can't even picture the envelope.

Summer ended and I started my sophomore year as a man

of leisure. No pressure for money. No night owl at Formica. No Hawthorne to maintain. Just an easy 21-hour class load with plenty of time for spiritual maintenance, physical development, and, now and then, work undercover. Plus, as needed, the station and pharmacy provided pocket change.

Within a month, work with my Handler intensified. It began with a slight increase in Pete's visits. We reacted routinely, he was top priority. However, in no time he went back to his more familiar now-you-see-me, now-you-don't and we realized his actions were subordinate to other activity and personnel we had never seen before. These personnel did not become temporary roommates, they became visitors and all of them followed a similar pattern. Some sort of introduction to George and Olga, followed by a request for a visit to Daytona and then continuations of varying numbers of visits for varying lengths of time involving varying combinations of these people and, now and then, Pete.

For the next eighteen months, my Handler and I were more active than we had ever been before and were convinced Pete was controlling a sophisticated and productive intelligence collection operation.

Sometime during this hubbub of undercover activity, late in my sophomore year, I was introduced to The Foreign Area Specialist Training Program. It is remarkable that I don't remember precisely when, how, or who made the introduction. I have vague images of being interviewed and advised by suits and uniforms but nothing specific. Because it was a classified program, I would have made myself forget at the time, but now, I should have some recollection. Nevertheless, because I can't remember, I feel strongly that my Handler orchestrated the whole thing. He would never let himself be linked to anything and was able to distance himself from everything. However, I knew he liked me and feel he pointed me to The FAST Program because it was the perfect place for me, something only he could fully know.

The Foreign Area Specialist Training Program had seven prerequisites that had to be satisfied in numerical order. The first prerequisite, or step, had to be successfully completed before you were permitted to attempt the second step. Then step two had to be achieved before starting on step three and so on. The steps were: Step 1, be commissioned in the Regular Army with Intelligence as your basic branch; Step 2, spend two years serving in a combat branch; Step 3, graduate the Intelligence Officers Basic Course; Step 4, graduate the Intelligence Officers Advanced Course; Step 5, develop fluency in a foreign language at the Monterey Language School; Step 6, return to a civilian institution and earn a master's degree, most often in business; Step 7, graduate the Intelligence Officers Career Course. After successfully completing all seven steps you would be assigned overseas, to your geographical area of specialty, where you were expected to run a legitimate business as your cover for the remaining years of your twenty-year commitment.

I couldn't believe my ears, Serbian me, in Yugoslavia, after years undercover with the FBI. This was the absolute of "hand in glove." I was hot to trot. Good, but my advisors and recruiters wanted to insure I fully understood the first two steps.

The First Step required me to earn a Regular Army Commission (RA). At the time, the Regular Army reported to Congress first and then the military hierarchy. RA Officers could not be rifted, that is demoted to lower ranks during one of the periodic military cutbacks. The concept was to insure a military "core" of expert professionals under civilian control. This adds understanding to General MacArthur's advocacy of, "The Corps, the Corps, the Corps".

The classic method for achieving a Regular Army Commission was to graduate The Military Academy at West Point. The RA distinction was not cosmetic but very powerful. Regular Army Commissions were awarded first in annual commissioning's. This insured RAs had date of rank over officers with any other types of commission. In a profession where rank is paramount, this seniority cemented the elite character of the RA.

However, there were other means of earning an RA. The Army's ROTC Distinguished Military Graduate Program was one. You had to be identified as qualified and then invited to join The DMG Program. Once in the Program, you had to excel in all the ROTC venues and graduate at certain levels of both your ROTC and graduating classes, to be a Distinguished Military Graduate and be commissioned Regular Army.

As for the second of the FAST Program's seven steps, I was strongly advised to be completely realistic and focus on the downside possibilities. Step Two required me to serve two years in a combat branch. The concept is to make the Intelligence Officer go as close as possible to combat. Go, and experience what it is the Intelligence Branch is supposed to prevent in the best case, and support in the worst case. In the current international environment, this could and probably would translate Step Two of the FAST Program as, service in combat.

I was realistic and I was enthralled. This was the end of my rainbow, a career that satisfied my definition of honorable, provided how I could pay off the various debts to America and, had a high probability that I would see combat and learn if I really believed what I thought I believed, and just how strong were my commitment and faith. Hallelujah.

Step 2 was the first time the Army demonstrated something I was to experience many times during my service, the sophistication of Army training and development systems. Step 2 of the FAST Program was the perfect way to get the performance needed on the job. Any job. Applied to business, industry, education, or government, this technique would provide provocative images. Accountants would have to survive as salesmen before they could move to the office to support salespeople. Engineers would have to work on the manufacturing floor and produce the designs of others before they could start designing things to be made. Teachers would have to make a living by applying what they wanted to teach before they could design curriculum. Legislators would have to live under the reality of their proposals before such proposals become law.

Okay, those that needed to be satisfied that I understood what I was getting into, were satisfied and pointed me back to Step 2. To be able to go as close as possible to combat I had to pick which combat branch I wanted to join. There were three, Armor, the tanks, Artillery, the big guns and Infantry, the foot soldiers. I felt that climbing inside an armored vehicle was merely putting on my coffin. I felt that firing artillery probably involved more math than I could comprehend. So, I picked the Infantry.

The spear carrier, ground pounder, mud hugger, grunt, foot soldier, Infantryman, fit my background. My roots were the mountain people of Serbia. I imagined that in positions of command in the Infantry you were primarily alone, and I was used to being alone. Further, many of my temporary roommates had provided me with first-hand experiences and education about survival in combat. They confirmed what I learned playing cowboys and Indians, you could always crawl into a ditch, bury yourself in the dirt, and survive on the ground. I would negotiate Step 2 of The FAST Program in the Infantry.

Congratulations, all the papers were signed, and I was on

board. Now, Step 1. How do I get invited to participate in The Distinguished Military Graduate Program? Very soon I got my answer. How it happened is neither forgotten nor vague.

Colonel Funk, The Commandant of the Corps of Cadets, wanted to see me. I had no previous contact with him and was surprised he even knew I existed. When I reported to his office, the XO was there as well. Right to business, the Colonel announced that he had received a call through channels from the Army. The message was that I should be accepted into The Distinguished Military Graduate Program. ASAP. And, most interestingly, without any questions. He glued his eyes to mine and wondered did I know anything about this?

I waited a long time to answer. This was most delicate. I didn't know how to handle this. I had to give it some thought. Fortunately, the Colonel was not patient. I imagined he was somewhat frustrated to receive such a directive about a mere underclassman when he had an entire Corps of cadets. He continued.

"Look, Cadet Marksity, the implication in this message I've received is that you're doing things that make you a priority to the Army, but things that I know nothing about. I think you need to bring us up to speed. What's this all about."

Bingo! I could see my Handler's hand, make something happen but be invisible when it does. I decided to try one of his answers on the Colonel. "Colonel, I'm sure you know that if I were involved in something of that nature, I would not be allowed to admit it whatsoever. And Sir, I don't know what else to say so as not to compromise the endorsement you're received."

He looked at me for a long time. I couldn't get a feeling of what was going on in his mind. He and the Major exchanged glances and time was dragging. Then the Colonel spoke. "Okay. That's that. Welcome to the DMG Program." We shook hands and I am happy to report that Colonel Funk was true to his word, the matter never came up again.

I was still a man of leisure as my education continued. I went into my junior year with a different boat load of classes, plenty of time for spiritual maintenance, physical development, and more pocket change, as income from the station and pharmacy was augmented by monthly paychecks from ROTC. Also, unseen, was a steady volume of work with my Handler.

Almost everyone remembers exactly where they were and what they were doing when President John Fitzgerald Kennedy was shot. I do not. However, I do remember exactly where I was and what I was doing during his Inaugural Address. Olga and I were in the living room so we could watch the ceremonies on TV, she was ironing, I was polishing my shoes. At one moment during his speech a small electrical flash came from under the podium and the scene around the President erupted. It was not a serious matter, order was quickly restored, and he continued his address. Only then did I realize Olga was on the couch sobbing while her iron burned the piece she had been working on. I took care of the iron and tried to comfort her but to no avail as her sobbing persisted. Finally, I understood what she was trying to say between the spasms. "Ronnie, he is going to be assassinated."

Well, it was November 22, 1963, and the President was dead. The Nation mourned. The funeral was appropriately somber and stately. I had the feeling that the majority of the population seemed honestly touched and everywhere people were actually contemplating things beyond themselves. Then, black comedy on the scale of a black hole suffocated our nation's conscientiousness as James Earl shot Lee Harvey in the middle of a pack of law enforcement specialists! This debacle moved me to look at my personal preparedness. Immediately after the burial, I added to my running and conditioning. I bought a speed bag and Uncle Lou showed me how to use it. I also made a heavy bag and tried my best to bruise it.

There was one more thing during this entire period of time my education was continuing. It was in a completely different curriculum.

CATHIE

"Marks, I'm tellin' ya, ya have to go out with her, she's good looking, a serious Christian, been in Job's Daughters a long time, senior in high school, cheerleader, real athletic, smart, sings in a choir, so-and-so dated her for a while and said when she French kissed..."

I've never been comfortable having a conversation while facing a urinal, but my buddy had no such inhibitions. He continued his laundry list of the attributes of the latest girl I "...had to go out with..." all the way to our next class where he concluded with what he felt would seal the deal, "...and she's got humongous tits."

He wasn't alone, everybody had been working to set me up and get me out and they were right, I had no social life. They understood that my various jobs and class load kept me busy, but I needed some fun time. They were probably right again, but there was the little matter of The FBI and, I wasn't a tit man. So, I'd think about it, but no thank you.

Not too much later, another buddy announced that he had the girl for me. He had met her under the auspices of Job's Daughters, nice-looking, senior in high school, cheerleader, smart, sings in some choir, one of those people who are involved in everything and oh yeah, she has a really big rack. He just knew we were meant for each other, or at least I should take her out to check out her boobs.

That I had heard about this same girl just recently made me wonder, had the guys been trying to set me up for so long that they were out of girls. It would be nice to have a date, my last one was with Nellie, in high school. Maybe it was time to change. I agreed and my buddy set it up. Her name was Cathie and we talked on the phone a few times before our first date.

Through Bridgetown it was a long way to her house, through Mack it was taking a lot of my time and I was almost to the damn river when I pulled into her drive. Once of this was going to be enough.

I liked that her father answered the door, introduced himself, and then introduced her mother. We chatted long enough for them to learn whatever it was they wanted to know about me and me to learn they cared about their daughter. Their reception was friendly and by the time they called to tell her I was there, the three of us were comfortable together.

Cathie Jo Hayes came down the steps and I was shocked, all my sensors were on alert telling me there was something about this girl, something special. More than good-looking, she had long dark hair, high cheek bones, dark eyes, and full lips. If she had a darker complexion, she might have been a Serb. She looked me straight in the eyes and had a firm handshake. The four of us said our goodbyes and by the time we got to the car we were talking ninety miles a minute and didn't stop until I brought her back home.

That was the start of a whirlwind. I called Cathie a few weeks later and enjoyed our conversation. A week later I called, and we talked a good while. A week and a half later I called and after a great chat, asked her out for the week after next. Actually, it was more than a whirlwind, it was a tornado. Wait, before you give up on the facts, keep in mind that prior to this it had been two years between my calls to a girl. Big time tornado.

Over the next who knows how long, I learned about her. She believed in God, had faith, and knew her relationship with Him was the most important thing in her life. She was very active in her church, sang in the choir, and Job's Daughters was important to her. A senior in high school, she was a cheerleader, excelled academically, was very athletic, and was involved in everything around her. In other words, she was exactly as advertised by my two buddies, which in itself was a wonder. And there was a lot of wonder around me, to include a steady growth of my original intuition that there was something about her, something special.

Her father worked hard and kept busy with church and volunteer activities. Madge was her stepmother; her mother had passed away two years ago. She had an older brother who was a hard case and had done some time, a younger brother who was a solid citizen, and the youngest brother who was of her father and stepmother.

Cathie was the answer to my buddies' prayers as she planted the seed and then nurtured the growth of my social life. It was ironic that as time passed, she got me to do all the things I didn't do when I was in high school and to have fun in the process. She wanted to know everything about me, especially my background and family so, except for my undercover work, I gave her all of it. She took it all in and I was captivated, I even had the inkling that she rather liked me. Then, about six months later, our relationship moved to a different level.

She wanted to go to our special place for being together. This was not unusual but that evening, everything about her felt unusual. Whatever it was that was weighing on her was very heavy and something I couldn't help her manage. We were quiet a long time after parking and then finally, she started speaking, simply and directly. She told me that as a young teenager, she had come home from school and found her mother hanging from the second-floor railing. She cut her mother down and from then on felt it was her responsibility to compensate for the family's loss. When she was finished, we just hung on to each other until I had to take her home.

As time passed, we reached the following conclusions about her disclosure. I now knew exactly what my sensors felt as she came down the steps on our first date. It was wonderful that she was able to share her burden, it reflected her trust in our relationship. Perhaps more importantly, now she no longer had to carry it alone. But the most significant conclusion we reached, was that her experience with her mother and my experiences with my mother were the ingredients that formed a glue between us. A glue that to this point we may have felt but certainly didn't understand.

At the start of my junior year, Cathie started her freshman year at Miami of Ohio, just up the road in Oxford. Her tutoring my fun self continued. I learned that she could do a legitimate belly-dance, filled in for her father's Church softball team, not only excelled academically, she was somewhat of a math whiz, loved to eat lemons like the rest of us eat oranges, and got me to a dance where there was a hypnotist, and my date was the one on stage reacting to a swinging pocket watch.

So, there was no question, at this point we were an item. Our primary activities were those during which we learned about each other and ourselves and watched our relationship evolve.

UNDERCOVER

We went on rides every which way and on walks to places where we could be together. We frequently went to Whitewater State Park where, lying in the middle of a field of high grass, she decided it was time I saw what all the fuss was about and for the first time in my life, I saw a woman's naked breasts.

BUY THE BARRACUDA

The arrival of the new model cars was an annual event during my youth. Sometime near the end of summer the automobile industry's rite of passage was celebrated as all the manufacturers introduced their new versions for the next year. Most years we would head over to Henry Sieve Pontiac in hopes of getting a glimpse of what the new Pony-tracks would look like because Sieve was notorious for being sloppy during unloading. The new models would come in at night all covered up on car carriers and we'd get a little peek and then frustration. This year's introductions had some surprises, including a completely new model from Plymouth, called the Barracuda. Its design was sporty, and its hatchback included the biggest glass window ever in a production car. On the performance side, the Cuda had potential.

On this afternoon I had been working in the yard when the backdoor slammed and I saw Pete coming down the steps. I was unaware he was home and as he headed directly to me, his bearing unsettled me, he seemed all business. He was all business, no chit-chat, no pleasantries.

"I want you to do me a favor."

I was eager as I hoped I hadn't caused his demeanor.

"Buy the Barracuda."

"What?"

My question was not about the Barracuda, like everyone else I knew about the Barracuda. My question was about buying it. He had to be joking. I already had a paid-off car...I didn't have enough money...I needed my money for college I...I...I composed myself and offered him a little smile, "Ha ha. Buy the Barracuda. Very funny."

That he had always treated me like an adult seemed, from his perspective, to enfranchise him to give me looks that became etchings on my being. This was such a look. With one tilt of his head, he reviewed all the times since we met that he trusted and confided in me, summarized the times I had made errors and he accepted them as part of my growing up, catalogued the things I said I gained from him, disdained mentioning my weaknesses, and wondered what it was that was making me treat him as I was now doing. He didn't see anything funny and with one look into his eyes, I knew he was dead serious.

After a slight pause he made a point of switching to Serbian and looking into me said, "To do me a favor. Buy the Barracuda."

The man could work me and did so as he observed that after all it was a simple enough request. Not assignment. Certainly not directive. Just a request. Now, what was it that was making me hesitate? What had he done or not done? He always tried to comply with my requests, didn't he?

At the moment, it did not occur to me to evaluate if I had ever made a request of him, but I was distracted from doing my best thinking and heard myself say, "Okay Pete, I'll do it."

He switched back to American with a smile. "Well then, there you are. That's the spirit. I knew I could count on you."

"Fine. Thanks. But, could you go over exactly how I'm supposed to do you this favor without being laughed out of the dealership?"

"Of course."

He looked at me amazed, how could I have such ideas.

"Don't be so negative. You should be happy."

His entire countenance changed to that of a light-hearted man enjoying being with a friend.

"So, you know the one I'm talking about? It was there yesterday and I'm sure it will be there until you take it. It's white with a red interior, the big engine, automatic, and that wonderful back window. You've seen it?"

"I've seen it."

"So, you go and buy it."

"Pete, you want me to go into Wullenweber Motors on Harrison Avenue and buy that new Plymouth Barracuda sitting alone in the center of their showroom?"

"Exactly. You go in, introduce yourself, and ask them to show you the car. Let them make their sales pitch."

"Excuse me, but what is it that makes you think they're going to make a sales pitch to me? Do you think I look like I can afford a new car?"

"They don't know what you can or can't afford. If they don't offer to give you their sales pitch, ask for it. If the salesman won't do it, ask to see the manager."

He gave me a sideways shot and seemed to conclude something. He leaned toward me and barked, "You're not afraid of any of those guys, are you? Some personal thing…"

"No! No, that's not it at all. It's just that I never imagined myself in this position and I'm not sure how I'm gonna act. I'm afraid of looking like a horse's ass."

He went silent, looked at me as if waiting to see if I understood the language and then continued.

"Just remember this talk. You're going to make them give you the sales pitch. When they're done, you ask for the price. No matter what they say, no matter how they twist and turn, you are going to say only these words, $2,520.00, title, tags, spotless, and ready Friday at noon. Nothing else. Period."

I waited.

He waited more.

"Okay, but what if they say no-can-do?"

"You repeat your words."

There was no use waiting again. It seemed there was only one thing left to ask. "Okay, what if they say yes?"

"You reach in your pocket, take out this roll of bills and ask for the paperwork." And with this commentary he handed me $2,520.00, said, "Go buy the Barracuda." turned and went back in the house.

MY BARRACUDA

The next day I went up to Wullenweber Motors and the Barracuda was still the only thing in the showroom. It dominated the facility like the last rose of summer dominates a trellis, there was nothing else worth looking at and everyone who passed knew it.

Once inside, no one was surprised I headed straight for their centerpiece. No one tried to alter my course. I figured that's what everyone did since the 'Cuda arrived. I thought I was around and in the car long enough for someone to at least come over and talk with me, but no one did.

I was going to have to get someone's attention, but I wasn't ready for that yet, so I picked up the fancy first class brochure, promotion flyers and testimonials, and read them cover to cover. They provided tons of mechanical and cosmetic facts, pictures, specifications, and all kinds of options to mix and match. I had fun putting combinations together, but of course the best combination was sitting on the floor in front of me and I was supposed to buy it.

I had already looked the car over and there was no more to read, I had to act. Unable to get eye contact with anyone, I asked the showroom in general if I could get some service. That turned a few heads and one of the salesmen dragged himself over. He was bored and I could identify with him because watching people watch your new model with no intention of buying had to be at least boring. But he made it hard for me to like him as his question to me did not sound like what could he do for me, it sounded like what could he do to me for making him get off his duff.

"I'd like to hear what you have to say about the car. Looking her over and reading the literature are nice, but I figure the real skinny will come from listening to you."

"You want me to put on a show for you?"

"No, just your normal sales pitch."

"Look, you seem nice enough, but this is a pain. You gonna buy this 'Cuda? Ha-ha."

"Could be. Right now, it depends on how I hear your sales pitch. When I bought my present car, several people gave me input on the pluses and minuses."

He was not pleased but he sort of steeled himself, looking like I imagined I looked on McMicken when we were having fresh cow brains for supper. He started very mechanically but as he continued, his appreciation for the car crept out and he got enthusiastic. It was a good sales pitch and I realized he wished he could buy the Barracuda.

The next part was easy. I parroted Pete. "When they're done with the sales pitch, you ask for the price. No matter what they say, no matter how they twist and turn, you are going to say only these words, $2,520.00, title, tags, spotless, and ready Friday at noon."

My salesman was having none of it and was no longer dragging. My offer was out of the question. Did I know how many people were on the list of interested buyers? Did I realize people were willing to pay a premium for this baby? He'd have to see his Sales manager. They had to have more money. They couldn't get all that paperwork done Friday by noon, hell, probably not by next Friday noon. They'd have to see the General Manager. The GM just made them a trio.

As for me, through it all, I just repeated Pete. At every objection, rejection, counter proposal, request for negotiation, pleas for me to be sensible, all they got was, "$2,520.00, title, tags, spotless, and ready Friday at noon."

Finally, the brain trust trio had enough. The General Manager pulled his shoulders back and said, "Okay. Okay to it all IF, and it's a big if, IF you can pay for it. Well, can you?"

And with that I reached in my pocket, took out the roll of bills and asked for the paperwork. There wasn't a person in that showroom or sales area who wasn't riveted to the money. I signed the papers they put in front of me and took my copies and the receipt for the payment. Learning that was it, I said, "Thank you. I'll be back Friday at noon." and left. I'm not sure how far I got before it hit me, "I own the Barracuda."

THE PROPOSITION

When I got home, Pete was waiting and looked like the cat that ate all the canaries. I gave him the picture, but he wanted the details, in detail. He loved them and was particularly interested in how I felt during the experience. Maybe it was because he asked that I didn't tell him how, for a minute or two, as I pulled the cash out of my pocket, I had a feeling I'd never had before. I couldn't exactly describe it but knew it was a feeling I should avoid.

He congratulated me for completing his favor and was sorry that he wasn't going to be available Friday at noon. On the other hand, he was certain I could get someone to drive me to Wullenweber Motors. He'd come by over the weekend and maybe I could give him a ride. Then, just before driving off, he handed me an envelope. When I opened the envelope, I found a year of paid-up car insurance, effective Thursday!

Friday morning, I wanted to be alone with my Barracuda and walked to the dealership. When I entered the showroom, I was swallowed by an experience I'd never imagined. It seemed the job of the day was to congratulate me. Everyone knew me. Everyone asked about my welfare. My Barracuda was all ready and everyone hoped I was satisfied. I had no idea how to deal with this kind of attention and then the Sales manager gave me a primer on using the manual and the Service manager gave me a primer on the mechanics, and finally they let me get in and get away.

That was just the start of it. From the very first stop, whoever ended up next to us couldn't ask enough questions and people we passed expressed their love of the design, pleaded for a ride, gave the thumbs up and on and on. I continued out Harrison Avenue thinking that in the country 'Cuda and I could get to know each other, bad thinking. Anyone who passed, either way, had to get a second look, honk, yell, wave, or just smile. I was not equipped for this attention, even though I knew it was for the 'Cuda, it was just too much fuss in my direction. I got her home and tried to stop feeling the eyes of the world on her, us, me.

I gave Olga and George the sales pitch, let them feel and touch and explained I was doing Pete a favor. That was all they needed and exactly what I needed because the attention that came with that car was overwhelming. I had no precedent in my background for such uninhibited wealth, and others linking it to me was terrifying.

Pete came over during the weekend and I flipped him the keys before we took off. Right off the bat it was clear he had no problems with the reactions of others. He knew how to drive and took 'Cuda through the paces and all the way to her limits. In time, satisfied with his shakedown drive, Pete pulled off the road and under a huge tree. We opened the doors and hatch and enjoyed the breeze wafting through the cabin.

In a mixture of Serbian and American, Pete reflected on the car and then on other matters. He hadn't missed that I flipped him the keys before we took off, just as he had done to me the day he taught me how to drive. Hey, that was not too far from this spot, we did spend a lot of time in Indiana. Just think how long we've known each other. We've been through some interesting situations. Done a lot together. Had a good relationship. Whitewater. Drive-Ins and cheesecake. Dave Frisch's piano. How about the house on Hawthorne.

And then he shifted gears and it was only Serbian and all specific. His assignment for President Tito was coming to fruition. He was into a very sensitive project, probably the biggest of his assignment, he finally had a deal that included some really important horses. The type of horses that could give Tito what he wanted, a world class line. But success was only to be achieved during a small-time window and he was going to need some serious help. Help from someone he completely trusted. Someone that he knew, inside and out.

"Understand Zoran, I have a proposition for you. I have to go to New York City to make the contacts and arrange for the purchase and export of these horses. You may not know it but not everyone wants to see Yugoslavia get on the world stage in any manner, including the Sport of Kings. To get this done, I need help that you have proven able to provide. I propose you go with me.

"Understand, I need some serious help driving. When everything falls into place and the timetable is announced, we will have to get to Manhattan immediately and with both of us driving it can be done.

"Also, in order to make all the contacts and arrangements, I need the support of an interpreter. There are many people behind the scenes who only speak Serb. What they are doing is very important, but I don't have the time to give them the attention they need and deserve. You have interpreted and know both my methods and my thinking. As my interpreter you can be my voice to them.

"You see you are perfect for the job. Will you go with me?"

Just for a moment I had a flash of satisfaction. He had been trying to read me from the moment he started his proposition but without success and now he was waiting for my decision without a clue as to what it would be. I didn't keep him waiting.

"Well, we have a history and friends should help friends. So, only because you're a friend and you need me, I'm willing to drive your four-door Lincoln yacht, that smoothes out at over ninety, to New York City and run around Manhattan for at least a week. Are you kidding me? When do we leave?"

He was sure it would be no sooner than a week. Then he emphasized that beyond that he couldn't be positive about any of the timing because so many other people and factors were involved. His best guess was that we would depart in less than two weeks and be in Manhattan for at least one week, but I needed to be flexible, we could be there a lot longer.

I drove home and, on the way, we laid out preliminary details. Once home, as we were getting out of the Barracuda, I handed him the keys and explained they were his set, she was his to drive anytime. The smile of satisfaction that creased the corners of his mouth had two sources, that I had keys made for him, that he knew that's what I'd do. He liked being right.

PREPARATIONS

As soon as he left, I contacted my Handler to set up a session. The call on a weekend established that something important was happening. The next day, he was surprised by my appearance.

"Well, hellllO! You look like a man who's had a red-letter...what? Week?"

I had no idea what was different about my looks, but I knew well what was different about my situation.

"You might say that. Since our last session I became the owner of a brand-new big engine Plymouth Barracuda. I paid for it with cash. Cash given to me by our Mr. Johnson who also paid for a year of my car insurance. In less than a week, I'll be driving my friend and his luxury liner Lincoln to New York City. We'll be gone at least a week, but I'll be flexible because it could be a lot longer. How about you since our last session?"

He smiled at the sarcasm and was lit up as I continued.

"The last few days with him makes me believe this is a major move. I wouldn't be surprised if it's The major move. We need to get me prepped so that if the timing changes and he wants to go now, I can go now."

He agreed wholeheartedly and we spent the rest of Monday

putting to use all the things he'd taught me for just such a situation.

I picked Greensleeves as my code name just because I liked the song. He established the procedure for me to prove I was Greensleeves and for others to prove they were who they were supposed to be.

He gave me a contact number, an emergency number, and a contingency number. Each included parameters for determining when to use that number and security steps for its use. This was very important to me as it addressed the matter of me not ending up in Yugoslavia with Mr. Dejurdjev.

Our preparation included close coordination between the New York and Cincinnati Bureau Stations. Things went smoothly until the issue of where and how I would meet my New York contact. Nothing seemed to fit so I suggested a porno theater. Dead silence. I took that to mean they wanted me to continue.

I explained my reasoning was based on my experience with porno theaters, where, unless it was a guy helping his girl have an adventure she wanted, it's only men in the audience and those men did not want to talk or be talked to. So, a man entering the place was nothing to notice and, didn't they agree that the last thing anyone would think of such a man was that he was an FBI agent passing the time.

A porno theater was also good cover for me. It was highly unlikely that I would run into any Slavic personnel at a porno theater, it's not good for a Slavic man to watch rather than act. But, in the unlikely event I was spotted, Pete knew I enjoyed porno and would merely agree it was me. If I had a bodyguard or chaperon, I was certain he wouldn't want to go in with me, so whether I was alone from the hotel or not, I would certainly be alone in the theater. Further, I truly believed that once inside, our talking together would be something all the other patrons would try to avoid, in effect we would have a secured conversation.

Again, no one had anything else to offer and so it was agreed that my first contact with the New York City Bureau would be in a porno theater. After a few odds and ends, everything was set and on my way home I determined that until we left, I would balance exaggerated displays of my normal routine with covert work preparing for the trip.

When I got home, Olga told me Pete had called so I rang the number he had left. He wondered if he could take the Barracuda the next morning. He wanted to show it to some of his acquaintances and a particular associate, all of whom would love to drive the hit of the new car year. Before I could agree, he continued that his Lincoln needed to be in the shop for a check-up and so my letting him drive the Barracuda would serve several purposes. I couldn't say 'of course' enough but eventually convinced him I'd love for him to take the car.

Tuesday, when I got home, the 'Cuda was gone. Looking at the empty garage, I had to admit there was something odd about last night's phone conversation. I mean, how hard is it to ask to drive the car you paid for? I didn't know but reasoned that I felt odd because this was another interruption of me and my Barracuda.

Then the very next evening, Wednesday, she was back in the garage. I guessed it had to do with keeping me on my toes, but then decided that all the acquaintances, associates, and others had been able to get their thrills quicker than expected and the Lincoln had passed muster, so Pete didn't need my Barracuda any longer. Maybe one day, I'd drive the damn thing.

As I had been doing, the next day I continued to work my plan. Covertly I memorized the agreed upon codes, numbers, contingencies, and related procedures and then mentally pictured successfully implementing each. To aid this exercise I studied maps of Manhattan until I was somewhat oriented to the island. As for my normal routine, if one looked closely, it could be noticed that it included abnormal emphasis on physical fitness, especially running.

Two days later, I was taking the day off and sleeping-in. At a certain moment I thought I heard something but just rolled over and went back to sleep. Then I knew I heard something coming from the back yard. Unhappy at being disturbed, I was startled when I opened my shade and saw Pete and the Barracuda. Intuitively I knew he shouldn't know I was there.

The car was in the middle of the two-car apron with the driver's door open. Pete was crouched down facing the inside of the open door. From my window I couldn't see exactly what he was doing, so I moved to the window in the other bedroom. From that vantage point I could see everything, but I certainly had no idea what it was I was seeing.

The door panel was off, and all the workings were exposed. He had a fancy tool kit, the everything you need in a carrying case type, and a piece of cushion material on which three or four uniquely shaped containers or canisters or cylinders were displayed. I couldn't determine what they were made of but could see that each had a screw cap on one end. Pete was trying to place one of the containers in the body of the door but couldn't seem to find the correct space for it. He looked like a guy working a puzzle that required putting the right shaped container in the right space in the door body.

It took him quite a while and I was able to witness his behavior, confident patience. He knew all those containers were going to fit in the door, it was just a matter of time until he'd make that happen. And, sure enough, in the end all the containers fit, and the door panel was secured. He then cleaned the door and put my Barracuda back in the garage before leaving in his Lincoln.

Fortunately, he didn't check the house after his little surgery on the 'Cuda and I assumed he hadn't checked it before he became preoccupied with his puzzle playing. I waited, to make certain he wasn't going to come back looking for something, and then went out to check-out the car. I looked over the driver's door and panel and rail and interior and in the vicinity...everywhere and anywhere there might be some shred of evidence that the door had been tampered with, nothing. Plus, the door and window worked perfectly. Absolutely nothing.

No, absolutely something, those containers were heavy duty important and the number of questions this posed was staggering. Why canisters or cylinders or containers or whatever they were? What could they contain? Who were they for? And oh yes, why put them in my Barracuda? Was I going to be driving around with this package of who-knows-what for who-knows-who for how long? Not too much later My Handler agreed, and we both began the business of waiting. We didn't have to wait long. It was just after supper when I answered the phone.

On the line, in Serbian, "Zoran, how about taking a little drive?"

He was all charisma but didn't need to be, I was still excited from the afternoon's puzzle playing.

"You bet. What's up?"

"The call I have been waiting for, about the horses, just came in and everything in New York is in order. All that's missing is us."

"That's great, I know you've been working on this a long time and I'm good to go, just say when."

"What I'd like to do is come over tomorrow evening and

spend the night so we can take off for New York early in the morning. You think Olga and George would mind?"

"Oh sure, they'd mind. Give me a break. You know they'll be glad to see you."

"Okay. But now, how about you. Are you sure you can leave that soon?"

"Pete, you know I'm ready and you know I was ready the day after you made the offer."

"Okay, okay. Well then, I'll see you tomorrow evening."

"Right. Thanks."... and just before I hung up...

"Oh, by the way, we need to take the Barracuda."

"My Barracuda?"

"Yes."

"But the Lincoln is made for this sort of drive, it's a high-speed cruiser. I mean it's okay with me if you want to take the Barracuda, but it doesn't make good sense."

"Well, you see, the other day when I took the Lincoln in, they found it needs work and we can't take a chance of something going wrong on this drive. Taking your car lets me give them the boat with plenty of time to get it right before we get back."

"Hey, don't get me wrong, it's not exactly a punishment to have to drive a brand-new pumped-up Barracuda. Where are you having the work done on the Lincoln? I'll pick you up after you drop her off, just tell me where and when?"

"Never mind that, you've got enough to do getting the Barracuda ready for the trip. I'll just have one of the service people bring me over."

"Really, it's no bother. I'd think you'd rather ride with me..."

He was having none of it. I was clearly not to know where the Lincoln was going to be parked or anything other than what I already knew.

"Okay then compatriot, I'll see you tomorrow."… and the line went dead.

I looked at the phone and heard "compatriot". This was a no nonsense message. Pete had explained to me that for a Serb, compatriot was a term of extremely high status and respect. That was how he was viewing me and that's the way he expected me to see myself, and act accordingly. I got the message and saw a lot more.

Now I saw the days since his proposition in a new light. "Acquaintances and a particular associate" my ass. He had taken my Barracuda to someone who could craft the containers that would fit in the door. As soon as those measurements were completed, he didn't need the car anymore and put her back. It obviously had taken two days for that someone to manufacture the containers and as soon as they were done, Pete brought them to the Barracuda to test how they fit. And they did fit, as I had witnessed. And, since we were leaving tomorrow, it was not an unreasonable assumption that the containers he was fitting in the door were already loaded for transport.

My Handler concurred and wished me well because it was also not an assumption that early in the morning, I would be on my own.

THE DRIVE

The next day, Pete was dropped off at our house much earlier than expected, so I didn't get to see who played chauffeur or the car. It would have been nice to at least have the plates from that car.

When I got home with the Barracuda, I had her dressed and fed. Pete wanted to give her his pre-trip check-up and was not surprised that everything was shipshape. He then asked me to help him load his things and as we were doing so, he announced that he had already had supper and wanted nothing so much as a relaxing night.

Good for him but I was not going to have a relaxing night. I got unrelaxed when I saw that the one item he didn't load into the car was my old friend, the valise he entrusted to me at the scene of his wreck. The valise I thought was going to be our breakthrough. The valise that had the naughty pictures. I had a bad feeling about that valise. No, that valise pissed me off.

During the evening I decided some chitchat might be useful. Yes, the Lincoln was in a place where it would be taken care of. Yes, it was nice of the person to drop him off. Yes, he knew I would have been more than happy to pick him up, but this way worked just fine. Zilch was the result of my chitchat; it didn't feel like I was experiencing a good start to our trip.

We were on the road before sun-up, switching off as usual, and only stopping for gas, eats, and the facilities. We used rabbits as much as possible but most of the time we were our own rabbit. The Barracuda absolutely could run and there was not much on the road able or willing to keep up, let alone lead.

The weather was excellent, bright sunshine and clear but very few drivers were looking at the weather, attention and lots of it, was focused on the Barracuda. Almost all the drivers reacted to the hatchback. Anyone we came up on was staring in the rear-view mirror and then stayed glued after we'd passed. Women absolutely loved it and truckers were obsessed, many would give us the thumbs up with their horns.

I drove a lot and Pete slept a lot. I felt this was his way of demonstrating his trust in me. Then we were about an hour out, and past the time for us to switch, when he said he'd like me to continue and get us on the island.

Maybe this kick-started my paranoia, but when he put the seatback as far down as possible and pretended to sleep, I got a not ha-ha funny feeling. By the time we got to the lower tunnel, I felt certain he was hiding, but from whom? Who would see him and so what if they did? And then I got a jolt. No one had seen him since we left Cincinnati. All focus had been on the car. In the Barracuda we were basically invisible. But it was more than that, there was absolutely nothing that could even link him to the car, nothing at Wullenweber Motors, the license bureau, the insurance agency, or any other place. He was invisible and riding in another person's car. This wasn't his car; this was my Barracuda. It was my car that was loaded with canisters that held I didn't know what, headed I didn't know where…

As soon as we came out of the tunnel in Manhattan, Pete took the wheel and drove directly to the docks. He seemed to know exactly where he was going and maneuvered through Manhattan as routinely as I had maneuvered through my grade school paper route.

When we hit the docks, my mind turned to the pile of books I'd read that painted the scene. I saw what Mike Hammer and others were talking about and recognized the docks, ships, warehouses, and longshoremen as if they were old acquaintances.

We came to a large ship out of La Havre, France. Pete went halfway past the vessel, turned left into a monster warehouse, and continued into the place toward a few cars where a group of people were standing. By the time we came to a stop, it was clear they were waiting for us, definitely all Slavs.

As we got out of our car, it was obvious this was not the first time these people had seen Pete. There was handshaking all round as our baggage was removed from my Barracuda and put in a big four-door, our baggage except for his valise, that he carried himself.

Pete was clearly the leader of this show. He turned my Barracuda's keys over to a stevedore who was built like a stove and a bunch of papers to a wiry bespectacled had-to-be accountant and then turned to the group. He thanked them for their help thus far, knew he could count on them in the future, and introduced me as his compatriot. Then he motioned me toward the big sedan whose rear doors were being held open for us.

As our driver headed out of the warehouse, the door panels of my Barracuda were being removed. This was a two-fold surprise. First, that they were dismantling the car and second, that both doors were being dismantled. Just a few days ago, I really had gone back to sleep after being awakened and had slept long enough for Pete to have completed his work on the passenger side door before I watched him from the second bedroom. So now I knew both doors held cylinders, another entire set of things I didn't have a clue about.

I wondered why they were dismantling the doors, but then we were in traffic until we stopped under the portico of a hotel. As on the docks, there were people waiting for us who could be described as henchmen, but for me they were distinguishable as knowing Pete, expecting both of us and mostly Serbians. Pete was sincerely welcomed, and the reception was not a show, these men were pleased to be working for him.

Off to the side of this scene were two very imposing guys. I was not an expert on hotels but these two were not doormen. I had to stop looking at this as a hotel and start looking at it as the center of operations and with that it was easy to see that these were the gatekeepers. During our visit, I learned that two imposing and very serious guys were always there, and somehow each pair seemed wider and more serious than the others.

A distinguished man who was obviously the local leader was seeing to Pete while others were taking our luggage, minus the valise, into the hotel. Before I entered, Pete pulled me aside and introduced me to this local chief as his compatriot. Just as he had done on the docks, Pete was making it clear I was special and was to get special treatment. Then, plainly directing me, he and the local leader explained that if anything happened, anything at all, and I needed help, of any kind, anytime, I was to get to this gentleman, and he would see to my needs. I nodded, and we entered the hotel like tourists.

The hotel was something of a blur in shades of orange and brown, very clean and neat, but certainly not new. Pete and I were in a two-bedroom suite with separate baths and a common room with couch, side chairs, coffee table, and writing desk. It was spacious and first class, offering more than the hotel's exterior promised.

We unpacked and went downstairs for a light supper. We were treated with respect and the only business was a review of tomorrow's schedule before we headed back upstairs to hit the sack. I didn't drift off, I needed to catalogue the day's experiences.

Unfortunately, I had to admit, "My Barracuda" had been a premeditated tool from the get-go. More unfortunately, I was pretty sure I was never going to see that car again.

Now, what was that at the docks? Why were they dismantling the doors? Pete must have put the contents into the canisters before we left Cincinnati, so why dismantle them? Once we hit the warehouse, I figured the car was going to be shipped to France on that big boat outside and thereby be the delivery vehicle for the contents of the canisters. So, dismantling the doors didn't make sense, unless, unless something else was going to be added. This was nuts, I had nothing but my fantasy.

On the plus side, they certainly trusted me. No one seemed surprised to see me with Pete, in fact they were expecting both of us. They started taking the doors off while I was still able to see them, if they didn't trust me, they would have waited until I was out of sight. Plus, I was welcomed in all the conversations I joined. Everyone took Pete at his word. I was his compatriot. That's solid.

Fine, but how about what was in the bunch of papers he gave to the had-to-be accountant? Who were the people in the warehouse? Who were the people at this hotel? I had seen no pictures or bios that might have helped me identify someone. Most annoying of all, what was in that damn valise?

Taking everything together, I had to recognize there was a

cloud over me. I was comforted to have the local chief to go to for help, any kind, anytime. On the other hand, having him to go to signified I might need help and there was the rub, you only get a safety net when you're flying the high trapeze.

MAELSTROM

…it's mid-morning of our first full day in Manhattan and the day is already full. I had a name and description for each of the three Slavic visitors who came through breakfast like a parade, one after the other, to welcome Pete and offer their services. These were three very hard men.

…can you believe it, a Yellow Cab. My very first ride in a cab is in New York City in an authentic Yellow Cab. Lots of room inside. I thought we'd be driven in the four-door.

…that was the first Embassy I ever saw, never mind visited. I got the names and faces but don't really understand the position or function of the man we met or his helpers.

As for me, so far, I have nothing to do but listen and remember…

…okay I know where it is and what it's called but, exactly what does that agency we spent two hours in do?

…Pete, what am I supposed to do when you introduce me as your personal assistant? "What you did. You may have been wondering on your inside, but your outside looked like you knew a secret. People think personal assistants know secrets. Help them think that."

…first an Embassy, now a Consulate. Are they all in first class locations? In grand buildings? What's the difference between a Consulate and an Embassy? I don't know squat about International Relations…

I do know this is one great supper. Our host makes today include Yugoslavs, Poles, and Czechs. I got enough addresses, names, faces, and tidbits to take a week of debriefing.

…it can't be morning already.

So, that operation specializes in international transport. I'm out of my depth, after all our time in there, I don't know if the endless chatter was about the horses or the Barracuda. I know where the car was but in fact, where are the horses? I talk like I know the horses; I don't know diddle…

…yet another cab. We're not going to see that four-door, it's tied to the hotel, only cabs for us.

…it's sure the horses aren't in this place; can I say impressive!

Fine, chalk up two more Embassies and add Rumanians and Hungarians and we're in another Yellow going somewhere, Whoa…Why did we leave that cab early…he wants to talk…

"Right now, you no longer speak or understand Serbian. When we enter the next place, I will introduce you as my liaison here in the United States, a college man who only speaks American. I want to know what those you will be sitting with have to say."

No sweat. How hard could that be? Oh Lord, I almost wrenched my back stopping my head from spinning around the first time one of them asked me to pass the coffee. This is a bitch. Some practice in this dance would have helped. Steady, here they come again. Excellent, I ignored them perfectly. I wonder if the face I'm making is convincing them that I'm thinking, "What the hell are these foreigners yapping about?" I think they bought it.

Serbs alright. Okay Zorana, pretend you're back on McMicken and listen...

New roles today. Confidant, reverse interpreter and this evening, subordinate, which was a gimme, I'm a natural.

...same old at the table, Pete and I are the only ones who don't drink or smoke.

I got to keep cataloging the places, functions, names, and faces, things are starting to get jumbled. Nice bed. Good bed...

It was late morning on our third day in Manhattan. We had visited two more impressive edifices, one housing another formidable International Bureaucracy and the other playing home to another Eastern European Agency. When we returned to the hotel, Pete decided we needed some time off and told everyone they were on their own till evening.

Amen and thank you brother. My roles as personal assistant, confidant, subordinate, interpreter, liaison, and compatriot were taking a toll. I needed to get the data I'd been memorizing off my brain before it explode, and Pete had just given me my chance to do so.

Back in our suite, I was preparing for my afternoon of sightseeing when Pete casually asked where I was headed. In the split second that followed I experienced an attack of guilt. I knew the purpose of my sightseeing and for some reason my guilt made me think that he knew as well. It took all I had for me to control myself. In the meantime, reflexively, I was answering, "To the movies, to see some porno. The best is supposed to be here." As he walked out, he agreed, and I took a deep breath. I waited, a little past long enough, for him to be off the elevators before I followed.

On my walk up-town I was thankful that since we arrived, I had never had a chaperon, bodyguard or tag along. Wait a minute,

I had never had any time alone to determine if I was being followed. I paid attention to my surroundings and once satisfied I was alone, I found an indoor payphone and set up my meeting with the New York Bureau.

As I continued my stroll, I couldn't shake the fact that, until the incident in our suite, I had never felt guilty about working undercover. So why did I react to Pete's simple question with the impulse to come clean? This was damn dangerous. I needed some way to cope with this development, to prevent such an internal reaction from ever happening again and, I had to do that now because I was in front of the theater where I was to make contact.

The two little band boxes that showed porno in Kentucky, across the river from Cincinnati, were no preparation for what I found on 42nd Street. It was a good thing we had picked a specific theater, or I could have been looking for my contact the rest of the day. Under the marquee, I bought my ticket and headed for the seat we had designated for our meeting, the middle of row 10. The row was empty, so I didn't have to start moving to the alternatives we had established. I took positive reinforcement for my idea to meet in a porno theater as the men that were there were spread as far apart as possible.

In no time a man sat down in the aisle seat to my right. I acknowledged that I had seen him before focusing back on the giant screen. If he was my contact, the next move was his. Directly, he moved from the aisle to the seat next to me. This was awkward. Why would the idiot plunk himself down so close, he would draw attention to us. Plus, it was likely we'd have to turn our heads to be able to hear each other and that would look like two guys talking. I expected an agent from New York City to know enough to take a seat in front of me so he could hear what

I had to report, and we would look like two guys watching the show.

I couldn't very well try to educate him at this point, and I needed to unload, so I gave him my prompt. He didn't react. I did. I was unhappy, why did I get some novice as my contact? This bozo was all wrong and this time I gave him my prompt with an edge on it. Believe it or not, his response was to sort of lean into my right arm. That was it. I turned to look him in the face and asked if he had anything to say to me. After his first four words I realized I wasn't sitting next to my FBI contact, I was in the middle of my first homosexual experience. This idiot fairy was trying to pick me up. He could mess up my mission. I moved from unhappy, in one giant step, to crazy. Had I caught him I would have killed him, I did neither.

Whoa! I returned to my seat in the middle of row ten and, with the huge screen grunting and moaning in my face, tried to regain my composure. It was hard to do. I had been infuriated, not because he was homosexual. I had never encountered a homosexual before and had no feelings one way or the other about their preferences. No, I had been infuriated because he was possibly compromising my mission and that caused my condition to surface, I was way too tightly wound. My emotions in handling this clown, coupled with the surprise guilt I had back at the hotel, showed me just how up-tight I was. I needed to get a grip. If my contact had seen this episode, his report to the locals would not be good, the operative from Cincinnati is a loose cannon. And then, a nondescript man stopped at row nine and after looking around to be sure he liked that row the best, entered row nine and ended up sitting in front of me.

Looking at my watch, I saw it was the time we had targeted for our contact. That was a break for me, if he were my contact and his actions said he was, he had not seen my behavioral breakdown. As an aside to myself, I wondered why it hadn't occurred to me to check the time when queeny sat down on the aisle.

Unlike my homo would be buddy, this man said and did all the right things to secure his identity and mine. It was an adjustment for me as I had never worked with anyone other than my Handler in Cincinnati, and now, here in Manhattan, I was working with a complete stranger who was going to tape my report. As the sounds from the giant screen covered our meeting, we began working. I leaned forward to tie my shoelace and asked what he knew. His last input was the canisters in the driver's door, so I started the night before we left Cincinnati and just kept rolling.

My Handler needed to know I had nothing about Pete's departure, where he spent the nights before, where he left his belongings, not even where he left the Lincoln or who dropped him off at our place. Nothing to help determine what this trip was all about.

When we left Cincinnati and the trip route. I saw no contact points.

Pete's behavior as we approached Manhattan. His obvious familiarity with the city.

The docks, ship from La Havre, warehouse, cars and plates inside, thumbnail sketches of the personnel with the importance of identifying the had-to-be-an-accountant as that might lead to what was in the papers Pete gave him, the four-door, its plates and driver, the dismantling of both Barracuda doors.

The hotel, more sketches of the personnel with emphasis on the leader, and then, I got into details. I reported every place we visited and everything I witnessed that might have value to the Bureau. It was good we had a double feature.

He was not a novice, and the session went smoothly with him

only asking questions that helped him understand, and me see things from new perspectives. When we were done, we set up a place for our next session and places as fallbacks. While giving me a new emergency number and codes, he remarked that the New York Office had everything about me and all their people could recognize me, so I shouldn't feel alone. Then stretching as if he had been sitting too long, he sort of worked his way to a standing position and ambled out. When he disappeared from my peripheral vision, I sat back to enjoy the show and fell asleep.

...I woke up and was back in the maelstrom...hustling my butt back to the hotel in time to clean up and be ready for supper and talk and sleep and it was the next morning and we were off again to another Eastern Block functionary.

Pete, how long we gonna be here doing this? "As I said in Cincinnati, I can't say how the politicians and pencil pushers will behave, but I expect at least one full week."...great, feels like two weeks already.

...was that Russian, Latvian, what?

...more role playing. I'd like another shot at playing dumb...I don't understand a word you're saying so talk so I can listen...

..how many agencies, sub units and functionaries is it going to take. We've certainly seen more than enough people to ship a Plymouth and some ponies.

Come to think of it, we haven't met with a single American...Of course, he could have had meetings with a pile of others, we weren't together all the time. Yes, like yesterday during my grunt and groan movie show.

...wait here comes another guest joining us for another part of another meal. Pete and I have spent more time in restaurants in NYC than during all the years we've known each other.

...so, what's that make, Yugoslavian, Hungarian, Rumanian,

Czechoslovakian, Polish. And then the one that got me because I couldn't exactly understand the language but did understand the odd portion now and then which was frustrating and annoying and interrupted my concentrating, could it have been Bulgarian...

How many Governments are in the Eastern Block? I thought I knew but there's got to be more in real life than shown on the map and we're going to visit every one...and now, Russians. I understood more than I expected. Course that could be due to the speaker who looked like a British gentleman whose Seville Row clothes were perfectly tailored yet couldn't hide the physical threat his body represented.

...so here's a twist, a representative of The Western Block, France, imagine that, geez, where is La Havre. The talk of horses was pronounced yet no mention of the car. Okay, I couldn't speak a word but neither La Havre nor Barracuda required translation.

...it seems our French friend knows the right place for our export/import questions and, Yankee Doodle Dandy, it's an American office full of Americans and it actually seems like straight forward business talk about getting horses from Kentucky to Europe. I forgot what straight talk sounded like.

...a bank. I'm getting a feeling things are about to change. Well maybe, but not right now. Now we're here at another point in the maelstrom.

OUT AND IN

I still had no idea about Pete's plans. Was he going, where, when, alone, with someone, who, for how long...? Regardless my futile musings about his plans, my reality remained the same, time was closing in on me. These feelings were real and had meaning, hell, lately everything had at least two meanings. I was unsettled, anxious.

On this afternoon I found myself alone in our suite and decided to take a chance. I went into his room, leaving the door half open so I could hear if anyone happened by and get out and close the door quicker than if it were all the way open. I made straight to Pete's valise, the same valise he entrusted to me after his wreck. The valise I thought would produce a breakthrough regarding his activities but only startled me by its pornographic contents.

I didn't have time to review my history with the valise because, this time, what was inside more than startled me. On top were multiple passports and multiple tickets—tickets for two—on four different airlines, to four different countries in Europe. Tickets that included Mr. Johnson and Mr. Marksity and, OH JOY, the departure date printed on the tickets, was tomorrow.

Tomorrow, somebody or some bodies were going someplace and today, The FBI were nowhere to be seen.

The key was that the departure times were very close together, which meant all four airlines would have to be covered by my safety net. There were all kinds of ways he and I could go, and in all but the one we would go, they would be in the wrong place. It didn't take a genius to figure that the FBI needed to know the details of all our travel options and even then, there were plenty of openings for me to fall through. I had to do something.

At this point, my experience with my Handler replaced my musings and I went about my business. I memorized everything, passport names, numbers, and dates, ticket numbers, departure airlines and times, arrival countries, airports and times.

Once finished, I closed the valise, opened his door completely, left his room and went to mine, leaving the door half open before sitting down with a magazine. Now I was set to plan.

There was no time to set up and conduct a meeting. I had to get to a phone, call the number established for such a situation, confirm my code and that of whoever would be taking the data and, once the confirmations were complete, transfer the information. I should expect some requests for review of points. This call would not be wham-bam-thank-you-ma'am. I will have to be patient, which means I must find a spot that affords cover and time for the call.

Any phone in the hotel was out. I didn't know anything about operators listening or listening devices but calling from the hotel, just felt wrong. There were two phone booths in the vicinity, but I couldn't use the closest. It was too near the hotel and in a bright area, making the chances of me being seen too high. If I were seen, it would eventually get to Pete and what would I say when he asked why I was making a call away from the hotel?

Why wasn't I calling from the hotel? Wasn't the hotel offering me anything I wanted, anytime? It was going to have to be the phone booth farther up the street near the adjacent business area.

Okay, but maybe not so good. I have to get out of the hotel, make the call and get back in, all without being noticed or missed. How am I going to get out of this hotel?

Plus, there's more to it, it's getting dark. There's no way they're going to let me go anywhere without some accompaniment, obvious or not so obvious. I liked the guys who followed me around but felt confident I could lose them. However, losing them would not be a success, it would be stupid. How do I explain to Pete why I lost my benefactor? Why I made my bodyguard look foolish? Shit, imagine explaining that to the bodyguard the next time we see each other, 'nuf said. I got to get out and in, alone.

So, what exit and entrance? The front entrance was out, the gatekeepers would notice me leaving and returning. The rear exit had a security alarm and there are no fire escapes. I hadn't noticed any other exits...wait, the lobby restroom. Did I see a window? I couldn't wait, and immediately took off for the lobby. At the elevator I made myself calm down. I had to get a grip. How lame would it be to blow this in the planning stage?

Exiting the elevator, I eased into the lobby and gave the place my best once over as I ambled toward the front doors. The elevator was visible from the front desk. The stairs were around the corner from the front desk and not visible from half of the lobby.

I said hello to the gatekeepers, walked to the street, looked around, stretched, returned and then, in Serbian, "Have you all noticed Pete?...blah...blah, Yes it is a good temperature....blah...blah. See you later." Nice. That explains why I'm out here and sounds usual.

Then I reversed my dance. On my way back into the hotel I

noted there was only one small section of the stairs visible from the front doors and from the outside the spot was hard to see. I made sure to get eye contact and say "hi" to all the personnel — on my way into the restroom — they had to see me use it.

Finally, inside the restroom, Thank God, there was a window, and it was a normal height from the floor. Also, thanks, the place was deserted.

I made myself time conscious. I had made the front desk and lobby people see me enter and didn't have all day before I had to reappear and reinforce their seeing me exit. Later, if asked, they would honestly report, "Oh yes, I've seen him use the lav." "Me too." "Yes, just the other day." and thereby, if I do get seen, make my being there nothing extraordinary.

Nervous, I listened for anyone joining me as I moved to the window. I needed three bits of info. Can the window be opened? How far below is the drop outside? Where would I be once out there? The window opened easily but there was a noise from the lobby, and I felt I had get out. It would have been nice to get the other two bits of information.

I tried to be natural as I passed the front desk and traversed the lobby. "Hello." I smiled, maintained eye contact but didn't get chatty. Standing in front of the elevator I pretended to push the button. I wanted more time to stand and be noticed. Suddenly, I developed an easy-to-be-heard-around-the-lobby cough. I pushed the up button and then, up I went. It may have been my imagination, but the lobby seemed particularly bright during this recon.

Back in our suite I continued my preparation. I had to be as clean when I exited the men's room as I was when I entered. Outside the window it must be filthy so maybe I should take a spare shirt. But where could I leave it while I was gallivanting to the phone? And if it were found, what are the chances of it being identified as mine? And if it was, how am I gonna explain my shirt being anywhere other than in my room or on me? No, I'll have to use my physical skills to get out and in clean. As a last resort, I can wash up in the restroom.

Okay, when? While they're at supper. Supper has not been a command performance so me not joining them would mean nothing. That is key, I've got to make my location and myself irrelevant.

Anyone who asks about my plans will get a subtle version of the age old man-speak that is heard as, my basic goal is to find a woman and spend the night doing everything it takes to satisfy—and here the listener inserts his sexual fantasy. Come to think of it, this will do my image some good. Maybe I don't smoke and drink, but at least I got one virtue.

Now I needed to picture the mechanics. I must wait long enough to be sure they have left for supper. Be patient. When I leave our suite, I'll take the elevator because if there is anyone in the hallway, they should wonder why I'm taking the steps. I haven't taken the steps since we arrived. However, I'll get off on the third floor.

From there, I'll take the steps to the landing above the lobby. There, I'll wait and listen to get a sense of how many people are in the lobby and their positions. The key is how many might have a line of sight on the restroom entrance. Once satisfied, I'll continue downstairs normally. I must stay to the inside of the stairs, the side closest to the front desk, this is where it is the hardest to be seen from any place in the lobby or the front doors.

If anyone happens upon me on my way down the steps, I'll immediately tie my shoe and the person will automatically look at my body rather than my face. The point is to avoid anyone being able to recall seeing me, even people not associated with Pete.

I need to give them time to get past the landing and then I'll take it up as before the interruption. Do not run. Do not hunch over. Do not tip toe, this isn't Spy vs Spy in Mad Magazine. Walk normally to the restroom.

The best is that no one sees me go in. The worst is that someone sees me go in, because that would start a timeline and me in the restroom for more than, what? ten minutes? longer? I don't know how long. I had to think.

I couldn't figure out how long in the restroom was too long but, I could try the following no matter my time in there. Vomit. "Man, I was sick as a dog. Don't know why. Nothing in the bowl to explain what happened. I'm just glad there was soap in there because it gave me a chance to clean my mouth. I just hate that smell and taste, don't you? I think I got rid of both. I felt like I was in there for hours."

I felt that could work plus it made me see, "Can you believe it. Not only did I get sick, but I got myself dirty vomiting. That floor in the far stall is filthy." Now I had no need for an extra shirt.

Okay, once inside, if someone is there, get into a stall as quickly yet naturally as possible hoping they didn't get a look at me as I went straight in to do my business. I've got to be prepared to wait and prepared to accept waiting will not be easy. But I will wait till they leave, making appropriate sounds if they are lingering. Once they've gone, move out and check the other stalls. If there is someone there, I'll use my judgment to decide if I have time to do things before the person exits or if I should return to my stall and wait for them to leave.

In either case, once alone, get to the window and open it. Once it's open, I'll get out and over the ledge and place the window so it is waiting to open for me when I come back. I figure I'll have to hang by both hands until oriented to the light—it's going to be dark—and then pick a spot to land, or if it's too high, pick a way to get down.

Hey, what about the window? Will that window close on me after I'm out? I didn't check that. Relax, just take several packs of matches to use as a wedge to prevent the window closing.

Once I'm down I'll have to go down the alley, or whatever it is, and start to the phone booth, staying in the shadows as much as possible. Once there make the call.

From this point I reversed the process and tried to visualize returning from the call.

Even though it looked like I was reading a magazine in my room, I was on full alert the entire time of this planning. The half open door to my room and where I was sitting let anyone entering the common room see me straight away. There would be no reason for them to wonder what I was doing.

And then Pete came in. After a few minutes of normal chit chat he asked if I wanted to eat with the group, I was welcome, but he could understand if I wanted to go elsewhere. I offered thanks but I'd just as soon skip their supper. That was fine by him and as he got ready, I was still reading, and when he eventually left, I was still planning.

After a long time, I waited a little longer. I was wound up and my sense of time could have been affected. I had to be sure I wasn't going to bump into anyone on their way to supper with Pete. It was a long wait...

WAIT!!! Oh, I'm very good. What a yo-yo. When was I going to think about having money to make the call? In the booth? How could I have overlooked thinking of change? Fortunately, in my drawer I collected more than enough change. I began to review to make sure there wasn't some other major oversight in my planning when I decided... that's it. I had to get going or my head would explode with my planning. I got up and worked my plan.

There was no one in the hall, in the elevator, on the landing to the lobby or on the steps. When I listened to the sounds of the lobby, I couldn't hear anyone close, so I walked normally to the restroom. I had the feeling it was a clean entry. There was no one in the restroom.

The window didn't need to be braced and I got out okay. My eyes didn't have to make a big adjustment because there was enough light in the alley, and I didn't have to hang at all before dropping the short distance to the ground. Getting in would be easy.

I headed to the street but before leaving the alley I listened, to make sure I wouldn't bump into anyone upon entering the street. I made a clean entry and had no trouble staying in shadows most of the walk. There were relatively few people about and the only challenge was not to run.

The phone booth was slightly lighted on a corner with everything else in the area muted, dark. Once at the phone booth I used my change and dialed the FBI.

"Hello."

"Hello, this is Greensleeves. I have a report to transmit. I need to talk to..."

"What? What are you talking about? Who is this?"

I lit up immediately. The last thing I had expected—no, the one thing I had not expected—was for The Bureau not to be ready for my call. Seething is the word!

"I told you. This is Greensleeves and I have a report to transmit and it's urgent."

She could tell I was pissed.

"Sir, I have never heard of a Greensleeves, is that your first or last name?"

Now it was my turn. "WHAT?"

By this point I was ready to hurt someone. Not the silly girl stuck with answering the phone but the assholes she worked for—I worked for.

"I'm sorry sir but I don't know what you're talking about. This is the—she told me some bullshit company name—and you have to have the wrong number."

I didn't calm down, but I did get a grip.

"Look, my life is in danger. I know you're the FBI, how do you think I got this number. You have to think. If my call is making you give me your cover answer I must know something. Think. Someone has screwed up and if you don't help me…"

Maybe she did think because, "Okay sir, give me a minute."

Standing in that phone booth, with my extra change and good ole plan, I had very little faith in the FBI and absolutely no respect. Then she came back on.

"Sir, please just be patient, there is a situation here and someone…" She didn't have to go on. Up to that point I hadn't considered that this reception was the way they were checking my status, authenticating my call. The more I thought about The FBI the more I thought of them as bastards, pompous bastards.

Someone came on the line who convinced me they were who I needed them to be and after exchanging codes the dumping of the data began. It was very slow. It's more likely that I was so uptight it all just seemed slow. In either case I asked why the hell they weren't ready for my call. Typical FBI of my experience in New York, no one knew anything. They all acted smug but when on the spot, didn't know their asses from their elbows. When it came to asking them questions, they were lucky they had that "need to know" panacea. Anything they didn't know; you didn't need to know.

My plan to expect a request for a review of the data—don't think this is going to be wham-bam-thank-you-ma'am, be ready to be patient—was a nice plan but didn't help one bit. Finally, it was done, and we agreed there would be no further contact until the airport but I wasn't done.

"Now for the hard part. Are you geniuses going to repeat your incompetent performance of answering my call tonight, at the airports tomorrow?"

They assured me The Mighty Bureau would cover me.

"At all four airlines?"

Of course, I needn't worry, they would cover me.

"You do realize cover me means, it doesn't imply but means, that you will prevent me from getting on an airplane with Pete Johnson. You understand?" Before he could make some Bureau Pavlovian response I whispered, "I sure hope you can." and hung up.

Getting back to the hotel was a welcome relief. I stayed in the shadows, walked casually and actually felt comfortable. Oh shit! My plan had a major hole and now I was about to fall into it. Think. How could I have missed this—stop—this ain't the time to ride myself. I hadn't considered that someone might be coming into the restroom just as I was climbing in through the window! So, think about it now.

Could this work? "Man, glad you're here, there was noise outside and a banging and when I opened the window to see, a guy tried to grab me. I managed to hang on until you scared him away. I don't know what the son-of-a-bitch was going to do."

Flimsy. If I look at it, opening the window for noise and

banging works, but what about my body? My feet being outside doesn't support this approach and my legs being outside kills it.

Okay, I'll have to go in feet first so he sees my bottom half is inside and my top half can be outside. That fits someone trying to pull me out. Yeah, that works but how do I get my feet and legs in first? Think.

By this time, even though I was walking too slowly trying to gain time to think about my problem, I was close by the entrance to the alley. There was nothing else to do, I entered the alley.

I crouched under the window and listened. I couldn't hear anything inside. I tried to picture my actions and realized I was stalling. That'd be perfect. Get caught in the alley crouching under the men's bathroom window. Special me would become pervert me and there was no explanation that would help. Get in the damn window.

I made a little jump to get one foot on the window ledge and the fingers of both hands under the window frame. I used the other foot on the brick wall for balance and kept pushing my fingers until my hands were in place, paused to ensure my balance and then pushed the window up. As soon as it was up, I put the foot that had been on the ledge inside and followed that with my backside. At this point I was safe because even if someone entered now, I'd have my other leg on the way in and I would look like I had been leaning out, not climbing in.

I completed the entry and immediately checked the stalls, no one. I returned to the window, closed it and was sweating. I went to one of the sinks and the mirror told me I looked hot and discombobulated. I had to get combobulated. It felt good to wash my arms and face and a wet paper towel on my neck helped me pull myself together. I was still alone in the restroom.

Not too much later, I listened at the door and hearing nothing opened it and walked smartly to the steps. Up the steps to the third floor and then the elevator to home. I was in, alone, and the data was with the Bureau. I took up my earlier position sitting with my door open to the common room. I sat staring and...

DEPARTURE

…I'm awake. What time is it? I'm still in the chair. I didn't spend the night in this stupid chair, did I?

Disoriented, I got up and opened my door, I didn't remember closing it. It was light and — wait a minute — I've never noticed those two windows in the common room, nice big windows which were now drenching the place with blaring brightness. How could I not have noticed them? I know I was focused, uptight, but come on, I had to have noticed. But I hadn't. Maybe up to yesterday I was just seeing things that the Bureau needed to see and now that I've unloaded to my contact I'm unwinding.

A noise interrupted my self analysis. Pete's door was open, and I followed the noise to his bathroom. He was shaving and saw me in his mirror.

"You don't like the bed anymore?"

"What? Oh, cute."

"You know, we have to pay whether you use the bed or not, it's all the same." And before I could get a shot in, "Or, maybe you feel sorry for the ladies who have to clean, very noble of you."

He was enjoying himself. I was not yet oriented.

"Oh please Mr. Wonderfully Clever, what the hell time is it?"

"Time for you to do what you have to so we can make our plane."

Holy shit, this is it. "Seriously?" A nod. "How much time do I have?"

"For you Mr. Organized, enough. Yesterday at supper I got confirmation that the horses are routed through and we're going to be there to meet them."

"Outstanding. I'll be ready." I turned back to my room and noticed his partially filled suitcase on the bed and next to it, my old buddy, the valise.

I smiled and was immediately shocked to be smiling. I was smiling because my history with the valise no longer intimidated me. I was standing in the door frame to Pete's room completely confident that I had rifled that valise in such a way no one would suspect it had been tampered with. I had learned my lesson during the wreck of his Oldsmobile, the valise was just small luggage.

When we were done packing, he called and two bellhops came to take our things. Ring-your-bellhops was more descriptive of these two. This hotel had a contingent of personnel built like fireplugs.

When the elevator opened on the lobby we were greeted by a group, with several faces I'd not seen before, wanting to see and be seen by my compatriot, Pete. He was something, these people honestly liked, respected, and were glad for the chance to see him, if not be of service to him. He had a magnetic charisma and rather than assume it as his birthright, he seemed to ask others to help him understand why he had been given such a gift, thus magnifying the endearment he engendered.

Having made our way across the lobby, one set of gatekeepers held the doors to the outside and another set held the doors to the loaded cab. We spent a little extra time with the local leader and the handshakes had more than a little extra meaning, he was an impressive individual. And, as it had always been, off to the side of the scene were two very imposing guys, I gave a high sign to the gatekeepers on duty.

On the way to the airport, it took a lot of self-discipline to keep myself from looking about for Bureau personnel. There was no excuse in the world for me to look like anything but a super happy tourist about to see Europe, at least France, with his buddy, for free.

Then we were at the airport passing terminals. French. TWA. British. PanAm. Eastern. French again. Were we just gonna drive in circles past this buffet of carriers? Seems like. We stopped. TWA.

Pete hailed a porter who loaded our baggage on his cart and led us inside. There were steps leading up to a next level and lines of counters representing and selling everything from rental cars to perfume. Our porter/guide managed us to the International Check-in, unloaded his cart, and thanked Pete for the tip.

The place was hopping, people everywhere and lots of things to see. From my personal perspective, which was totally sweet-sour, too much to see. Sweet to finally see the FBI was there. Sour to see the FBI agent standing behind the TWA counter. He was so Bureau I wondered if he'd been a recruiting campaign poster boy. I hoped Pete hadn't noticed me watching dark-suit white-shirt dark-tie, but I couldn't imagine he didn't see this sore thumb.

And then we hit the head of the line and the counter. Our passports and tickets were checked, everything was okay until we got to seat selection. We didn't have what we requested, and no TWA Charm School Graduate was going to smooth talk Pete into anything but the two spots he had picked. No, that wouldn't do either, she may have been a supervisor with tons of TWA Let Me Talk You Into This experience but Pete wanted our seats. The TWA, I Will Manage This, executive was up to the task, he gave Pete exactly what had been promised in the first place. Now, let's check the baggage, get you your boarding passes, and aren't we all the best of buddies here in TWA Land.

I'm really not so sure the preceding was exactly how it went but I was so busy trying to get the FBI Representative to hide from sight that I'm not as objective as I'd like to be.

We pulled away from International Check-in and returned to the center of the terminal where two corridors formed a giant Y, with one leg to the left and one leg to the right. These corridors had curved ceilings and were long and huge. I imagined a marching band coming down one corridor and doing some fancy foot work to turn and march up the other. As for Pete and me, we marched up the left corridor to the gates for International Departures.

As we walked to our gate, on one hand it was embarrassing, they were so obvious they might as well have been neon signs promoting FBI presence. On the other hand, it was good to feel I wouldn't be going to Paris today, but good Lord, unbutton a button or two.

The atmosphere was jovial as we were funneled this way and that on our way to our departure gate. As the corridors got smaller as they branched off, the atmosphere became more intense and real excitement filled the air as people got closer and closer to their planes.

Other people. The closer we got to our plane the closer I got to my nightmare because as blatant as their presence was before we entered the Departure Corridor, that's how huge was the void of any Bureau presence since. I hated it, but I couldn't stop myself from recalling my desperation phone call, "Greensleeves? Never heard of you."

And then we were in the queue going past the TWA attendant who was checking boarding passes before she turned good-boys-and-girls-waiting-in-line, into passengers-to-Paris. I sure hoped Pete took my nerves as signs of anticipation to make the flight and not as signs of apprehension to make the flight.

I wondered about him. He must have noticed the Agents just as I had but he didn't show it. From this morning, when he was shaving, to this very minute he was cool, calm, and collected. He had obviously done this before, as his Passport, the Yugoslavian one he was using for this trip, proved. His behavior and appearance were that of a man sunning on a beach, a beach he owned.

When we were three people from the attendant's station at the gangway, a door I hadn't noticed flew open next to us and smooth as silk we were surrounded by four men. This happened so quickly that I hadn't even identified their uniforms when the one in front of Pete asked, "Mr. Johnson? Mr. Marksity?" He didn't wait for an answer. "Please don't be alarmed, you'll make your flight. It's just that there's a misunderstanding about your luggage and we need your help to clear it up. Won't be a minute."

This guy should have been on Broadway, if being a ham and sounding like a megaphone is what it takes. He wanted everyone to hear what he was saying but I knew what he meant. "Look folks you have no need to know, so just let me put you at ease while my buddies yank these two miscreants out of your lives. Now, before we have to bounce any of you on your melons, forget what you saw and stay in line." The sad part was that not one of the people in that line had a clue or could have cared less. The ones past us were boarding and those behind us were two places closer to boarding because of our exit. Pete and I weren't there, he needn't have said a thing.

While ham had been doing crowd control, two suits appeared behind our queue, and another was there beside the TWA attendant. I had noticed them in the terminal, all wearing the suit and tie uniform I was familiar with and now, not unhappy to see.

We were ushered by our four new friends through the door I hadn't noticed into a large well-lit room. There were chairs and one extremely long table on which our luggage, including Pete's valise, was centered and open. The sight of that valise reminded me of the role I was playing.

"Okay group, what the hell's going on?"

No answer so I tried again.

"Let me get this straight, it takes four of you to help us clear up a misunderstanding about our luggage? I'm still in school but this don't figure from any way. Who are you lug nuts and what's going on?"

The uniform nearest me took my arm, as if to help me to a seat, and was shocked when I pushed him against a chair. I didn't like being helped.

"Get your hands off me and someone tell me what's this about?"

Finally, the ham who had entertained in the corridor found his line. "Everybody settle down, and you sit down."

"I don't want to settle down, I don't want to sit down, I don't like being manhandled and I want to know who you are and what you want. Do we need to start by clearing up any misunderstanding you might have about how I feel?"

As I finished, a suit and tie entered and I realized he was who the four uniforms were waiting for, the FBI agent behind the International Check-in counter. He waited till I was done and without a flicker began. "Marksity. Ronald E. hum...Mr. Marksity what is your relationship with this man, Mr. Johnson, Mr. Dejurdjev?"

He was good. His one question made it clear he knew Pete very well but wasn't so sure about me so that's where he would start. But before he did, I had more role to play. My character was way too stubborn to suddenly fit in.

"Before that let's start with my relationship with you. I don't know any of your names, first or last. And, are you with these clowns, maybe the head bozo? Why are you doing this to me and my friend? Do you just randomly yank people out of line to meet some sort of quota, like traffic cops in small towns who hide behind the lone billboard?"

In truth, our group already had a ham and it helped when Pete told me in Serbian to cooperate.

With me in check, the FBI agent continued. He explained he was so-and-so with the Bureau while the four gentlemen were with Customs and Immigration. He admitted this was not a random action and luggage was not the key. However, before broaching the facts of the matter, he needed to know where I stood, was I involved. Now, how about my relationship with Pete.

I gave him the overview from our initial meeting to this trip. I emphasized how long a time it had taken for the evolution of our friendship and tied it up by sharing how long we had been looking forward to this day.

As soon as I finished, Pete's voice reflected boredom with the activities. "Leave him alone. He has given you his truth. He doesn't know a thing about any of this. He's the son of two Reverends who are friends of mine in Cincinnati and was travelling with me for vacation." He emphasized that I was naive in matters of interest to them and playing the 'his parents are Samaritans' card as master trump, closed the deal.

While Pete was speaking, another agent that I had spotted in the terminal came in and gave a file folder to the first agent. He looked the file over, then looked at me, Pete, the folder and finally reached a decision. "Okay Mr. Marksity, it does appear that things are as you suggest, and you don't have a role to play in our proceedings. Unfortunately, or fortunately, you're not going to be making a trip to Paris. You are not going to be seeing your friend, Mr. Johnson Dejurdjev any time soon and I would advise you to go home."

With this he motioned for one of the Customs agents and asked him to collect my luggage and escort me out.

"Wait." It was Pete again. "A moment. My compatriot came with me to New York and since I can't go home with him, he should at least go home on me. I want to give him a pleasant trip to Cincinnati."

FBI nodded ascent and Pete reached in his breast pocket and took out his wallet. This time, unlike the flamenco tattoo, he made sure everyone could see it was just a wallet. He put together a small wad of bills as I was declining his offer, but he insisted so I put the wad in my pocket and said thanks. We shook hands and then hugged. As we backed away, I knew I'd miss him. I didn't know what to do with that truth, so I just headed for the exit door my escort was holding. Once in the doorframe, I stopped and turned around for one last look and saw him being handcuffed as the door closed.

Customs led me through a series of doors and passageways until we came to a stop. He told me a contact was waiting and then pushed a panel which opened behind the International Departures section of the main terminal where one step forward put me back in the middle of all the other travelers who, like me, wanted to be somewhere else.

I knew there was going to be much about this experience that I would not understand until later. The first example was Pete giving me the wad from his wallet. He could have given me many things folded in the wad, yet the agents weren't interested in finding out what he actually gave me. Well, I was plenty interested. I stepped out of the flow of people and checked the wad; it was $200 and there was no message. Securing it in my wallet I reentered the flow of people.

I looked around and saw no attempt at contact or control, so I decided to stay in my role as Pete's compatriot and head back to the hotel. There I'd report to my safety net and let him help me. That valise was working for me now, my experience mishandling its contents after Pete's wreck, taught me how to react and to do so immediately. I didn't miss a beat as I took the nearest exit and headed for the cabs.

FOUL AIR

As soon as I exited the terminal, a suit came up beside me and stayed there for a few paces. Making sure not to look at me, he said he was my contact and told me to get into the back seat of the blue Ford station wagon three cabs up on the curb. As he veered away, I wondered if he thought I needed him to identify himself, he was so Bureau he might as well have had a name tag.

When I got to the wagon, the back door was opened by a man in the front passenger seat who told me to lay down on the floor, he was the agent who had been behind the TWA check-in counter. I did so even though I couldn't imagine a purpose for such bizarre behavior. We drove around and I got the impression that we were heading into Manhattan by some circuitous route. This made no sense, but the noise and traffic seemed to confirm my reasoning. Eventually, we entered a parking garage and continued our trip by going underground into the bowels of the building on what felt like an elevator.

Finally, we stopped, and I was told to get out. When I got out there were three of them, as someone from the building had joined my chauffeurs. Riding on the floor of the wagon hadn't put me in a good mood and unfortunately this got worse. Each of this trio reminded me of my first contacts at Gamble Junior Hi, the two suits that didn't respect my being open and honest with them. As it turned out, most of the suits I was about to meet didn't respect my being open and honest with them.

There was no attempt at hello or introductions as I followed them to a nice-sized room. There was no common courtesy or questions of my circumstance, they were all business. This crew was worse than my first two, these beauties treated me as if I was an insect they were prohibited from squashing.

The check-in counter agent was the one who was going to lead the debriefing and he made a point of not talking to me. Instead, he talked to the room in general, as if there were 'lights camera and action' to set him off. Finally, he got to the end of his self-serving performance and finished by introducing himself as the head of the show. He could have just dressed up like a Ringmaster and saved a lot of time. He was more than a little pompous and, considering my relationship with his Bureau, he was happy to let me know he was a lot skeptical. He gave the assemblage a soliloquy about the difficulty of getting good operatives; but if he had a point I missed it.

By this time, several more agents had joined us and our crazy route from the airport explained itself. They were jerking me around to give the agents who were at the terminal time to get back to this debriefing. I got the distinct impression I was the curiosity, since not one mention had been made of Pete. From this perspective, it was a short think to understand that they wanted the agents from the airport present to evaluate my responses as to what happened. I was not amused.

Blowhard in charge, finally asked rhetorically if I was ready to begin the session. He did this purposefully in a tone that made it clear his expectations could not be lower.

I nodded.

"Well young man, why don't you tell us what you saw so we get an idea of your skills. You know, just tell us what, if anything, you noticed. We're all waiting."

I was not a happy young man. I waited, honestly weighing whether I was going to participate with this clown. I decided to do the job I signed on to do.

"Well, one of the first things I saw was you standing behind the TWA counter acting like you were an employee. Do you think anyone was fooled by you in your Bureau costume? And please don't tell me you were sticking out like a sore thumb, so I'd be sure to know The Mighty Bureau was near. Anyway, after you, I saw six more like you in various areas around the terminal and specifically, I 'noticed' him, and him, and him. Would you have a better idea of 'what if anything I noticed,' you know, of my 'skills' of observation, if I told you where each of the others were stationed?"

By the time I finished answering and pointing, Pompous was angry and very red. The others pointed out were embarrassed. Those in the room who had not been pointed out were uncomfortable, not knowing whether to laugh or cringe at their 'noticed' associates.

"Now I got a question. I was wondering why I had to be on the floor of that wagon after we pulled into this building or, after we were away from the airport and, more to the matter, why was I on the floor at all? What was I going to see? Who do you imagine was going to see me?" Before Blowhard could respond, I continued.

"Could it have been that you needed time to have your henchmen here get themselves to this session. Could it be that you want to have them evaluate my report? Or could it be that you feel having me ride upside down for a while would make me easier to interrogate?" There was no response and I continued.

"Following your lead, I wonder if you could just tell me what, if anything, you noticed about my condition. I'll wait."

He was seriously burned, and his face was having a tough time deciding between being red and being purple. I loved it. I had a deep-seated feeling of anger and realized I didn't like any of this and any of them. And particularly, I didn't like him. So, I went on.

"In your observing did you notice my condition. If or when are you going to let me go to the bathroom? And, agent, I forgot your name…no, I didn't forget it, you didn't give it to me, you just gave me your function. So, agent whoever, are you ever going to offer me something to eat and drink seeing as how the last couple days I've kind of been up tight and am more than a little bit tired and thirsty? You are aware I just saw a man I've been close to for years handcuffed and taken away?"

I was tired, thirsty, full of thoughts of Pete and what could have been, and altogether not up to par. I failed to notice that during my last little monologue someone had entered the room who had a different demeanor and as he did, the demeanor of the room changed.

Now, they were all over me being nice, cordial. We took a break. I visited the head and washed up a little. When I returned to the room, there were sodas and a couple sandwiches for me to pick from. I was invited to sit and get comfortable.

What I expected to happen next was a professional debriefing that would reflect the standards of my relationship with my Handler, a review and exchange of information wherein I would add nuances from my unique perspective inside the operation. What actually happened was anything but what I expected. It was not professional. I was there to be used and it was immediately obvious that their questions were more than leading, they were directing. I let them direct until they were done and then came the rub, I started asking questions.

I was right, it had been an interrogation, not a debriefing. They were not going to answer any of my questions. For example, I asked if Pete was arrested as a spy? Their song and dance was Fred and Ginger in dark suits and white shirts. This tip tap toe was all I got until I was fed up. The last straw was their unwillingness to confirm things that I obviously already knew, things that I had reported to them.

I reminded them that I was the one who saw Pete put the documents in the door of the Barracuda. I was the one who had all the passports, tickets, and schedules memorized and then had to jump through hoops to get out the bathroom window and call the all-knowing Bureau. Were they aware that when I called, their Bureau wasn't ready, had not been alerted for my code? Did they think I didn't realize the position that put me in? Nothing. They just sat there like a group of lug nuts.

As for me, my feelings were hurt. Plain and simple, they had hurt my feelings. Only I knew that I was the most dangerous when my feelings were hurt, much more unpredictable than when I was mad or anxious. I pulled myself tight and spoke with resignation.

"So help me, if I honestly knew you guys were going to treat me this way when I got started, I would have told you to deport my parents and put me in a home, cause I ain't working for people like you miserable bunch of manipulators. You guys are real sweethearts. I bust my butt to do something you can't do — you have been using me since the eighth grade — and now you won't tell me squat and are surprised I have expectations of you."

While I was finishing, another suit came in with my luggage. He had seen the last of the calm me and spoke up with the intent of cheering up the joint. He was just too sweet when he offered, "I've brought your luggage and we'll get you back to your hotel and…" I cut him off.

"Are you going to answer my questions?"

Fred and Ginger. Fine.

"Are any of you going to answer any of my questions?"

Mostly like a waltz.

"We're done. Not one of you is taking me to the hotel or any other place. I want out of here and I want out now."

They looked around at each other and then, without another word, just a nod from the top dog's noggin, someone carried my luggage and led me through the labyrinth of corridors, elevators, and doors until we finally hit a door that opened on an alley. As I stepped out, I recognized that I was in the heart of Manhattan and, so help me, the air was fresh and clean compared to the foul air where I'd just been.

BENEFACTOR

I'd been inside with the Bureau too long and my spirit felt like an ashtray smells, a damp ashtray that's never been emptied.

"You the ride I'm here for?"

It was a cabby not six feet across the sidewalk on the curb. I assured him I was not and picked up my suitcase and started walking. He didn't care and continued waiting. I didn't care but wondered who arranged for him to be there.

My Manhattan map study and our days of crisscrossing the city made it easy for me to pick the best route to the hotel. After spending the day being disoriented by the Bureau, it felt good to know where I was and where I was going. In no time, the exercise produced the boost I needed and a few blocks later I had calmed down enough to evaluate my situation.

The positives. I was not in a plane over the Atlantic. I was applying my experience and training. I knew that under stress exercise was a route to self-control and clear thinking, and my decision to walk served up good exercise. I recognized that my only option was to keep playing my role as Pete's compatriot and that's what I was doing. Only in that role could I continue my relationship with Pete's friend, my Benefactor, and the key to my future in Manhattan. Only as Pete's compatriot could I continue being of value to the Bureau.

The negatives. There really didn't seem to be any, but wait, what exactly had I been doing? I paused to think and had to admit that I hadn't been walking, I had been avoiding being followed. Since I left the Bureau building, I had been stopping to look in windows to see who was behind me, taking wide turns at corners and then tucking myself close against the wall to see who made the turn too quickly, and all the other techniques practiced with my Handler. But why was I acting this way? If I was followed by Pete's people, great, they would see Pete's compatriot doing exactly what he was told to do. If by the Bureau, what for, they knew everything about me and the locals.

And then the negative came into focus, I had a real hard-on for the FBI. I hated them for the way they used me. I hoped they were following me so I could compromise them and point up their stupidity. Let them give it a shot. From my current perspective, I honestly doubted they could follow anyone, even if they knew where the anyone was headed. I thought back to the first two agents who approached me in the eighth grade, they were the real FBI, pompous suits who believed I was an insect while they were parts of The Federal Bureau of Idolatry. This was negative and dangerous. I was behaving as if I wanted to satisfy one of my strongest negative characteristics, the desire for revenge.

It was time for me to get walking. More blocks and I became aware people were looking at me. It was no accomplishment to realize eye contact was not a commodity in Manhattan, so there was something about me that made them look. I found a store window and this time, looked at me. Looking back was the Statue of Liberty-Ellis Island-DP-Poster Boy, a Slavic immigrant trudging across the lower West Side hauling a suitcase that had been back and forth to Europe many times. Well, so be it. Hell, I looked pretty good considering what I was hauling on the inside.

I kept walking and then rounded a corner and smiled, the hotel was halfway down the block. As far as I knew, I had no company at any point of the walk but really didn't care. Before I got to the driveway, one of the gatekeepers saw me, gestured to his partner, and headed toward me. When he was in front of me, he asked in Serbian, "Are you okay?"

"Yeah. Sure."

Taking my suitcase he offered, "You don't look okay."

His partner held the door for us and as we passed into the lobby asked, "What in the world happened to you?"

I was getting the picture I didn't look okay. I was also getting the picture that only the top man was qualified to broach the question, "Where's Pete?"

Someone else took my suitcase as the gatekeepers returned to their posts and almost immediately the local leader, the man I was to contact if anything happened, my Benefactor, was in the lobby.

"You look inside out. Let's go to my office." Leading the way he ordered ice, soft drinks, and water which got to his office almost as we did. He asked if I needed to use the bathroom and what could be done to get me comfortable.

As if I wasn't cranked up enough, now I had to witness the people I'd been spying on treating me better than the Bureau for whom I was doing the spying. The locals caring about my welfare roiled my bitterness toward the Bureau. I had to pull myself together, so I took a bathroom break. This was less than perfect as it was the lobby bathroom, with the exit window leading to the little lady on the Bureau phone, explaining she had never heard of Greensleeves, the FBI, or me. I washed up and once back in his office saw we had been joined by a few other men I had seen before. We did the hellos and I got settled with a glass of ice water and began my report.

"We got to the airport fine but at the departure check-in learned TWA had changed our seats. Pete explained he had specifically arranged for those seats, but TWA didn't get it, so Pete demonstrated his, 'I've got my mind made up as to how things should be and that is how things will be.' As we would expect, the TWA big-shot functionary did get it and Pete got the seats he wanted."

I think for an instant everyone in the office had a personal flashback of Pete controlling a scene. I held the pause before continuing.

"We looked around the terminal until we heard the call for boarding of our flight. We got in the queue and three people from the gangway, a door I hadn't noticed flew open next to us and four men surrounded us. One of these guys asked if we were Mr. Johnson and Mr. Marksity but it was plain as day, they knew who we were. This same guy then tells us, in a voice everybody in New York could hear, that everything was okay, there was just a misunderstanding regarding our luggage, and we'd make our flight. Meanwhile we were being motioned through the door I hadn't noticed. As soon as the door closed, Pete told them to leave me alone and…"

I gave it all to them, making sure not to miss one detail of the events or any of my emotions during the experience. They could see the honesty of my feelings and listened without interruptions, comments, or questions.

As I laid out the story, I wished Pete and my Handler were there to witness my actions and see the results of their training me in the artistry of the lie. I was telling the entire truth with as much of the detail and feelings as existed with one exception, the lie, which in this case was that I worked for the FBI.

Finally, I was finished and actually needed to use the head. When I returned, I got some more water and was ready for whatever my Benefactor had in mind.

He started, but not about Pete or my report, he started about my welfare. He reasoned I must feel better having unloaded because I didn't look inside out anymore. Was water enough or did I want something to eat, a snack. Only when he was satisfied that I was okay did he turn to business, and they started asking questions.

Was I okay? Had they hurt me in any way, for example when they took us out of the queue? Was there any warning the men were coming after us? Did I notice any of the men earlier, in the airport for example? Did it seem to me that Pete knew any of the men? Did I recognize any of the men? Who did the men work for, Police, Customs, Immigration? Was I sure it had been our luggage on the long table? Did Pete say anything that might have been intended for my Benefactor, something no one else would notice as such? Did I say they were handcuffing Pete? Was it one of the four who surrounded us in the queue who led me to the terminal lobby? So, on the way to get a cab the door to a station wagon opens and they offered you a ride, why didn't you have the wagon drop you off at the hotel?

An internal caution light flashed, either I had done a miserable job on the facts of my wagon ride, or this was quicksand.

"It's clear I did a poor job on this point. This was not an offer to give me a ride, this was a snatch. When I left the terminal to get a cab, a man in a suit and tie came up beside me and, without looking at me, said he was the FBI, and I was to get in the station wagon three cabs up on the curb. When I got next to the wagon the back door opened, blocking my route, and someone helped me into the wagon from behind. The guy in the front passenger seat told me to get on the floor, shut up, and stay put. Only when we got to their building did I realize they were taking me in for interrogation.

"Then, once they were done with me, they still didn't offer me a ride in their wagon but put me out on the sidewalk. Since this was the place I was to come to if I needed help, and I need help, I picked up my suitcase and walked directly here."

I was on edge. My answer was okay, but I could see that the way I delivered it was unnecessary, almost defensive. No matter, the man who asked the question felt he had misunderstood me, and they were off and running with questions that focused on my time in FBI custody.

As we dissected this topic, I let it all hang out. The Bureau's refusal to tell us who they were, what they wanted, anything about what was going on, why we were being detained, where they were taking us, what I was supposed to do once they decided to let me go, and where they were taking Pete. My emotions were like a boil that burst, putrid and unable to be ignored. I kept it up as I related the trip downtown and the interrogation, with particular emphasis on the fact the bastards never told me one thing about my friend Pete. To this minute, I had no idea about his welfare or whereabouts.

People who live and work in partial truths can sense the real truth before they can smell it, and they can smell it before the air pushes it out of the lungs. The group in that office knew to their cores that my feelings about the FBI were real. Further, selfishly, it was fantastic to be able to vent the truth about my hatred, the whole truth, and nothing but the truth.

The questions were followed by a general discussion with me

only answering specific questions for clarification or review. They were concerned about Pete but were realists, there was nothing they could do but wait. They were also pragmatists, they had to assess all the possible consequences of this development on their current and future activities and adjust accordingly. And then my Benefactor took over.

There was a lot of work before them and they would see to it, but now I was his priority. He thanked them and each of them made a point of shaking my hand and wishing me well. Then they were gone, and he and I were alone.

"You have any sense for where Pete might be?"

"I really can't say. At no time, and I mean not even for an instant or by mistake, did anyone say or hint anything about him. From the time the four surrounded us until they led me away, they acted like Pete wasn't there, with him right there they talked about him as if he wasn't there. Downtown it was the same. During the entire interrogation they never mentioned him and when I brought him up, they didn't hear me. In total, none of them ever heard of any Pete."

He seemed lost in thought, so I sat and watched. Maybe it was because the day was over and I felt safe, maybe it was because I was vented, or maybe I'll never know why, but he underwent a metamorphosis as I studied him. I saw his features differently and his bearing and demeanor had new depth. He grew in stature and substance until I knew he was a big deal.

"Too bad about your car. I bet you'll miss it."

Good God! He had snapped out of his contemplation before I snapped out of my observation and, for sure, he was a very big deal. The fate of the Barracuda fell off his lips so casually and matter-of-factly that I realized he had everything else on his lips as well. He had played the contact so Pete could do his bit. He had played support man so no one would place his real position. But this man was in place as the kingpin for the long haul. Sum-bitch. A twist on the play dumb stunt Pete had me play, my Benefactor acted like a subordinate to avoid being watched and to be able to watch. I got real focused.

"You know, that was one thing that didn't make sense. Those bozos badgered me half a day about everything and nothing but never even mentioned the Barracuda. And I'm not sure I can miss it; I didn't drive it five times other than the trip."

He smiled and I believed he read my mind and was pleased I had figured out the reality.

The slight nodding of his head made it clear we were done with any and all business. Everything to follow would be focused on getting me where I wanted to be, in a manner that would satisfy Pete's labeling me his compatriot. Also, I had gotten as close to my Benefactor as I ever would and my being able to intuit his techniques, did not give me access to anything else.

"Now, what would you like? Some of the others will be going for supper. You'd be welcome. How about something to eat?"

"Thank you, but I'd really rather just get cleaned up and get some sleep."

"As you wish. Your suitcase is up in the suite you used; it has been made available for you. Same arrangements, call for anything you might want, anything. After this little adventure it's better to sleep in a bed you know."

Before I could bring up what should come next, he closed the evening. "The morning is soon enough to look down the road. Laco notch." As he got up, his office door was opened from the outside by one of his people and he motioned me through it.

As we shook hands at the elevators, I looked him in the eye and meant it when I told him how much I appreciated what he had been and was still doing for me. Then in Serbian I asked him to accept my formal thanks and told him good night, Sir.

The next morning, we met in his office. It was time to look down the road. He asked what I had in mind, and I said I'd welcome his advice. He felt it wasn't his place to make advice but suggested we think of what Pete would want me to do. After a brief review of the options, we agreed there was nothing I could accomplish by remaining in Manhattan, I should go home. He offered to arrange for a plane back to Cincinnati, but I didn't want to get on a plane, I didn't want to go to that airport, I didn't want to go to any airport, I'd rather ride a bus.

"As you wish. Relax while you get ready to go. You'll get a call when things are set. Now, one last thing."

He pulled open the middle drawer of his desk and I couldn't imagine what was going to be in his hand when it reappeared. It was an envelope.

"Pete left this for just such a situation as we now have, it will serve you as you see fit."

I took the offered envelope and looked inside. It was a stack of bills. I didn't look long enough to count them and closed the envelope.

"No sir. I can't take this. Pete's already given me money. You know, at the airport. I can't take more."

He smiled as he moved around the desk and put his hand on my shoulder.

"Yes, you can. It's not difficult."

His actions matched his words as he continued.

"You just take the envelope and push it in your pocket. This is what Pete wanted. As you reported yesterday, once he's got his mind made up as to how things should be, that's how things will be. Take the money."

That was the last I saw of my Benefactor, but not the last I felt of his influence. Right after noon I was called and told my travel arrangements were complete. They asked me to call when I was ready for someone to collect my luggage. I said I didn't need help with my suitcase, and I'd be down directly.

In the lobby, an off-duty gatekeeper was waiting to see me off. He didn't ask if I needed help with my suitcase, he just took it and led the way outside to the blue four-door I hadn't seen since the docks. I waved to him and the two gatekeepers on duty. They all waved back as the driver pulled out from under the portico.

When we pulled into the depot, I wasn't nervous and shouldn't have been. The driver told me I was to go directly to the bus. He wanted to help me with my luggage and offered to accompany me to the bus, but I insisted he had done enough. When I got to the bus, another of my Benefactor's friends was waiting with my ticket and a window seat he had been securing for me with the help of the driver.

I thanked them both and right on time, the bus left for Cincinnati.

THE BUS TO REALITY

Things came to me piece by piece. I was in the front seat. We were underway. The silence was broken sporadically, by silhouettes of sounds. There was no one in the seat next to me. The windshield was in front of me, yet I couldn't see a thing. I wasn't looking through the windshield, I was looking at it. I looked through the windshield. Everything was black and white.

What if we had boarded that plane? Where would I be right now? What would be my circumstance? Wait! Is it possible? Yes, it is. This is the first time I ever thought those questions. This thought from somewhere in my brain rushed across the black and white in full color and volume, then was gone.

And so it went all the way to Cincinnati. The thoughts came randomly, without introduction, reference, or explanation. Their colors and sounds were magnified as they interrupted the black and white, then, once they passed, all that remained was black and white.

My Benefactor had that man come hours before departure to buy my ticket and sit in the best seat until I showed up. I should have let the gentleman stow my luggage, that was part of his day's work.

...black and white...

The way I was treated since returning to the hotel, after leaving the FBI offices, made me feel incredibly guilty. They were honestly concerned about helping me even though I wasn't their compatriot, I was Pete's compatriot. They were taking care of me for him, and their attentiveness amplified my guilt and made the whole episode harder to stomach. I had been spying on them and their Pete, for Christ's sake,

...black and white...

I have $400. Pete's $200 at the airport and $200 in the envelope from my Benefactor. I have been working for The FBI for over seven years and they have never given me one red cent.

...black and white...

Stupid, stupid, stupid. The entire ensemble in the bowels of their building suggested I go home to Cincinnati. What did they expect me to say to Pete's other compatriots when they caught up with me at home and asked why I had run away—after—Pete was detained? Was it possible they were so stupid they forgot I was undercover?

...black and white...

It's funny though, just by being what it had been in New York, the FBI did help me. I was disillusioned that they were not ready for my call. I was disgusted by their unprofessional performance at the airport. I was angry with their treatment of me once I left the airport. I was incensed with their debriefing song and dance. By the time I got to the hotel, I was honestly out for blood from The Full of Bullshit Idiots, and the emotions I vented while giving my report were my actual feelings.

...black and white...

I wonder where he is right now, what's happening to him? What's going to happen to the horses? I never did see any horses, maybe there never were any horses. Well, there sure was a car, 'My' Barracuda.

Pete is, or do I say was, a pro. The 'Cuda was an example of his brilliance. The objective was to get intelligence to Europe. Working for Marshal Tito was his cover story and horses were the hook for catching outside interest, and the vehicle for transporting intelligence. Now, about an emergency exit.

Start by giving me $2,520 cash, to buy myself the 'Cuda. From that moment on I was compromised. More than distracted by the car, I was preoccupied and for much of the time had no clue of who, what, when, where, or, was it night or day. With me in that state he went about creating an exit.

Man, I was so slow. The same people who arranged the car insurance policy for me, had everything about the purchase of the 'Cuda arranged with Wulleneber Motors before I walked in the first time. When I picked up the car, all I did was sign and drive. By doing so, I insured there was absolutely no link between Pete and my car.

Then he used the exit. It was at the last minute that I learned we were driving my car and couldn't learn who, what, or where about his Lincoln. Then on the road, people didn't notice him, they only saw the car and once on the island, it was directly to the docks and goodbye Barracuda, exit Pete.

…black and white…

It was the couple in the seats behind me talking. "I have to say I liked the Empire State Building the best." "That's okay for you but for me, The Statue of Liberty was my numero uno." "You sure? You seemed to like the boat ride around the island a whole bunch. How about that?" "Maybe. But how about imagery, you think anything comes close to the streets being described as canyons?"

As I listened, a sadness overwhelmed me. I was sliding down

an incline into nothingness, alone. As they went on, I realized my Manhattan was made up of microscopic attention to everything related to my job and not one hint of what was all around me. I was sad because I had never been to the place the couple had just visited.

...black and white...

He was a pro and practiced what he preached. Loading the doors of the 'Cuda in the middle of the day in our yard was the perfect application of his maxim, "Don't be afraid to do things in the open. People assume you aren't doing anything irregular because everyone knows it would be insane to do something irregular right out in the open. Acting in the open makes others less suspicious and the less suspicion you arouse the more apt you are to be ignored."

And everyone did ignore him, except for me, which was another instance of Something Bigger taking care of me, putting me in the right place at the perfect time.

...black and white...

Where is that Barracuda? Is it heading to La Havre? What else went on at that dock after we drove off? What else went on there routinely, and is the Bureau on top of it? I wish I had even a little faith in the New York office.

...black and white...

His family porno photo album! I have never been so faked out in my life. It had never been about the packets, it had always been about the valise. His first step was to plant the packets in my mind, so he made them the target of my actions, "...in the glovebox...two packets, get them out of here...no one to see...keep for me." Then, if I did get nosy, he was set to dictate my action by having the contents of the packets be a pornographic portfolio of the man who had been sharing my room. He knew me and knew that when I saw the contents of the packets, I would try to get away from them as fast as possible. I did just that and bingo! his main objective was accomplished. I didn't look inside the valise and whatever was in that valise was what mattered.

...black and white...

I have to stop thinking about those bastards putting me on the floor of the station wagon at the airport. That just stirs me up. I'm beginning to feel my old weaknesses, the need for justice and revenge, influencing my attitude and behavior.

...black and white...

He was able to keep everything about his personal life from me. For example, was the woman in the pictures with him his ex-wife? Did he have a current wife? How many wives had he had? I never saw him with a woman the entire time we spent together.

...black and white...

The more time after an experience with Pete, the more I learn what I had missed at the time of the experience, like the witnessing of shrewdness at the genius level. I pictured him on the car of the big angry six. The dance was an integral part of his plan and specifically flamenco dancing with his metal tapped heels. His denting of their car was so preposterous it froze the six, they didn't know what to do and therefore did nothing. In this way, he insured they didn't just accelerate and make him fall off and break his ass. Only when he was off the car and headed to the nearest door did they awake and leave.

...black and white...

I can be unbelievably naive. I really don't know a damn thing about Hawthorne. Why did I have it? Who handled the renting? How? What happened to the rent money? Who were the tenants? Was it just another way to pay back Olga and George? Was it his safe house?

...black and white...

Pete was generous with positive reinforcement and awarded it sincerely for both major successes and the slightest plus. He had countless ways of disarming me when he delivered these at-a-boys. But I cherished most those that made him tell me not to be phobic. He knew there was nothing else, no hidden fact, no concealed reality, no nuance, no anything, no nothing that I had missed, he knew I had it all.

...black and white...

Canada. Do any Mounties wear red coats?

...black and white...

He could read me at the start. He could not read me as time progressed. But there's no way I'll ever forget him. Every time I cut my toenails; I'll think of him.

When he learned I was Army bound he focused his tidbits on survival. I still can't believe the production he made on how to cut toenails. The threat was ingrown nails, the survival technique was to make a rounded 'v' of the cut with the bottom of the 'v' pointed toward the cuticle. This ensures the nails grow toward the middle of the toe. "Okay now Zorana, you try it." He was at the least, exotic. Also rich, connected, and different from any other DP or temporary roommate or anyone at all, in every way. I liked Pete and in some convoluted part of my reality, I felt that we were friends.

...black and white...

Josip Broz Tito. Marshal Josip Broz Tito. Minister of Defense Josip Tito. Prime Minister, President, the Leader of Yugoslavia, the Tito in The Encyclopedia Britannica. The Petar I have been working, worked for Josip Broz Tito.

...black and white...

Unimaginable. We never talked about Tito. It is incredible to me that I never had him discuss Tito, never asked him questions or begged for his firsthand experiences. How could this be? And if I did, how come I can't remember?

...black and white...

Has the Bureau made a decision about my parents? Do they still think The Reverend and The Missionary are espionage material? When...

..."Sir? Sir, excuse me. Are you alright Sir?"

"What? Oh, yes. Yeah, sure."

"Good. Thanks for riding with Greyhound and welcome to Cincinnati."

It was the driver. We were parked in the terminal. Tomorrow I'll start debriefing the FBI.

...black.

FINAL DEBRIEFING

Everything was different. We met downtown. It was my first time in the Cincinnati home of The Federal Bureau of Investigation and my Handler's office.

We got settled and brought each other up to date. There was no question I had developed an intense disrespect for all the FBI personnel I met in New York, and I cited reasons for my attitude every chance I got. My Handler surprised me, not because he wasn't surprised, he surprised me because he let me see he wasn't surprised.

I took a long look at him and wondered if my deference to him was because I wanted him to be capable and special, after all he was working in my life. No, he was capable and special. Of all the Bureau personnel I had any dealings with, he was the only one I respected. To a man, the others thought of themselves as superior and didn't do much to hide their opinion, while he treated me like an individual and our work together as important.

Back to the task at hand, he explained there were more than a few people who anticipated something related to what they were working on might surface in my report. For the first time, we would not be debriefing alone.

We met in a spacious meeting room where there were several different types of agents, supervisors, and who knew what. Prior to this, except for my Handler, the only local FBI I had ever seen were the two suits who'd approached me in the eighth grade.

Before the meaningless introductions were complete, a rush of questions was evidence that everyone wanted something from this debriefing. Unsolicited opinions were offered for where and how to start.

My Handler took control and explained that he and I agreed, I would go through every single act and nuance that I could remember of the trip, starting with the last time he and I had talked before the trip. There were to be no questions or interruptions until my report was completely finished, and then all manner of participation was welcome. And from the beginning, a retinue of various Bureau types came and went depending on the phase or substance of my debriefing.

Then it was my turn. For the rest of the day, I reported chapter and verse and word. Over the next few days, in bits and pieces, I did it again. Then, in addition to the trip, I was asked to review aspects of the work my Handler and I had done leading up to the trip. And then more reviewing of specifics regarding Pete.

Finally, with all the possible information gathered, everything, every single thing, I had been reporting was dissected, reviewed, looked at from every conceivable perspective by a host of different eyes, cataloged, discarded, related to, or distinguished from, labeled, and run through the ringer that was The FBI way.

As for me, I didn't give a shit.

I was just doing my job. A job I had little choice not to take. I had signed on to clear my parents, help my Handler and the Bureau, and be of service to my Country. I had done my part. Now it was time to be honest and see what had resulted.

For me, not much. I still believed my parents incredible naivete in worldly matters and Christian devotion to helping others had put them in this pickle. But I didn't know what the FBI thought any more now than I did seven years ago.

This lack of knowing went way past the status of my parents, it encompassed most of what we did together, and particularly everything about Pete. Taking a wider view, I could not deny that I knew zilch about most things the Bureau had me doing. It was this refusal to put me in the know that had started me boiling.

I had been percolating for some time and now, as a result of this debriefing experience, I was finished brewing. While the hours and days of debriefing progressed, I saw, right in front of me, countless examples of every type of Bureau mentality, and resulting behavior, that had turned me against them. More significantly, I was buried in countless — "You have no need to know." Maybe I was finished brewing during the New York debriefing but no matter exactly when, the what was clear and unassailable. I was done with the FBI.

Oh, I would continue to do my duty, mechanically, without interest or belief, but I have no memories of our activities after this debriefing, no happenstance, no recalls popping up to visit me. Everything with the FBI from here on was reflex. In my mind, my actions, and my heart, this was my final debriefing. No one in the FBI had a need to know that I was done working undercover.

EPILOGUE

As time passed, I began to notice other things I hadn't noticed before. My life now had only three categories. First and by far most, the bedrock foundation that had always been there, my belief and total faith in God. Second, my commitment to my career. Third, Cathie. Beyond those three was everything else and I didn't have much interest in any of everything else.

My life had no pressure and tons of free time and I had something I had never had before, someone who wanted to be with me and who I wanted to be with. We were together whenever possible and she continued to educate me as she crammed an adolescence worth of social experience into our time together. Now, she was my focus.

I was obsessed and in no time, Cathie became the third woman on a pedestal in my life. Life, and those around them, put The Matriarch and The Reverend on their pedestals, while I put Cathie on hers.

13 June 1965, I graduated the University of Cincinnati as a Distinguished Military Graduate (DMG) and had the same feelings for UC as I did for Formica, a factory where I could earn what I needed. At the same ceremony I was commissioned

Second Lieutenant, Regular Army, with a 9 June Date of Rank that was identical to that of the graduates of The United States Military Academy at West Point.

Cathie and I were married 19 June 1965 and left Cincinnati for Fort Benning, Georgia, where I started my Army career by attending Infantry Officers' Basic Course. After completion of the course, we drove across country in October to Fort Lewis, Washington to join the 4th Infantry Division. After training our troops in the first half of 1966, I found myself on a troop ship bound for my next adventure—Vietnam.

ABOUT THE AUTHOR

Ronald E. Marksity was born in Cincinnati, Ohio. He majored in Modern European History at the University of Cincinnati and completed the ROTC program. Upon graduation, Ron was commissioned in the Regular Army as 2nd Lieutenant, Infantry.

Soon after, Ron was assigned to Vietnam, where he served as a platoon leader, a liaison to special forces, a general's aide and intelligence officer in Saigon. Upon returning, he was assigned to the US Army Intelligence School at Fort Holabird, Maryland. There, he led the QV Program, which prepared intelligence officers from all branches for service in Vietnam.

After leaving the Army, Ron joined the Institute for Training Management as a partner. He worked with clients from local, state, and federal governments and the private sector.

He returned to Cincinnati and joined another consulting firm, which led to a position with Senco, where Ron developed their training department, The Learning Center.

As a result of his years at Senco, he started his own company, Success Strategies, where more than half of his business was with international clients.

In 2000, Ron retired and began writing full time.

Today, Ron is still in Cincinnati with his wife, Pam. They have two grown sons, Burke and Drew.

www.ingramcontent.com/pod-product-compliance
Lightning Source LLC
Chambersburg PA
CBHW030315100526
44592CB00010B/438